20,000 WORDS

for the use of

STENOGRAPHERS
STUDENTS
AUTHORS
AND
PROOFREADERS

Compiled by

LOUIS A. LESLIE

Fourth Edition

GREGG PUBLISHING DIVISION

McGraw-Hill Book Company

New York Chicago Dallas
Corte Madera, Calif. Toronto London

20,000 WORDS

Fourth Edition

7 8 9 0 KP-59 9 8 7 6 5 4

Library of Congress Catalog Card No. 59-13205

Published by the Gregg Publishing Division

McGraw-Hill Book Company, Inc.
Printed in the United States of America

FOREWORD

Because this volume represents a new idea in dictionaries, an explanation of its purpose may be helpful. In nine cases out of ten when you go to the dictionary it is to find how to spell a word or how to divide it at the end of a line. If you do want to uncover some of the finer shades of meaning, usually only the unabridged dictionary will answer.

It is difficult, if not impossible, in a small volume to give definitions without using very small type and a crowded page. Even when the attempt is made, the definitions are necessarily brief and unsatisfactory.

The present volume solves the problem by omitting the unwanted definitions, thus making it possible, even in so small a book, to print the word lists in large type. Much space has also been saved by the omission of unnecessary words of two classes—thousands of short, easy words (*cat, dog*) that present no spelling difficulty, and the many rare, archaic, obsolete, and obsolescent words included in the ordinary dictionary for the sake of lexicographical completeness and, for most users, serving only to clutter up the pages.

Therefore, because of very careful selection, the present list of approximately 20,000 words represents the *useful* part of an ordinary dictionary vocabulary of several times that number. Restricting the list to the words actually needed by the user of the book makes those words much more quickly found, because there are fewer words to look through and those words are in larger type that is easier to read.

In this Fourth Edition the list has been revised to include many additional words for which users have asked. A great many derivative forms have been included, such as *occurred,* in which the question is always "How many *r*'s?" Also, the "Spelling Helps" given at the end of this book will be useful in explaining general principles of derivatives so that you may not have to look for so many of them; but when you want them now, you will find them listed alphabetically in the general vocabulary.

In response to many requests, much more space has been given to words in which there is a question about hyphenation and to expressions written as two words, such as: *air pump, air raid, air space* (but compare similar expressions like *airmail, airbrush, airfield*).

It is never safe to rely on analogy in English spelling, and especially in the matter of deciding problems involving the use of one word, two words, or a hyphen. One cow lives in a one-word cowshed; the other lives in a two-word cow barn. A one-word businessman is taken up to his office by a two-word elevator man. Your typewriter may be dustproof (one word), but it is not error-proof (with a hyphen). Moral: to be sure, look it up.

Many place names have been included in this edition, but only those known to be difficult, such as *Pittsburgh, Pennsylvania,* and *Pittsburg* (without the *h*), *California* and *Kansas.*

Short definitions have been included for some words like *capital* and *capitol.*

In order to keep the book small and useful, many words, which experience proved were not necessary, have been omitted. Thus the revision of the vocabulary has in no way lessened the usefulness and convenience of *20,000 Words*.

Syllables are indicated by

A heavy accent mark (*her′mit*) to show strong emphasis in pronouncing the word

A light accent mark (*net′work′*) to show less emphasis in pronouncing the word

A centered period (*pit′i·ful*) to show the end of a syllable on which there is no stress in pronunciation

Rules for dividing a word at the end of a line are given on pages 232–233.

A

ab′a·cus
a·baft′
ab′a·lo′ne
a·ban′don
a·ban′don·ment
a·base′
a·bash′
a·bat′a·ble
a·bate′
a·bate′ment
a·bat′ing
ab′at·toir′
ab′bé′
ab′bess
ab′bey
ab′bot
ab·bre′vi·ate
ab·bre′vi·at′ing
ab·bre′vi·a′tion
ab′di·cate
ab′di·cat′ing
ab′di·ca′tion
ab·do′men
ab·dom′i·nal
ab·duct′
ab·duc′tion
ab·duc′tor
a·beam′
ab·er′rance
ab·er′rant
ab′er·ra′tion
a·bet′
a·bet′ting
a·bey′ance
ab·hor′
ab·horred′
ab·hor′rence
ab·hor′rent
ab·hor′ring
a·bide′
a·bil′i·ties
a·bil′i·ty
ab′ject
ab·jure′
ab′la·tive
a·blaze′
a′ble
a′ble–bod′ied
ab·lu′tion
a′bly
ab′ne·ga′tion
ab·nor′mal
ab·nor·mal′i·ties
ab′nor·mal′i·ty
ab·nor′mal·ly
ab·nor′mi·ty
a·board′
a·bode′
a·bol′ish
ab′o·li′tion
ab′o·li′tion·ism
ab′o·li′tion·ist
a·bom′i·na·ble
a·bom′i·nate
a·bom′i·na′tion
ab′o·rig′i·nal
ab′o·rig′i·nes
a·bor′tive
a·bound′
a·bout′
a·bove′
a·bove′board′
ab′ra·ca·dab′ra
ab·rade′
ab·rad′ing
ab·ra′sion
ab·ra′sive
a·breast′
a·bridge′
a·bridg′ing
a·bridg′ment
ab′ro·gate
ab′ro·gat′ing
ab′ro·ga′tion
ab·rupt′
ab′scess
ab·scond′

ab·scond′er
ab′sence
ab′sent, *adj.*
ab·sent′, *v.*
ab′sen·tee′
ab′sinthe
ab′so·lute
ab′so·lute·ly
ab′so·lu′tion
ab′so·lut·ism
ab′so·lut·ist
ab·solve′
ab·solv′ing
ab·sorb′
ab·sorb′ent
ab·sorb′ing
ab·sorp′tion
ab·sorp′tive
ab·stain′
ab·stain′er
ab·ste′mi·ous
ab·sten′tion
ab′sti·nence
ab′sti·nent
ab′stract, *n.*
ab·stract′, *v.*
ab·stract′ed
ab·strac′tion
ab′stract·ly
ab·struse′
ab·surd′
ab·surd′i·ty

a·bun′dance
a·bun′dant
a·buse′
a·bus′ing
a·bu′sive
a·bu′sive·ly
a·bu′sive·ness
a·but′
a·but′ment
a·but′ter
a·but′ting
a·bysm′
a·bys′mal
a·byss′
ac′a·dem′ic
a·cad′e·mi′cian
a·cad′e·my
A·ca′di·an
ac·cede′
(to agree. *cf.* *exceed.*)
ac·cel′er·ate
ac·cel′er·a′tion
ac·cel′er·a′tive
ac·cel′er·a′tor
ac′cent, *n.*
ac·cent′, *v.*
ac·cen′tu·ate
ac·cept′
ac·cept′a·bil′i·ty
ac·cept′a·ble
ac·cept′ance

ac′cep·ta′tion
ac′cess
ac·ces′si·bil′i·ty
ac·ces′si·ble
ac·ces′sion
ac·ces′so·ry
ac′ci·dence
ac′ci·dent
ac′ci·den′tal
ac′ci·den′tal·ly
ac·claim′
ac′cla·ma′tion
ac·cli′mate
ac·cli′ma·tize
ac′co·lade′
ac·com′mo·date
ac·com′mo·dat′-ing
ac·com′mo·da′-tion
ac·com′pa·nies
ac·com′pa·ni-ment
ac·com′pa·nist
ac·com′pa·ny
ac·com′plice
ac·com′plish
ac·com′plished
ac·com′plish-ment
ac·cord′
ac·cord′ance

ac·cord′ing
ac·cor′di·on
ac·cost′
ac·count′
ac·count′a·bil′-
i·ty
ac·count′a·ble
ac·count′an·cy
ac·count′ant
ac·count′ing
ac·cou′ter·ment
ac·cred′it
ac·cre′tion
ac·cru′al
ac·crue′
ac·cru′ing
ac·cu′mu·late
ac·cu′mu·lat′ing
ac·cu′mu·la′tion
ac·cu′mu·la′tive
ac·cu′mu·la′tor
ac′cu·ra·cy
ac′cu·rate
ac′cu·sa′tion
ac·cu′sa·tive
ac·cu′sa·to′ry
ac·cuse′
ac·cus′ing
ac·cus′tom
ac·cus′tomed
a·cer′bi·ty
ac′e·tate

a·ce′tic
ac′e·tone
a·cet′y·lene
a·chieve′
a·chieve′ment
a·chiev′ing
ach′ro·mat′ic
ac′id
a·cid′i·fied
a·cid′i·fy
a·cid′i·ty
ac′id·proof′
a·cid′u·late
a·cid′u·lous
ac·knowl′edge
ac·knowl′edg·ing
ac·knowl′edg-
ment
ac′me
(highest point)
ac′ne
(a disease)
ac′o·lyte
ac′o·nite
a′corn
a·cous′tic
a·cous′ti·cal
a·cous′tics
ac·quaint′
ac·quaint′ance
ac′qui·esce′
ac′qui·es′cence

ac′qui·es′cent
ac·quire′
ac·quire′ment
ac·quir′ing
ac′qui·si′tion
ac·quis′i·tive
ac·quit′
ac·quit′tal
ac·quit′ted
ac·quit′ting
a′cre
a′cre·age
ac′rid
a·crid′i·ty
ac′ri·mo′ni·ous
ac′ri·mo′ny
ac′ro·bat
ac′ro·bat′ic
ac′ro·nym
a·crop′o·lis
a·cross′
a·cros′tic
a·cryl′ic
act′ing
ac·tin′ic
ac′tion
ac′tion·a·ble
ac′ti·vate
ac′tive
ac′tive·ly
ac·tiv′i·ties
ac·tiv′i·ty

ac′tor
ac′tu·al
ac′tu·al′i·ty
ac′tu·al·ly
ac′tu·ar′i·al
ac′tu·ar′ies
ac′tu·ar′y
ac′tu·ate
ac′tu·at′ing
a·cu′i·ty
a·cu′men
a·cute′
a·cute′ness
ad′age
a·da′gio
ad′a·mant
a·dapt′
(adjust. cf. *adept* and *adopt.*)
a·dapt′a·bil′i·ty
a·dapt′a·ble
ad′ap·ta′tion
a·dapt′er
ad·den′dum
ad′der
ad·dict′, *v.*
ad′dict, *n.*
ad·dict′ed
ad·dic′tion
ad·di′tion
ad·di′tion·al
ad·dress′, *v.*
ad·dress′, *n.*
ad′dress·ee′
ad·dress′ing
Ad·dres′so·graph
ad·duce′
ad·duc′ing
ad′e·noid
ad′ept, *n.*
a·dept′, *adj.*
(skillful. cf. *adapt.*)
ad′e·qua·cy
ad′e·quate
ad′e·quate·ly
ad·here′
ad·her′ence
ad·her′ing
ad·he′sion
ad·he′sive
ad·he′sive·ly
a·dieu′
ad′i·pose
ad·ja′cent
ad′jec·tive
ad·join′
(to be next to)
ad·journ′
(suspend)
ad·journ′ment
ad·judge′
ad·judg′ing
ad·ju′di·cate
ad·ju′di·cat′ing
ad·ju′di·ca′tion
ad·ju′di·ca′tor
ad′junct
ad′ju·ra′tion
ad·jure′
ad·just′
ad·just′a·ble
ad·just′er
ad·just′ment
ad′ju·tant
ad′–lib′, *v.* and *adj.*
ad·min′is·ter
ad·min′is·tra′tion
ad·min′is·tra′tive
ad·min′is·tra′tor
ad′mi·ra·ble
ad′mi·ral
ad′mi·ral·ty
ad′mi·ra′tion
ad·mire′
ad·mir′ing
ad·mis′si·bil′i·ty
ad·mis′si·ble
ad·mis′sion
ad·mit′
ad·mit′tance
ad·mit′ted
ad·mit′ting
ad·mix′ture
ad·mon′ish
ad′mo·ni′tion

ad·mon′i·to′ry
a·do′be
ad′o·les′cence
ad′o·les′cent
a·dopt′
(accept. cf. *adapt* and *adept.*)
a·dop′tion
a·dop′tive
a·dor′a·ble
ad′o·ra′tion
a·dor′ing
a·dorn′
a·dorn′ment
ad·re′nal
ad·ren′al·ine
a·drift′
a·droit′
ad·sorp′tion
ad′u·late
ad′u·la′tion
a·dult′
a·dul′ter·ant
a·dul′ter·ate
a·dul′ter·a′tion
a·dul′ter·er
a·dul′ter·ous
a·dul′ter·y
a·dult′i·cide
ad va·lo′rem
ad·vance′
ad·vanced′
ad·vance′ment
ad·vanc′ing
ad·van′tage
ad′van·ta′geous
ad′vent
ad′ven·ti′tious
ad·ven′ture
ad·ven′tur·er
ad·ven′ture·some
ad·ven′tur·ous
ad′verb
ad·ver′bi·al
ad′ver·sar′ies
ad′ver·sar′y
ad·verse′
ad·ver′si·ty
ad·vert′
ad′ver·tise
ad·ver′tise·ment
ad′ver·tis′er
ad·vice′
ad·vis′a·bil′i·ty
ad·vis′a·ble
ad·vise′
ad·vised′
ad·vise′ment
ad·vis′ing
ad·vi′so·ry
ad′vo·ca·cy
ad′vo·cate
ae′on
a′er·ate
a′er·a′tion
a·e′ri·al
a′er·o·dy·nam′ics
a′er·o·sol′
aes·thet′ic
aes·thet′i·cal·ly
aes·thet′i·cism
aes·thet′ics
af′fa·bil′i·ty
af′fa·ble
af·fair′
af·fect′
af′fec·ta′tion
af·fect′ed
af·fec′tion
af·fec′tion·ate
af·fi′ance
af·fi′ant
af′fi·da′vit
af·fil′i·ate
af·fin′i·ties
af·fin′i·ty
af·firm′
af′fir·ma′tion
af·firm′a·tive
af·firm′a·to·ry
af·fix′, *v.*
af·flict′
af·flic′tion
af′flu·ence
af′flu·ent
af·ford′

af·fray′
af·front′
a·field′
a·fire′
a·float′
a·foot′
a·fore′said′
a·fore′thought′
a·fore′time′
a·fraid′
a·fresh′
Af′ri·can
aft′er
aft′er·burn′er
aft′er·care′
aft′er·ef·fect′
aft′er·glow′
aft′er·math
aft′er·noon′
aft′er·taste′
aft′er·thought′
aft′er·ward
a·gain′
a·gainst′
ag′ate
ag′ate·ware′
a′gen·cies
a′gen·cy
a·gen′da
a′gent
ag′gran·dize
ag·gran′dize-
ment
ag′gra·vate
ag′gra·vat′ing
ag′gra·va′tion
ag′gre·gate
ag′gre·gat′ing
ag′gre·ga′tion
ag·gres′sion
ag·gres′sor
ag·grieve′
ag·grieved′
a·ghast′
ag′ile
ag′ile·ly
a·gil′i·ty
ag′i·tate
ag′i·tat·ing
ag′i·ta′tion
ag′i·ta′tor
a·glow′
ag·nos′tic
ag′o·niz′ing
ag′o·ny
a·grar′i·an
a·gree′
a·gree′a·bil′i·ty
a·gree′a·ble
a·greed′
a·gree′ing
a·gree′ment
ag′ri·cul′tur·al
ag′ri·cul′ture
ag′ri·cul′tur·ist
a·gron′o·my
a·ground′
a′gue
a′gue·weed′
a·head′
a·hoy′
ai′ler·on
air base
air brake
air′brush′
air′–con·di′tion,
v.
air′craft′
air′drome′
air′drop′
air express
air′field′
air′foil′
air force
air′freight′
air hole
air′lift
air line
air′mail′
air′–mind′ed
air′plane′
air′port′
air′proof′
air pump
air raid
air′ship′
air space
air′strip′
air′tight′

air′way′
air well
air′wor′thy
aisle
al′a·bas′ter
a·lac′ri·ty
a·larm′
a·larm′ist
al′ba·tross
al·be′it
Al′bert Lea, Minn.
al·bi′no
al·bi′nos
al′bum
al·bu′men
Al′bu·quer·que, N. M.
al′co·hol
al′co·hol′ic
al′cove
al′der·man
al·fal′fa
al′ge·bra
al′ge·bra′ic
al′ge·bra′i·cal
a′li·as
al′i·bi
al′ien
al′ien·ate
al′ien·at·ing
al′ien·a′tion
al′ien·ist

a·lign′
a·lign′ment
a·like′
al′i·men′ta·ry
al′i·men·ta′tion
al′i·mo′ny
al′i·quot
al′ka·li
al′ka·line
al′ka·loid
al·lay′
al·lay′ing
al′le·ga′tion
al·lege′
Al′le·ghe′nies
Al′le·ghe′ny
al·le′giance
al·leg′ing
al′le·gor′i·cal
al′le·go′ries
al′le·go′ry
al·le′vi·ate
al·le′vi·a′tion
al′ley
al′leys
al·li′ance
al·lied′
al·lies′
al′li·ga′tor
al·lit′er·a′tion
al′lo·cate
al′lo·cat′ing
al′lo·ca′tion

al′lo·path′ic
al·lop′a·thy
al·lot′
al·lot′ment
al·lot′ted
al·lot′ting
al·low′
al·low′a·ble
al·low′ance
al·lowed′
al·low′ed·ly
all right
al·lude′ (refer to. cf. *elude.*)
al·lure′
al·lu′sion
al·lu′vi·al
al·ly′
al·ly′ing
al·might′y
al′mond
al′most
al′ni·co
a·loft′
a·lone′
a·long′
a·loud′
al·pac′a
al′pha·bet
al′pha·bet·ize
al·read′y (but: *all right.*)

al′tar
al′ter
(change)
al′ter·a′tion
al′ter·ca′tion
al′ter·nate
al′ter·nat·ing
al′ter·na′tion
al·ter′na·tive
al·though′
al·tim′e·ter
al′ti·tude
al′to·geth′er
al′tru·ism
al′tru·ist
al′tru·is′tic
al′um
a·lu′mi·num
a·lum′na, *sing.*
fem.
a·lum′nae, *pl.*
fem.
a·lum′ni, *pl.*
masc.
a·lum′nus, *sing.*
masc.
al′ways
a·mal′gam
a·mal′gam·ate
a·mal′gam·a′tion
a·man′u·en′sis
am′a·teur′
a·maze′
a·maze′ment
Am′a·zon
am·bas′sa·dor
am′ber·gris
am′bi·dex′trous
am′bi·gu′i·ty
am·big′u·ous
am·bi′tion
am·bi′tious
am·bro′si·a
am′bu·lance
am′bus·cade′
am′bush
a·mel′io·rate
a·mel′io·ra′tion
a·mel′io·ra′tive
a·me′na·ble
a·mend′
a·mend′ment
a·men′i·ties
a·men′i·ty
A·mer′i·can
am′e·thyst
a′mi·a·bil′i·ty
a′mi·a·ble
am′i·ca·bil′i·ty
am′i·ca·ble
a·mid′ships
a·midst′
am′i·ty
am′me′ter
am·mo′ni·a
am′mu·ni′tion
am·ne′si·a
am′nes·ty
a·moe′ba
a·mong′
a·mongst′
am′o·rous
a·mor′phous
a·mor′ti·za′tion
a·mor′tize
a·mor′tiz·ing
a·mount′
am·per′age
am′pere
am·phib′i·an
am·phib′i·ous
am′phi·the′a·ter
am′pho·ra
am′ple
am′pli·fi·ca′tion
am′pli·fied
am′pli·fi′er
am′pli·fy
am′pli·fy′ing
am′pli·tude
am′ply
am′pu·tate
am′pu·ta′tion
am′u·let
a·muse′
a·muse′ment

a·mus′ing
a·nach′ro·nism
a·nach'ro·nis′tic
an'a·con′da
an′a·gram
an'a·log′i·cal
a·nal′o·gies
a·nal′o·gous
a·nal′o·gy
a·nal′y·ses, *pl.*
a·nal′y·sis
an′a·lyst
an'a·lyt′i·cal
an′a·lyze
an′a·lyz·ing
an′arch·ism
an′arch·ist
an′arch·y
an·as'tig·mat′ic
a·nath′e·ma
an'a·tom′i·cal
a·nat′o·mist
a·nat′o·mize
a·nat′o·my
an′ces'tor
an·ces′tral
an′ces'try
an′chor
an′chor·age
an·cho'vies
an·cho′vy
an′cient
an′cil·lar'y
and′i'ron
an′ec·dote
a·ne′mi·a
a·ne′mic
an'e·mom′e·ter
a·nem′o·ne
an′er·oid
an'es·the′si·a
an'es·the'si·ol′o-
gist
an'es·thet′ic
an·es′the·tist
an·es′the·tize
an′gel
an·gel′ic
an′ger
an′gle
an′gler
An′gli·can
An'glo–Sax′on
An·go′ra
an′gri·ly
an′gry
an′guish
an′gu·lar
an'gu·lar′i·ty
an′i·line
an'i·mad·ver′-
sion
an′i·mal
an'i·mal′i·ty
an′i·mate
an'i·ma′tion
an'i·mos′i·ty
an′i·mus
an′ise
an′kle
an′klet
an′nal·ist
an·neal′
an·nex′, *v.*
an′nex, *n.*
an'nex·a′tion
an·ni′hi·late
an·ni'hi·la′tion
an·ni′hi·la'tor
an'ni·ver′sa·ries
an'ni·ver′sa·ry
an′no·tate
an'no·ta′tion
an·nounce′
an·nounce′ment
an·nounc′ing
an·noy′
an·noy′ance
an·noyed′
an·noy′ing
an′nu·al
an·nu′i·ty
an·nul′
an′nu·lar
an·nulled′
an·nul′ling

an·nul′ment
an·nun′ci·a′tion
an·nun′ci·a′tor
an′o·dyne
a·noint′
a·nom′a·lous
a·nom′a·ly
an′o·nym′i·ty
a·non′y·mous
an·oth′er
an′swer
an′swer·a·ble
ant·ac′id
an·tag′o·nism
an·tag′o·nist
an·tag′o·nis′tic
an·tag′o·nize
ant·arc′tic
an′te·ced′ent
an′te·cham′ber
an′te·date′
an′te·di·lu′vi·an
an′te·lope
an·ten′na
an′te·pe′nult
an·te′ri·or
an′te·room′
an′them
an·thol′o·gy
an′thra·cite
an′thrax
an′thro·poid
an′thro·pol′o·gy
an′ti·bi·ot′ic
an′tic
an·tic′i·pate
an·tic′i·pat·ing
an·tic′i·pa′tion
an·tic′i·pa′tive
an·tic′i·pa·to′ry
an′ti·cli′max
an′ti·dote
an′ti·ma·cas′sar
an′ti·mo′ny
an·tip′a·thy
an·tiph′o·nal
an·tip′o·des
an′ti·quar′i·an
an′ti·quar′y
an′ti·quat′ed
an·tique′
an·tiq′ui·ty
an′ti·sep′sis
an′ti·sep′tic
an′ti·so′cial
an·tith′e·sis
an′ti·tox′in
ant′ler
an′to·nym
ant′proof′
an′trum
an′vil
anx·i′e·ty
anx′ious
an′y
an′y·bod′y
an′y·how
an′y·one
an′y·thing
an′y·way
an′y·ways
an′y·where
a′o·rist
a·or′ta
a·pace′
a·part′
a·part′ment
ap′a·thet′ic
ap′a·thy
ap′er·ture
a′pex
a·pha′si·a
aph′o·rism
Aph′ro·di′te
a′pi·ar′y
ap′i·cal
a·piece′
a·poc′a·lypse
A·poc′ry·pha
a·poc′ry·phal
ap′o·gee
a·pol′o·get′ic
a·pol′o·get′i·cal
a·pol′o·get′ics
a·pol′o·gies
a·pol′o·gize

a·pol′o·giz′ing
ap′o·logue
a·pol′o·gy
ap′o·plec′tic
ap′o·plex′y
a·pos′ta·sy
a·pos′tate
a′pos·te′ri·o′ri
a·pos′tle
a·pos′to·late
ap′os·tol′ic
a·pos′tro·phe
a·pos′tro·phize
a·poth′e·car′ies
a·poth′e·car′y
a·poth′e·o′sis
Ap′pa·lach′i·an
ap·pall′
ap·palled′
ap·pall′ing
ap′pa·ra′tus
ap·par′el
ap·par′ent
ap′pa·ri′tion
ap·peal′
ap·pear′
ap·pear′ance
ap·pease′
ap·pel′lant
ap·pel′late
ap′pel·la′tion
ap′pel·lee′
ap·pend′
ap·pend′age
ap′pen·dec′to·my
ap·pen′di·ci′tis
ap·pen′dix
ap′per·ceive′
ap′per·cep′tion
ap′per·tain′
ap′pe·tite
ap′pe·tiz′ing
ap·plaud′
ap·plause′
ap′ple
ap′ple·jack′
ap·pli′ance
ap′pli·ca·bil′i·ty
ap′pli·ca·ble
ap′pli·cant
ap′pli·ca′tion
ap·plied′
ap′pli·qué′
ap·ply′
ap·ply′ing
ap·point′
ap·point′ee′
ap·point′ment
ap·por′tion
ap·por′tion·ment
ap′po·site
ap′po·si′tion
ap·prais′al
ap·praise′
ap·praise′ment
ap·prais′ing
ap·pre′ci·a·ble
ap·pre′ci·ate
ap·pre′ci·a′tion
ap·pre′ci·a′tive
ap′pre·hend′
ap′pre·hen′si·ble
ap′pre·hen′sion
ap′pre·hen′sive
ap·pren′tice
ap·pren′ticed
ap·pren′tice·ship
ap·prise′
ap·proach′
ap′pro·ba′tion
ap′pro·ba′tive
ap′pro·ba′tive-
ness
ap′pro·ba·to′ry
ap·pro′pri·ate
ap·pro′pri·ate·ly
ap·pro′pri·ate-
ness
ap·pro′pri·a′tion
ap·prov′al
ap·prove′
ap·prov′ing
ap·prox′i·mate
ap·prox′i·ma′tion
ap·pur′te·nance
ap·pur′te·nant

a'pri·cot
a'pri·o'ri
a'pron
ap'ro·pos'
ap'ti·tude
apt'ly
apt'ness
aq'ua·ma·rine'
a·quar'i·um
A·quar'i·us
a·quat'ic
aq'ua·tint'
aq'ue·duct
a'que·ous
aq'ui·line
ar'a·besque'
A·ra'bi·an
Ar'a·bic
ar'a·ble
a·rach'noid
ar'bi·ter
ar'bi·tra·ble
ar'bi·trage
ar·bit'ra·ment
ar'bi·trar'y
ar'bi·trate
ar'bi·tra'tion
ar'bi·tra'tive
ar'bi·tra'tor
ar'bor
ar·bo're·al
ar'bo·re'tum
ar·bu'tus
arc'ing
ar·cade'
ar'chae·o·log'i-
cal
ar'chae·ol'o·gist
ar'chae·ol'o·gy
ar·cha'ic
arch'an'gel
arch'bish'op
arch'dea'con
arch'du'cal
arch'duch'ess
arch'duch'y
arch'duke'
arch'er
arch'er·y
arch'fiend'
ar'chi·e·pis'co·pal
ar'chi·pel'a·go
ar'chi·pel'a·goes
ar'chi·tect
ar'chi·tec'tur·al
ar'chi·tec'ture
ar'chi·trave
ar'chives
arch'ness
arch'priest'
arch'way'
arc'tic
Arc·tu'rus
ar'dent
ar'dor
ar'du·ous
a're·a
a·re'na
Ar'gen·tine
ar'gon
ar'go·naut
ar'go·sy
ar'gue
ar'gued
ar'gu·ing
ar'gu·ment
ar'gu·men·ta'tion
ar'gu·men'ta·tive
Ar'gy·rol
a'ri·a
ar'id
a·rid'i·ty
Ar'i·el
a·rio'so
ar'is·toc'ra·cy
a·ris'to·crat
a·ris'to·crat'ic
Ar'is·to·te'li·an
a·rith'me·tic
ar'ith·met'i·cal
a·rith'me·ti'cian
ar·ma'da
ar'ma·dil'lo
ar'ma·ment
ar'ma·ture
arm'chair'

arm′ful
arm′hole′
ar′mies
ar′mi·stice
ar′mor
ar′mor·er
ar·mo′ri·al
ar′mor·y
arm′pit′
ar′my
a·ro′ma
ar′o·mat′ic
a·round′
ar·peg′gio
ar·raign′
ar·raign′ment
ar·range′
ar·range′ment
ar·rang′ing
ar′rant
ar′ras
ar·ray′
ar·rayed′
ar·ray′ing
ar·rear′
ar·rear′age
ar·rest′
ar·riv′al
ar·rive′
ar·riv′ing
ar′ro·gance
ar′ro·gant
ar′ro·gate
ar′row
ar′row·head′
ar′row·root′
ar·roy′o
ar′se·nal
ar′se·nate
ar′se·nic
ar′son
ar·te′ri·al
ar′ter·ies
ar·te′ri·o·scle·ro′-
sis
ar′ter·y
ar·te′sian
art′ful
art′ful·ly
ar·thri′tis
ar′ti·choke
ar′ti·cle
ar′ti·cled
ar·tic′u·late
ar·tic′u·la′tion
ar′ti·fice
ar·tif′i·cer
ar′ti·fi′cial
ar′ti·fi′ci·al′i·ty
ar·til′ler·y
ar′ti·san
art′ist
ar·tiste′
ar·tis′tic
art′ist·ry
art′less
Ar′y·an
as·bes′tos
as·cend′
as·cend′an·cy
as·cend′ant
as·cend′ing
as·cen′sion
as·cent′
as′cer·tain′
as′cer·tain′ment
as·cet′ic
as·cet′i·cism
as·cribe′
as·crib′ing
as·crip′tion
a·sep′sis
a·sep′tic
a·shamed′
ash bin
ash cart
ash′en
ash–free
ash′y
ash′man′
A′sian
A′si·at′ic
a·side′
as′i·nine
as′i·nin′i·ty
a·skance′

a·skew′
a·sleep′
as·par′a·gus
as′pect
as′pen
as·per′i·ty
as·perse′
as·per′sion
as′phalt
as·phyx′i·a
as·phyx′i·ate
as·phyx′i·at′ing
as·phyx′i·a′tion
as′pic
as·pir′ant
as′pi·rate
as′pi·ra′tion
as′pi·ra′tor
as·pir′a·to′ry
as·pire′
as′pi·rin
as·pir′ing
as′sa·gai
as·sail′
as·sail′ant
as·sas′sin
as·sas′si·nate
as·sas′si·na′tion
as·sault′
as·say′
as·sayed′
as·say′ing
as·sem′blage
as·sem′ble
as·sem′bling
as·sem′bly
as·sem′bly·man
as·sent′
as·sert′
as·ser′tion
as·ser′tive
as·sess′
as·sess′a·ble
as·sess′ment
as·ses′sor
as′set
as·sev′er·ate
as·sev′er·a′tion
as′si·du′i·ty
as·sid′u·ous
as·sign′
as·sign′a·ble
as′sig·nat
as′sig·na′tion
as′sign·ee′
as·sign′er
as·sign′ment
as·sim′i·la·ble
as·sim′i·late
as·sim′i·lat′ing
as·sim′i·la′tion
as·sim′i·la′tive
as·sim′i·la·to′ry
as·sist′
as·sist′ance
as·sist′ant
as·size′
as·so′ci·ate
as·so′ci·at′ing
as·so′ci·a′tion
as·so′ci·a′tive
as′so·nance
as′so·nant
as·sort′
as·sort′ment
as·suage′
as·suag′ing
as·sume′
as·sum′ing
as·sump′tion
as·sur′ance
as·sure′
as·sured′
as·sur′ing
as′ter
as′ter·isk
as′ter·oid
as·the′ni·a
asth′ma
as′tig·mat′ic
a·stig′ma·tism
as·ton′ish
as·ton′ish·ment
as·tound′
as′tral
a·stride′

as·trin′gent
as′tro·labe
as·trol′o·ger
as·trol′o·gy
as·tron′o·mer
asʹtro·nom′ic
asʹtro·nom′i·cal
as·tron′o·my
as·tute′
a·sun′der
a·sy′lum
at′a·vism
at′el·ier
a′the·ism
a′the·ist
aʹthe·is′tic
athʹe·nae′um
ath′lete
ath·let′ic
ath·let′ics
a·thwart′
At·lan′tic
at′las
at′mos·phere
atʹmos·pher′ic
at′om
a·tom′ic
at′om·ize
a·tone′ment
a·ton′ing
a′tri·um
a·tro′cious
a·troc′i·ty
at′ro·phied
at′ro·phy
at·tach′
atʹta·ché′
at·tach′ment
at·tack′
at·tain′
at·tain′a·ble
at·tain′der
at·tain′ment
at·taint′
at′tar
at·tempt′
at·tend′
at·tend′ance
at·tend′ant
at·ten′tion
at·ten′tive
at·ten′u·ate
at·tenʹu·a′tion
at·test′
atʹtes·ta′tion
at′tic
at·tire′
at′ti·tude
at·tor′ney
at·tract′
at·trac′tion
at·trac′tive
at·trib′ute′, *v.*
at′tri·bute, *n.*
at·trib′u·tive
at·tri′tion
au′burn
auc′tion
aucʹtion·eer′
au·da′cious
au·dac′i·ty
auʹdi·bil′i·ty
au′di·ble
au′di·ence
au′di·o·phile
au′dit
au·di′tion
au′di·tor
auʹdi·to′ri·um
au′di·toʹry
au′ger
(tool)
aught
aug·ment′, *v.*
aug′ment, *n.*
augʹmen·ta′tion
au′gur
(predict)
au′gu·ry
Au′gust
(month)
au·gust′
(majestic)
auk
au′ra
au′ral

au′re·ate
au′re·ole
au′re·o·my′cin
au′ric
au·ric′u·lar
au·rif′er·ous
au·ro′ra
aus′cul·tate
aus′cul·ta′tion
aus′pice
aus·pi′cious
aus·tere′
aus·ter′i·ty
Aus·tral′ian
Aus′tri·an
au·then′tic
au·then′ti·cate
au′then·tic′i·ty
au′thor
au·thor′i·tar′i·an
au·thor′i·ta′tive
au·thor′i·ty
au′thor·i·za′tion
au′thor·ize
au′thor·iz′ing
au′thor·ship
au′to·bi′o-
graph′i·cal
au′to·bi·og′ra-
phy
au·toch′tho·nous
au·toc′ra·cy
au′to·crat
au′to·crat′ic
au′to–da–fé′
au′to·graph
au′to·graph′ic
au′to·in·fec′tion
au′to·mat′ic
au·tom′a·tism
au·tom′a·ton
au′to·mo·bile′
au′to·mo′tive
au·ton′o·mous
au·ton′o·my
au′top·sy
au′to·sug·ges′-
tion
au′tumn
au·tum′nal
aux·il′ia·ry
a·vail′
a·vail′a·bil′i·ty
a·vail′a·ble
av′a·lanche
av′a·rice
av′a·ri′cious
a·venge′
av′e·nue
a·ver′
av′er·age
a·ver′ment
a·verred′
a·ver′ring
a·verse′
a·ver′sion
a·vert′
a′vi·ar′y
a′vi·a′tion
a′vi·a′tor
a′vi·cul′ture
av′id
a·vid′i·ty
av′o·ca′do
av′o·ca′dos
av′o·ca′tion
a·void′
a·void′a·ble
a·void′ance
av′oir·du·pois′
a·vow′
a·vow′al
a·vowed′
a·vun′cu·lar
a·wait′
a·wake′
a·wak′en
a·ward′
a·ware′
a·ware′ness
a·wash′
a·way′
a·weigh′
awe′some
aw′ful
a·while′

awk'ward
awl
awn'ing
a·woke'
a·wry'
ax
ax'i·om
ax'i·o·mat'ic
ax'is
ax'le
aye
a·zal'e·a
az'i·muth
Az'tec
az'ure

B

bab'bitt
bab'ble
bab'bling
ba'bies
ba·boon'
ba'by
ba'by·ing
bac'ca·lau're·ate
bac'ca·rat'
bac'cha·nal
bac'chant
Bac'chus
bach'e·lor
ba·cil'li, *pl.*
ba·cil'lus
back'bite'
back'bone'
back'break'ing
back'door'
back'gam'mon
back'ground'
back'hand'
back'hand'ed
back'lash'
back'log'
back'stairs'
back'stitch'
back'ward
back'ward·ly
back'ward·ness
back'wash'
back'wa'ter
back'woods'
ba'con
bac·te'ri·a
bac·te'ri·al
bac·te'ri·cide
bac·te'ri·o·log'i-cal
bac·te'ri·ol'o·gy
badg'er
bad'i·nage'
bad'min·ton
baf'fle
baf'fle·ment
baf'fling
bag'a·telle'
bag'gage
bag'gage·man
bag'gage·mas'ter
bag'gage room
bag'ging
bag'pipe'
bailed
(set free. cf. *baled.*)
bail'ee'
bail'iff
bail'i·wick
bail'ment
bail'or'
ba'ke·lite
bak'ing
bal'ance
bal'anc·ing
bal'co·nies
bal'co·ny

bal′der·dash
baled
(packaged. cf. *bailed.*)
bale′ful
bal′ing
balk
Bal′kan
bal′lad
bal′lad·ry
bal′last
bal′let
bal·lis′tics
bal·loon′
bal·loon′ist
bal′lot
ball′room′
balm
balm′i·ness
Bal·mor′al
bal′sa
bal′sam
Bal′tic
bal′us·trade′
bam·boo′
bam·boo′zle
ba′nal
ba·nal′i·ty
ba·nan′a
band′age
band′ag·ing
ban·dan′na
band′box′
ban·deau′
ban′de·role
ban′dit
band′mas′ter
ban′do·leer′
band′stand′
ban′dy
bane′ful
ban′gle
ban′ish
ban′ish·ment
ban′is·ter
ban′jo
ban′jos
bank′book′
bank draft
bank′er
bank note
bank′rupt
bank′rupt·cy
ban′ner
ban′ner·et
ban′nock
ban′quet
Ban′quo
ban′shee
ban′tam
ban′ter
ban′yan
ban′zai′
bap′tism
Bap′tist
bap′tis·ter·y
bap·tize′
bar·bar′i·an
bar·bar′ic
bar′ba·rism
bar·bar′i·ty
bar′ba·rize
bar′ba·rous
bar′be·cue
bar′ber
bar′ber·shop
bar·bette′
bar′bi·tu′rate
bar′ca·role
bard′ic
bare′back′
bare′faced′
bare′foot′
bare′head′ed
bare′ly
bar′gain
barge ca·nal′
barge′load′
barge′man
barge′mas′ter
bar′i·tone
bar′i·um
bar′keep′er
bark′en·tine
bark′er
bar′ley
bar′ley·corn′
bar′maid′
bar′na·cle

barn′storm′er
barn′yard′
bar′o·graph
ba·rom′e·ter
bar′o·met′ric
bar′on
(nobleman. cf. *barren.*)
bar′on·age
bar′on·ess
bar′on·et
bar′on·et·cy
ba·ro′ni·al
bar′o·ny
ba·roque′
bar′o·scope
ba·rouche′
bar′rack
bar′ra·cu′da
bar·rage′
bar′ra·trous
bar′rel
bar′ren
(sterile. cf. *baron.*)
bar′ri·cade′
bar′ri·er
bar′ris·ter
bar′room′
bar′row
bar′tend′er
bar′ter
ba·salt′
bas′cule

base′ball′
base′board′
base′born′
base′heart′ed
base′less
base′ment
base′–mind′ed
base′ness
ba′ses, *pl.*
bash′ful
bas′ic
bas′i·cal·ly
ba·sil′i·ca
bas′i·lisk
ba′sin
bas′i·net
(helmet. cf. *bassinet.*)
ba′sis
(plural: *bases*)
bas′ket
bas′ket·ball′
bas′ket·ful
bas′ket·ry
bas′ket·work′
bas′–re·lief′
bas′si·net′
(cradle. cf. *basinet.*)
bas·soon′
bas′so–re·lie′vo
bass′wood′
bas′tion

ba·teau′
bat′fish′
bath
bathe
ba·thet′ic
bath′house′
bath′ing
ba′thos
bath′robe′
bath′room′
bath′tub′
ba·tiste′
ba′ton′
Bat′on Rouge, La.
bat·tal′ion
bat′ten
bat′ter
bat′ter·ies
bat′ter·y
bat′tle
battle cry
bat′tle·field′
bat′tle flag
bat′tle·ground′
bat′tle·ment
bat′tle–scarred
bat′tle·ship′
Ba·var′i·an
bay′ber′ry
bay′o·net
Ba′yonne′, N. J.
bay′ou

ba·zaar′
(market. cf. *bizarre.*)
ba·zoo′ka
beach′comb′er
bea′con
bea′dle
bead′work′
bear′a·ble
bear′skin′
be′a·tif′ic
be·at′i·fi·ca′tion
be·at′i·tude
beau′te·ous
beau′ties
beau′ti·fied
beau′ti·ful
beau′ti·fy
beau′ti·fy′ing
beau′ty
bea′ver
be·calm′
be·came′
be·cause′
beck′on
be·cloud′
be·come′
bed′cham′ber
bed′clothes′
bed′ding
be·deck′
be·dev′il
bed′fel·low
bed jacket
be·dight′
be·diz′en
bed′lam
Bed′ou·in
bed′post
be·drag′gle
bed′rid′den
bed′rock′
bed′room′
bed sheet
bed′side′
bed′sore′
bed′spread′
bed′staff′
bed′stead
bed′time
bed′warm·er
beech′nut′
beef′eat′er
bee′hive′
Be·el′ze·bub
bee′tle–browed′
be·fall′
be·fit′
be·fog′
be·fool′
be·fore′
be·fore′hand′
be·fore′time′
be·friend′
be·fud′dle
beg′gar
beg′gar·ly
beg′gar·weed′
beg′gar·y
be·gin′
be·gin′ning
be·grime′
be·grudge′
be·guile′
be′gum
be·gun′
be·half′
be·have′
be·hav′ing
be·hav′ior
be·head′
be·held′
be·he′moth
be·hest′
be·hind′
be·hind′hand′
be·hold′
be·hoof′
be·hoove′
beige
be·la′bor
be·lat′ed
be·lay′
bel′fry
Bel′gi·an
Be′li·al
be·lie′
be·lief′
be·liev′a·ble

be·lieve′
be·liev′ing
be·lit′tle
bel′la·don′na
belles′–let′tres
bell′flow′er
bel′li·cose
bel·lig′er·ence
bel·lig′er·ent
bel′lows
bell–shaped
bell tow′er
bell′weth′er
bel′ly
bel′ly·band′
be·long′
be·lov′ed
be·low′
belt
bel′ve·dere′
be·moan′
be·neath′
ben′e·dic′tion
ben′e·fac′tion
ben′e·fac′tor
ben′e·fice
be·nef′i·cence
be·nef′i·cent
be·nef′i·cent·ly
ben′e·fi′cial
ben′e·fi′ci·ar′ies
ben′e·fi′ci·ar′y
ben′e·fit
ben′e·fit′ed
ben′e·fit′ing
be·nev′o·lence
be·nev′o·lent
be·night′ed
be·nign′
be·nig′nan·cy
be·nig′nant
be·nig′nant·ly
be·nig′ni·ty
be·nign′ly
ben′i·son
Be′o·wulf
be·queath′
be·quest′
ber′ceuse′
be·reave′
be·reave′ment
ber′i·ber′i
Berke′ley, Calif.
Berk′ley, Mich.
ber·lin′
ber′ries
ber′ry
(fruit. cf. *bury.*)
ber′serk
ber′serk·er
berth
(bed. cf. *birth.*)
ber′yl
be·ryl′li·um
be·seech′
be·side′
be·sides′
be·siege′
be·smear′
be·smirch′
be·speak′
Bes′se·mer
bes′tial
bes′ti·al′i·ty
best–known
best–liked
be·stow′
best–paid
best sel′ler
best–sell′ing
Be·thes′da
be·tide′
be·times′
be·to′ken
be·tray′
be·tray′al
be·troth′
be·troth′al
bet′ter
bet′ter·ment
be·tween′
be·twixt′
bev′el
bev′eled
bev′el·ing
bev′er·age
bev′ies
bev′y
be·wail′

be·ware′
be·wil′der
be·wil′dered
be·wil′der·ment
be·witch′
be·wray′
be·yond′
bez′ant
bi·an′gu·lar
bi·an′nu·al
bi′as
bi′ased
Bi′ble
Bib′li·cal
bib′li·og′ra·pher
bib′li·og′ra·phy
bib′li·o·phile
bib′u·lous
bi·cam′er·al
bi·car′bon·ate
bi·cen′te·nar′y
bi′cen·ten′ni·al
bi′ceps
bi·chlo′ride
bi·chro′mate
bi·cus′pid
bi′cy·cle
bi′cy·clist
Bid′de·ford,
Maine
Bid′e·ford,
England
bi·en′ni·al
big′a·mist
big′a·mous
big′a·my
big–head′ed
big′heart′ed
bight
big′ot·ed
big′ot·ry
big′wig′
bi′jou
bi·la′bi·al
bi·lat′er·al
bilge
bi·lin′gual
bil′ious
bill′board′
bil′let
bil′let–doux′
bill′fish′
bill′head′
bil′liards
bil′lings·gate′
bil′lion
bil′lion·aire′
bil′lionth
bil′low
bil′low·y
bill′post′er
bill′stick′er
bi′me·tal′lic
bi·met′al·lism
bi·met′al·list
bi·month′ly
bi′na·ry
bind′er
bind′er·y
bind′ing
bind′weed′
bin′na·cle
bin·oc′u·lar
bi·no′mi·al
bi′o·chem′is·try
bi·og′ra·pher
bi′o·graph′ic
bi′o·graph′i·cal
bi·og′ra·phy
bi′o·log′i·cal
bi·ol′o·gy
bi′o·scope
bi·par′ti·san
bi′ped
bi′plane′
bi·po′lar
bird′call′
bird′lime′
bird′man′
bird′s′–eye′
birth
(beginning. cf. *berth.*)
birth′day′
birth′mark′
birth′place′

birth rate
birth′right′
birth′stone′
bis′cuit
bi′sect′
bish′op
Bis′marck, N. D.
bis′muth
bi′son
bisque
bis·sex′tile
bit′stock′
bit′ter
bit′tern
bit′ter·ness
bit′ter·root′
bit′ter·sweet′
bit′ter·weed′
bi·tu′mi·nous
bi·va′lent
bi′valve′
biv′ou·ac
biv′ou·acked
bi·zarre′ (odd. cf. *bazaar.*)
black′a·moor
black′ball′
black′ber′ry
black′bird′
black′board′
black′cap′
black′ened
black′guard
black′head′
black′jack′
black lead
black′leg′
black list, *n.*
black′-list′, *v.*
black′mail′
black′ness
black′out′
black′poll′
black′smith′
black′thorn′
blad′der
blam′a·ble
blame′ful
blame′less
blame′wor′thy
blam′ing
blanc·mange′
blan′dish
blank′book′
blan′ket
blank′ness
blar′ney
bla·sé′
blas·pheme′
blas·phem′ing
blas′phe·mous
blas′phe·my
bla′tan·cy
bla′tant
blath′er·skite
blaze
blaz′ing
bla′zon
bla′zon·ry
bleach′er
blem′ish
bless′ed·ness
blind′er
blind′fish′
blind′fold′
blind′ing
blind′ly
blink′er
bliss′ful
blis′ter
blithe
blithe′some
bliz′zard
bloat′er
block·ade′
block′head′
block′house′
blood
blood′ed
blood′hound′
blood′i·est
blood′i·ly
blood′i·ness
blood′less
blood′let′ting

blood money
blood′root′
blood′shed′
blood′shot′
blood′stain′
blood′stone′
blood′suck′er
blood′thirst′y
blood vessel
blood′wort′
blood′y
bloom′er
blos′som
blot′ter
blot′ting
blouse
blow′er
blow′fish′
blow′fly′
blow′gun′
blow′hole′
blow′out′
blow′pipe′
blow′torch′
blow′tube′
blowz′y
blub′ber
blub′ber·y
blu′cher
bludg′eon
blue′bell′
blue′ber′ry
blue′bird′
blue′bon′net
blue′book′
blue′bot′tle
blue′coat′
blue′–eyed′
blue′fish′
blue′jack′et
blue jay
blue laws
blue moon
blue′–pen′cil, *v.*
blue′print′
blue′stock′ing
blu′et
blu′ing
blu′ish
blun′der
blun′der·buss
blunt′ly
blunt′ness
blus′ter
blus′ter·ous
bo′a
board′er
board′ing·house′
board′walk′
boast′ful
boast′ing·ly
boat′bill′
boat′build′er
boat club
boat hire
boat hook
boat′house′
boat′man
boat′swain
bob′bin
bob′bi·net′
bob′cat′
bob′o·link
bob′sled′
bob′stay′
bob′tail′
bob′white′
bo·cac′cio
bod′ice
bod′i·less
bod′i·ly
bod′kin
bod′y
bod′y·guard′
Boer
bo′gey
bog′gle
bo′gus
bo′gy
Bo·he′mi·an
boil′er
bois′ter·ous
bold′–faced′
bold′ly
bold′ness
bo·le′ro

bol'i·var
Bo·liv'i·an
boll weevil
boll'worm'
bol'ster
bolt'er
bolt'head'
bolt'rope'
bo'lus
bomb
bom'bard, *n.*
bom·bard', *v.*
bom'bard·ier'
bom·bard'ment
bom'bast
bom·bas'tic
bom'ba·zine'
bomb'proof'
bomb'shell'
bomb'sight'
bo'na fi'de
bo·nan'za
bon'bon'nière'
bond'age
bond'ed
bond'hold'er
bond'maid'
bond servant
bonds'man
bond'wom'an
bon'fire'
bo·ni'to
bon' mot'
bon'net
bon'ny
bo'nus
bon' vi'vant'
bonze
boo'bies
boo'by
boo'dle
book
book a'gent
book'bind'er
book'case'
book club
book col·lect'or
book'deal'er
book end
book'ish
book'keep'er
book'keep'ing
book'let
book'mak'er
book'mark'
book'plate'
book'rack'
book re·view'
book'shelf'
book'shop'
book'store'
book'worm'
boom'er·ang
boon'dog'gle
boor'ish
boost'er
boot'black'
boot'ed
boot'ee'
booth
boot'jack'
boot'leg'
boot'less
boot tree
boo'ty
booze
booz'y
bo·rac'ic
bo'rate
bo'rax
Bor'deaux'
bor'der
bo're·al
Bo're·as
bore'dom
bor'ing
bo'ron
bor'ough
bor'row
bosk'y
Bos'ni·an
bos'om
bo·tan'i·cal
bot'a·nist
bot'a·nize
bot'a·ny

botch
both
both'er
both'er·some
bot'tle
bot'tled
bot'tle–fed
bot'tle·nose'
bot'tler
bot'tling
bot'tle wash'er
bot'tom
bot'tom·less
bot'tom·ry
bou'doir
bough
bough'pot'
bought
bouil'la·baisse'
bouil'lon'
(soup. cf. *bullion.*)
boul'der
bou'le·vard
bounce
bounc'er
bounc'ing
bound
bound'a·ries
bound'a·ry
bound'en
bound'er
bound'less

boun'te·ous
boun'ti·ful
boun'ty
bou·quet'
Bour'bon
bour·geois'
bour'geoi'sie'
bourse
bou'ton·niere'
bo'vine
bowd'ler·ize
bow'el
bow'er
bow'er·y
bow'fin'
bow'knot'
bowl'der
bowl'er
bow'line
bowl'ing
bow'man
bow'shot'
bow'sprit
bow'string'
bow'yer
box'ber'ry
box coat
box'er
box'ing
box kite
box'thorn'
box'wood'

bo·yar'
boy'cott
boy'hood
boy'ish
brace'let
brac'er
brack'et
brack'et·ing
brack'ish
brag
brag'ga·do'ci·o
brag'gart
brag'ging
Braille
brain cell
brain'less
brain'pan'
brain'sick'
brain'wash'ing
brain'work'
brake'man
bram'ble
bran'died
bran'dish
brand'–new'
bran'dy
bras'sard
brass'ware'
brass'work'
bra·va'do
brave·heart'ed
brave–mind'ed

brav′er·y
brav′est
bra′vo
bra·vu′ra
brawl
brawn′i·est
brawn′y
bra′zen
bra′zen·faced′
bra′zier
Bra·zil′ian
bra·zil′wood′
breach
(violation. cf. *breech.*)
bread′fruit′
bread pan
bread′root′
bread′stuff′
breadth
(size. cf. *breath.*)
bread′win′ner
break′a·ble
break′age
break′down′
break′er
break′fast
break′neck′
break′wa′ter
breast
breast′bone′
breast′pin′

breast′plate′
breast′work′
breath
(of air. cf. *breadth.*)
breath′a·ble
breathe
breath′er
breath′ing
breath′less
breech
(rear. cf. *breach.*)
breech′es
breech′load′er
breech′–load′ing
breed
breed′ing
breeze
breeze′way′
breez′y
breth′ren
bre·vet′
bre′vi·ar′y
brev′i·ty
brew
brew′er·y
brew′ing
bribe
brib′er·y
brib′ing
bric′–a–brac′
brick
brick′bat′

brick′kiln′
brick′lay′er
brick′lay′ing
brick′work′
brick′yard′
brid′al
(wedding. cf. *bridle.*)
bride
bride′groom′
brides′maid′
bride′well
bridge
bridge′head′
bridge′work′
bri′dle
(harness. cf. *bridal.*)
brief
brief′less
bri′er
bri′er·root′
bri′er·wood′
bri·gade′
brig′a·dier′
brig′and
brig′an·tine
bright
bright′en
bright′–eyed′
bright′ly
bright′ness

bright–wit′ted
bril′liance
bril′lian·cy
bril′liant
bril′lian·tine
bril′liant·ly
brim
brim′ful′
brimmed
brim′ming
brim′stone
brin′dle
bring
brink
brin′y
bri·quette′
brisk
bris′ket
bris′tle
bris′tle·tail′
bris′tling
Bris′tol board
Bri·tan′ni·a
Bri·tan′nic
Brit′ish
Brit′ish·er
Brit′on
brit′tle
broach
broad
broad′ax′
broad′brim′
broad′cast′
broad′cloth′
broad′en
broad′ly
broad′–mind′ed
broad′–mind′-
ed·ness
broad′side′
broad′sword′
broad′tail′
bro·cade′
broc′co·li
bro·chette′
bro·chure′
brogue
broi′der
broil
broil′er
broke
bro′ken
bro′ken·heart′ed
bro′ker
bro′ker·age
bro′mate
bro′mide
bro′mine
bron′chi·al
bron·chi′tis
bron′cho
bronze
brooch
brood
brood′er
brook
brook′let
Brook′line, Mass.
Brook′lyn, N. Y.
broom′stick′
broth
broth′er
broth′er·hood
broth′er–in–
law′
broth′er·ly
brougham
brought
brow
brow′beat′
brown bread
brown′ish
brown′out′
brown′stone′
bru′in
bruise
bruis′er
bruis′ing
bruit
bru·nette′
brunt
brush
brush′wood′
brush′work′
brusque
bru′tal

bru·tal′i·ty
bru′tal·ize
brute
brut′ish
bub′ble
bu·bon′ic
buc′ca·neer′
Bu·ceph′a·lus
buck′board′
buck′et
buck′eye′
buck′hound′
buck′le
buck′ler
buck′ling
buck′ram
buck′saw′
buck′shot′
buck′skin′
buck′thorn′
buck′wheat′
bu·col′ic
Bud′dha
Bud′dhism
budg′et
budg′et·ed
budg′et·ing
buf′fa·lo
buf′fa·loes
buf′fet
buf·foon′
buf·foon′er·y

bug′bear′
bu′gle
bu′gling
bug′proof′
build′er
build′ing
bulb′ous
Bul·gar′i·an
bulge
bulg′ing
bulk′head′
bulk′y
bull′dog′
bull′doze′
bull′doz′er
bull′doz′ing
bul′let
bul′le·tin
bul′let·proof′
bull′fight′
bull′finch′
bull′frog′
bull′head′
bul′lion
(gold or silver. cf. *bouillon.*)
bull′ock
bull pen
bull′pout′
bull's′–eye′
bul′ly
bul′ly·rag′

bul′rush′
bul′wark
bum′ble·bee′
bum′boat′
bump′er
bump′kin
bump′y
bunch
bun′combe
bun′dle
bun′ga·low
bun′gle
bun′gled
bun′gling
bun′ion
bunk
bunk′er
bun′ting
buoy
buoy′age
buoy′an·cy
buoy′ant
bur′den
bur′den·some
bur′dock′
bu′reau
bu·reauc′ra·cy
bu′reau·crat
bu·rette′
bur′geon
burgh′er
bur′glar

bur′gla·ries
bur·glar′i·ous
bur′glar·ize
bur′glar·proof
bur′gla·ry
bur′go·mas′ter
Bur·gun′di·an
Bur′gun·dy
bur′i·al
bur′ied
bur′ies
bur′lap
bur·lesque′
bur′ly
Bur′mese′
burn′er
bur′nish
bur·noose′
burn′sides′
burnt
bur′ro
(donkey)
bur′row
(dig)
bur′sar
burst
bur′weed′
bur′y
(conceal. cf. *berry*.)
bur′y·ing
bush′el, *n.* and *v.*
bush′rang′er
bush′whack′er
bus′ied
bus′i·er
bus′i·est
bus′i·ly
busi′ness
busi′ness·like′
busi′ness·man′
bus′kin
bus′tle
bus′tled
bus′tling
bus′y
bus′y·bod′y
bus′y·work′
butch′er
butch′er·y
butte
but′ter
but′ter·cup′
but′ter·fat′
but′ter·fish′
but′ter·fly′
but′ter·milk′
but′ter·nut′
but′ter·scotch′
but′ter·weed′
but′ter·y
but′tock
but′ton
but′ton·hole′
but′ton·hook′
but′ton·mold′
but′ton·wood′
but′tress
bux′om
buy′er
buy′ing
buzz
buz′zard
buzz′er
buzz saw
by′–e·lec′tion
by′gone′
by′law′
by′–line′
by′pass
by′path′
by′play′
by′–prod′uct
by′road′
By·ron′ic
bys′sus
by′stand′er
by′way′
by′word′
By·zan′tine

C

ca·bal′
cab′a·lis′tic
cab′a·ret
cab′bage
cab′in
cab′i·net
cab′i·net·mak′er
cab′i·net·work′
ca′ble
ca′ble·gram
ca′bling
cab′man
ca′bo′chon′
ca·boose′
cab′ri·o·let′
cab′stand′
ca·ca′o
cach′a·lot
cache
ca·chet′
cach′in·na′tion
ca·cique′
cack′le
ca·coph′o·ny
cac′tus
(plural: *cacti*)
ca·dav′er
ca·dav′er·ous
ca′dence

ca·den′za
ca·det′
cad′mi·um
Cad′mus
ca·du′ce·us
Cae′sar
cae·su′ra
ca′fé′
caf′e·te′ri·a
caf′fe·ine
cais′son
cai′tiff
ca·jole′
ca·jol′er·y
cake′box
cake mix′er
cake pan
cake′walk′
cal′a·bash
cal′a·boose
ca·lam′i·tous
ca·lam′i·ty
cal·car′e·ous
cal′ci·fi·ca′tion
cal′ci·fy
cal′ci·mine
cal′ci·na′tion
cal·cine′
cal′ci·um

cal′cu·la·ble
cal′cu·late
cal′cu·lat′ing
cal′cu·la′tion
cal′cu·la′tor
cal′cu·lus
(plural: *calculi*)
cal′dron
cal′en·dar
(for dates)
cal′en·der
(machine)
calf
(plural: *calves*)
calf′skin′
Cal′i·ban
cal′i·ber
cal′i·brate
cal′i·co
cal′i·per
ca′liph
cal′is·then′ics
calk
call′er
cal·lig′ra·phy
call′ing
cal·los′i·ty
cal′lous, *adj.*
cal′low

cal′lus, *n.*
calm
calm′ly
calm′ness
cal′o·mel
ca·lor′ic
cal′o·rie
cal′o·ries
cal′o·rim′e·ter
ca·lum′ni·ate
ca·lum′ni·a′tion
ca·lum′ni·a′tor
cal′um·nies
ca·lum′ni·ous
cal′um·ny
Cal′va·ry
Cal′vin·ism
Cal′vin·ist
Cal′vin·is′tic
Ca·lyp′so
ca′lyx
ca′ma·ra′de·rie
cam′ber
cam′bric
cam′el
ca·mel′li·a
ca·mel′o·pard
Cam′e·lot
Cam′em·bert′
cam′e·o
cam′e·os
cam′er·a
cam′er·a·man′
cam′i·sole
cam′o·mile
Ca·mor′ra
cam′ou·flage
cam·paign′
cam′pa·ni′le
camp′fire′
camp′ground′
cam′phor
cam′pus
Ca·na′di·an
ca·naille′
ca·nal′
ca·nal′boat′
ca·nal′i·za′tion
ca′na′pé′
ca·nard′
ca·nar′ies
ca·nar′y
can′cel
can′celed
can′cel·er
can′cel·ing
can′cel·la′tion
can′cer
can′cer·ous
can′did
can′di·da·cy
can′di·date
can′did·ly
can′did·ness
can′died
can′dies
can′dle
can′dle·ber′ry
can′dle·fish′
can′dle grease
can′dle·light′
Can′dle·mas
can′dle·nut′
can′dle·pin′
candle power
can′dle shade
can′dle·stick′
can′dle·wood′
can′dor
can′dy
ca′nine
can′is·ter
can′ker
can′ker·ous
can′ker·worm′
can′ner
can′ner·y
can′ni·bal
can′ni·bal·ism
can′ni·ly
can′ni·ness
can′ning
can′non
(gun. cf. *canon.*)
can′non·ade′
can′non·eer′

can′not
ca·noe′
ca·noe′ing
ca·noes′
can′on
(rule. cf. *cannon.*)
ca·non′i·cal
can′on·ize
can′o·pies
can′o·py
can·ta′bi·le
can′ta·loupe
can·tan′ker·ous
can·ta′ta
can·teen′
cant′er
can′ti·cle
can′ti·le′ver
can′to
can′ton′
can′ton·al
Can′ton·ese′
can·ton′ment
can′tor
can′vas, *n.*
(cloth)
can′vass, *v.*
(solicit)
can′yon
ca′pa·bil′i·ties
ca′pa·bil′i·ty
ca′pa·ble
ca′pa·bly
ca·pa′cious
ca·pac′i·ty
cap′–a–pie′
ca·par′i·son
ca′per
cap′il·lar′i·ty
cap′il·lar′y
cap′i·tal
(city, property)
cap′i·tal·ism
cap′i·tal·ist
cap′i·tal·ize
cap′i·tol
(building)
ca·pit′u·late
ca·pit′u·la′tion
ca·price′
ca·pri′cious
cap·size′
cap·siz′ing
cap′stan
cap′sule
cap′tain
cap′tion
cap′tious
cap′ti·vate
cap′ti·va′tion
cap′tive
cap·tiv′i·ty
cap′tor
cap′ture
cap′tur·ing
ca′ra·ba′o
car′a·mel
car′at
(weight. cf. *caret, carrot.*)
car′a·van
car′a·van′sa·ry
car′a·vel
car′a·way
car′bide
car′bine
car·bol′ic
car′bon
car′bo·na′ceous
car′bon·ate
car·bon′ic
car′bon·if′er·ous
car′bon·ize
car′bo·run′dum
car·box′yl
car′boy
car′bun·cle
car′bu·ret′or
car′cass
car′ci·no′ma
car′da·mom
card′board′
card′case′
car′di·ac
car′di·gan
car′di·nal

car′di·nal·ate
car′di·o·graph′
car·di′tis
card′play·er
card′room
card ta′ble
card writ′er
ca·reen′
ca·reer′
care′ful
care′ful·ly
care′less
ca·ress′
car′et
(sign of insertion. cf. *carat, carrot.*)
care′worn′
car′go
car′goes
Car′ib·be′an
car′i·bou
car′i·ca·ture
car′il·lon
car·min′a·tive
car′mine
car′nage
car′nal
car·nal′i·ty
car·na′tion
car·nel′ian
car′ni·val
car·niv′o·rous
car′om
ca·rot′id
ca·rous′al
ca·rouse′
car′pen·ter
car′pen·try
car′pet
car′pet·bag′
car′pet·bag′ger
car′pet·beat′er
car′pet clean′ing
car′riage
car′ri·er
car′ri·on
car′rot
(vegetable. cf. *carat, caret.*)
car′rou·sel′
car′ry
car′ry·all′
car′ry–o′ver
cart′age
carte′ blanche′
car′tel
Car′tha·gin′i·an
car′ti·lage
car′ti·lag′i·nous
car·tog′ra·phy
car′ton
(box)
car·toon′
(picture)
car·toon′ist
car·touche′
car′tridge
carve
carv′ing
car′y·at′id
cas·cade′
case′hard′en
ca′se·in
case′mate
case′ment
ca·sern′
cash′book′
ca·shew′
cash·ier′
cash′mere
ca·si′no
cas′ket
Cas′pi·an
casque
Cas·san′dra
cas·sa′tion
cas′se·role
cas′si·a
Cas′si·o·pe′ia
cas′sock
cas′so·war′y
cast
(throw)
cas′ta·net′
cast′a·way′
caste
(social class)
cas′tel·lat′ed
cas′ti·gate

cas'ti·ga'tion
Cas·til'ian
cas'tle
cast'off'
cas'tor
cas'tra·me·ta'tion
cas'u·al
cas'u·al·ty
cas'u·ist
cas'u·ist·ry
cat'a·clysm
cat'a·comb
cat'a·falque
Cat'a·lan
cat'a·lep'sy
cat'a·lep'tic
cat'a·logue
ca·tal'pa
ca·tal'y·sis
cat'a·lyt'ic
cat'a·ma·ran'
cat'a·mount
cat'a·pult
cat'a·ract
ca·tarrh'
ca·tarrh'al
ca·tas'ta·sis
ca·tas'tro·phe
cat'a·stroph'ic
Ca·taw'ba
cat'bird'
cat'boat'
cat'call'
catch'all'
catch'er
catch'pen'ny
catch'word'
cat'e·chism
cat'e·chist
cat'e·chize
cat'e·chu'men
cat'e·gor'i·cal
cat'e·go'ry
cat'e·nar'y
cat'er–cor'nered
ca'ter·er
cat'er·pil'lar
cat'er·waul
cat'fish'
cat'gut'
ca·thar'sis
ca·thar'tic
ca·the'dral
cath'e·ter
cath'ode
cath'o·lic
ca·thol'i·cism
cath'o·lic'i·ty
ca·thol'i·cize
cat'like'
cat'nip
cat'–o'–nine'–
tails'
cat's'–eye'
cat's'–paw'
cat'tail'
cat'tle
cat'walk'
Cau·ca'sian
cau'cus
cau'dal
caul'dron
cau'li·flow'er
caus'al
cau·sal'i·ty
cau·sa'tion
caus'a·tive
cau'se·rie'
cause'way'
caus'ing
caus'tic
cau'ter·i·za'tion
cau'ter·ize
cau'ter·y
cau'tion
cau'tion·ar'y
cau'tious
cav'al·cade'
cav'a·lier'
cav'a·lier'ly
cav'al·ry
ca'va·ti'na
cav'ern
cav'ern·ous
cav'i·ar
cav'i·ties
cav'i·ty
ca·vort'
cay'man

cease
ceased
cease′less
ceas′ing
ce′dar
cede
(yield)
ced′ed
ce·dil′la
ced′ing
ceil
ceil′ing
cel′e·brant
cel′e·brate
cel′e·brat′ed
cel′e·bra′tion
cel′e·bra′tor
ce·leb′ri·ty
ce·ler′i·ty
cel′er·y
ce·les′ta
ce·les′tial
cel′i·ba·cy
cel′i·bate
cel′lar
cel′lar·age
cel′lar·er
cel′lar·et′
cel′list
cel′lo
Cel′lo·phane
cel′lu·lar
cel′lu·loid
cel′lu·lose
Cel′si·us
ce·ment′
ce′men·ta′tion
cem′e·ter′ies
cem′e·ter′y
cen′o·bite
cen′o·taph
cen′ser
(for incense)
cen′sor
(examiner)
cen·so′ri·al
cen·so′ri·ous
cen′sor·ship
cen′sur·a·ble
cen′sure
cen′sur·ing
cen′sus
cen′taur
cen·ta′vo
cen′te·nar′y
cen·ten′ni·al
cen′ter·board′
cen′ter·piece′
cen′ti·grade
cen′ti·gram
cen′ti·li′ter
cen′time
cen′ti·me′ter
cen′ti·pede
cen′tral
cen′tral·i·za′tion
cen′tral·ize
cen·trif′u·gal
cen·trip′e·tal
cen·tu′ri·on
cen′tu·ry
ce·phal′ic
ce·ram′ic
ce·ram′ics
Cer′ber·us
ce′re·al
cer′e·bel′lum
cer′e·bral
cer′e·bro·spi′nal
cer′e·mo′ni·al
cer′e·mo·nies
cer′e·mo′ni·ous
cer′e·mo′ny
Ce′res
ce·rise′
ce′ri·um
cer′tain
cer′tain·ly
cer′tain·ties
cer′tain·ty
cer·tif′i·cate
cer′ti·fi·ca′tion
cer′ti·fies
cer′ti·fy
cer′ti·fy′ing
cer′ti·o·ra′ri

cer'ti·tude
ce·ru'le·an
cer'vi·cal
cer'vix
ce'si·um
ces·sa'tion
ces'sion
(yielding)
cess'pit'
cess'pool'
chaf'finch
cha·grin'
cha·grined'
chain gang
chain mail
chain shot
chain stitch
chain'work'
chair'man
chal·ced'o·ny
cha·let'
chal'ice
chal'lenge
cham'ber
cham'ber·lain
cham'ber·maid'
cha·me'le·on
cham'fer
cham'ois
cham·pagne'
cham'per·ty
cham'pi·on
cham'pi·on·ship'
chance'ful
chan'cel
chan'cel·ler·y
chan'cel·lor
chan'cer·y
chan'de·lier'
chan'dler
chan'dler·y
change'a·bil'i·ty
change'a·ble
changed
change'less
change'ling
chang'ing
chan'nel
chan'neled
chan'nel·ing
chan'son
chan'te·relle'
chan'ti·cleer
cha'os
cha·ot'ic
chap'ar·ral'
chap'book'
cha'peau'
(plural: *chapeaux*)
chap'el
chap'er·on
chap'fall'en
chap'lain
chap'let
chap'ter
char'ac·ter
char'ac·ter·is'tic
char'ac·ter·i·za'-
tion
char'ac·ter·ize
cha·rade'
char'coal'
charge'a·ble
char'gé' d'af-
faires'
charg'ing
char'i·ot
char'i·ot·eer'
char'i·ta·ble
char'i·ties
char'i·ty
char'la·tan
Charles'ton,
S. C., W. Va.
Charles'town,
Mass.
charm'ing
char'nel
char'ter
char·treuse'
chart'room
char'wom'an
Cha·ryb'dis
chasm
chasse'pot'
chas'sis

chas′ten
chas·tise′
chas′tise·ment
chas′ti·ty
chas′u·ble
châ·teau′
(plural: *châteaux*)
chat′e·laine
chat′tel
chat′ter
chat′ter·box′
chat′ter·er
chat′ting
chauf·feur′
Chau·tau′qua
cheap′en
cheap′ened
check′book′
check′er·ber′ry
check′er·board′
check′ered
check girl
check′mate′
check′rein′
check′room
cheek′y
cheer′ful
cheer′ful·ness
cheer′less
cheer′y
cheese′cake′
cheese′cloth′
cheese knife
cheese′par′ing
chef
chef′–d'oeu′vre
chem′i·cal
che·mise′
chem′ist
chem′is·try
che·nille′
cher′ish
Cher′o·kee′
che·root′
cher′ries
cher′ry
cher′ub
(plural: *cherubs* or *cherubim*)
chess′board
chess′man
chest′nut
chev′a·lier′
Chev′i·ot
chev′ron
Chi·an′ti
chi·can′er·y
chick′a·dee
chick′en
chick′en·heart′ed
chicken pox
chick′–pea′
chick′weed′
chi′cle
chic′o·ry
chief′ly
chief′tain
chif′fon
chif′fo·nier′
chi′gnon
chil′blain′
child′bed′
child′hood
child′ish
child′less
child′like′
chil′dren
Chil′e·an
chill
chill′ing
chill′y
chi·me′ra
chi·mer′i·cal
chim′ney
chim′pan·zee′
chi′na·ber′ry
Chi′na·man
Chi′na·town′
chi′na·ware′
chin·chil′la
Chi′nese′
Chi·nook′
chip′munk
chip′ping
chi·rog′ra·phy
chi·rop′o·dist

chi'ro·prac'tor
chis'el
chis'el·er
chit'chat'
chiv'al·ric
chiv'al·rous
chiv'al·ry
chlo'ral
chlo'rate
chlo'ric
chlo'ride
chlo'rin·ate
chlo'rine
chlo'rite
chlo'ro·form
chlo'ro·phyll
chlo'rous
chock'–full'
choc'o·late
Choc'taw
choir
choke'ber'ry
choke'bore'
choke'cher'ry
choke'damp'
chok'er
chol'er
chol'er·a
chol'er·ic
choose
choos'ing
chop'house'
chop'per
chop'ping
chop'stick'
chop' su'ey
cho'ral
chord
(music. cf. *cord.*)
chore
cho·re'a
chor'is·ter
chor'tle
cho'rus
cho'sen
chow'der
chrism
chris'ten
Chris'ten·dom
Chris'tian
Chris'ti·an'i·ty
Chris'tian·ize
Christ'like'
Christ'ly
Christ'mas
Christ'mas·tide'
chro'mate
chro·mat'ic
chrome
chro'mite
chro'mi·um
chron'ic
chron'i·cle
chron'o·graph
chron'o·log'i·cal
chro·nol'o·gy
chro·nom'e·ter
chron'o·met'ric
chrys'a·lis
chrys·an'the-
mum
chrys'o·ber'yl
chrys'o·lite
chrys'o·prase
chuck'le
chuck'le·head'
chuk'ker
chum
chump
church'go'er
church'man
church'ward'en
church'yard'
churl
churl'ish
churn
chut'ney
chyle
chyme
ci·bo'ri·um
ci·ca'da
ci·ca'la
cic'a·trix
ci'der
ci'–de·vant'
ci·gar'

cig'a·rette'
ci·gar'–shaped
Cim·me'ri·an
cin·cho'na
Cin'cin·nat'i, Ohio
cinc'ture
cin'der
Cin'der·el'la
cin'e·mat'o·graph
cin'na·bar
cin'na·mon
cin'que·cen'to
cinque'foil'
ci'pher
Cir·cas'sian
Cir'ce
cir'cle
cir'cled
cir'clet
cir'cling
cir'cuit
cir·cu'i·tous
cir'cu·lar
cir'cu·lar·ize
cir'cu·late
cir'cu·la'tion
cir'cu·la'tive
cir'cu·la'tor
cir'cu·la·to'ry
cir'cum·am'bi·ent
cir'cum·cise
cir'cum·ci'sion
cir·cum'fer·ence
cir'cum·flex
cir'cum·lo·cu'-tion
cir'cum·nav'i-gate
cir'cum·scribe'
cir'cum·scrip'-tion
cir'cum·spect
cir'cum·spec'tion
cir'cum·stance
cir'cum·stan'tial
cir'cum·stan'-tial·ly
cir'cum·stan'ti-ate
cir'cum·vent'
cir'cum·vent'er
cir'cum·ven'tion
cir'cus
cir·rho'sis
cir'ro–cu'mu·lus
cir'ro–stra'tus
cis'tern
cit'a·del
ci·ta'tion
cite (quote)
cit'ies
cit'ing
cit'i·zen
cit'i·zen·ry
cit'i·zen·ship'
cit'rate
cit'ric
cit'ron
cit'ron·el'la
cit'rus
cit'y
civ'et
civ'ic
civ'il
ci·vil'ian
ci·vil'i·ty
civ'i·li·za'tion
civ'i·lize
civ'i·liz'ing
civ'il·ly
claim'ant
clair·voy'ance
clair·voy'ant
cla'mant
clam'bake'
clam'ber
clam'mi·ness
clam'my
clam'or
clam'or·ous
clam'shell'
clan·des'tine
clan'gor
clan'nish

clans′man
clap′board
clap′per
clap′trap′
claque
clar′et
clar′i·fi·ca′tion
clar′i·fied
clar′i·fy
clar′i·fy′ing
clar′i·net′
clar′i·on
clar′i·ty
clas′sic
clas′si·cal
clas′si·cism
clas′si·cist
clas′si·fi′a·ble
clas′si·fi·ca′tion
clas′si·fied
clas′si·fy
clas′si·fy′ing
class′mate′
class′room′
clat′ter
clat′tered
clause
clav′i·chord
clav′i·cle
cla′vi·er
clay′more′
clean′er
clean′ly
clean′ness
cleanse
cleans′ing
clear′ance
clear′–cut′
clear′–eyed′
clear′ing·house′
clear′ly
clear′ness
clear′–sight′ed
cleav′age
cleav′er
clem′a·tis
clem′en·cy
clem′ent
clep′sy·dra
clere′sto′ry
cler′gy
cler′gy·man
cler′ic
cler′i·cal
clev′er
clew
cli·ché′
cli′ent
cli′en·tele′
cli·mac′ter·ic
cli′mate
cli·mat′ic
cli′max
cling′stone′
clin′ic
clin′i·cal
cli·ni′cian
clink′er
clip′per
clip′ping
clique
clo·a′ca
cloak′room
clock tow′er
clock′wise′
clock′work′
clod′hop′per
clog′ging
cloi′son·né′
clois′ter
close′fist′ed
close′–hauled′
close′–lipped′
close′ness
clos′et
close′–up′
clo′sure
cloth, *n.*
clothe, *v.*
clothes′pin′
cloth′ier
cloth′ing
cloud′burst′
cloud′–clapped′
cloud′less
clout

clo′ven
clo′ven–foot′ed
clo′ver
club′bing
club′foot′
club′room
clum′si·er
clum′si·ly
clum′si·ness
clum′sy
clus′ter
clut′ter
coach′man
co·ad′ju·tant
co·ad′ju·tor
co·ag′u·late
co·ag′u·la′tion
co·ag′u·la′tive
co′a·lesce′
co′a·les′cence
co′a·les′cent
co′a·lesc′ing
coal barge
coal′bin
coal′box
coal car
coal cel′lar
coal chute
coal′deal·er
coal field
coal gas
coal hod
coal′hole′
co′a·li′tion
coal mine
coal scuttle
coal shov′el
coal tar
coal′yard′
coarse
(rough. cf. *course*.)
coars′en
coast′al
coast′er
coast guard
coast′wise′
coat′ee′
coat′room
coat′tail
co·au′thor
coax
co′balt
cob′ble·stone′
co′bra
cob′web′
co·caine′
coc′cyx
Co′chin
coch′i·neal′
cock′a·too′
cock′a·trice
cock′boat′
cock′chaf′er
cock′ney
cock′pit
cock′roach′
cock′spur′
cock′tail′
co′coa
co′co·bo′lo
co′co·nut′
co·coon′
co′de·fend′ant
co′dex
cod′fish′
cod′i·cil
cod′i·fi·ca′tion
cod′i·fied
cod′i·fy
co′ef·fi′cient
co·erce′
co·er′cion
co·er′cive
co·e′val
cof′fee
cof′fee·house′
cof′fee·pot′
cof′fer
cof′fer·dam′
cof′fin
co′gen·cy
co′gent
cog′i·tate
cog′i·ta′tion
cog′i·ta′tive
co′gnac

cog′nate
cog′ni·zance
cog′ni·zant
cog·no′men
cog′way′
cog′wheel′
co·hab′it
co·heir′
co·here′
co·her′ence
co·her′en·cy
co·her′ent
co·he′sion
co·he′sive
co′hort
coif′feur′
coif·fure′
coin
(money)
coin′age
co′in·cide′
co·in′ci·dence
co·in′ci·den′tal
co′in·sure′
co·i′tion
col′an·der
cold′–blood′ed
cold chisel
cold cream
cold′proof
co′le·op′ter·ous
col′ic
col′ic·root′
col′ic·weed′
co·li′tis
col·lab′o·rate
col·lab′o·ra′tion
col·lab′o·ra′tor
col·lapse′
col·lapsed′
col·laps′i·ble
col′lar
col′lar·band′
col′lar·bone′
col′lar but′ton
col·late′
col·lat′ing
col·lat′er·al
col·la′tion
col′league, *n.*
col·league′, *v.*
col·lect′
col·lect′ed
col·lect′i·ble
col·lec′tion
col·lec′tive
col·lec′tive·ly
col·lec′tor
col′lege
col·le′gi·ate
col·lide′
col′lie
col′lier
col′lier·y
col·li′sion
col·lo′di·on
col′loid
col′lop
col·lo′qui·al
col·lo′qui·al·ism
col·lo′qui·al·ly
col′lo·quy
col·lu′sion
col·lu′sive
co·logne′
co′lon
colo′nel
colo′nel·cy
co·lo′ni·al
col′o·nies
col′o·nist
col′o·ni·za′tion
col′o·nize
col′on·nade′
col′o·ny
col′o·phon
col′or
col′or·a′tion
col′o·ra·tu′ra
col′or–blind′
col′ored
col′or·less
co·los′sal
Col′os·se′um
co·los′sus
col′umn

co·lum′nar
col′um·nist
co′ma
com′a·tose
com′bat
com′bat·ant
com′bat·ing
com′ba·tive
com′bi·na′tion
com·bine′
com·bin′ing
com·bus′ti·ble
com·bus′tion
co·me′di·an
co·me′di·enne′
com′e·dies
com′e·dy
come′li·ness
come′ly
co·mes′ti·ble
com′et
com′fit
com′fort
com′fort·a·ble
com′fort·er
com′ic
com′i·cal
com′ing
com′i·ty
com′ma
com·mand′
com′man·dant′
com′man·deer′
com·mand′er
com·mand′ing
com·mand′ment
com·man′do
com·man′dos
com·mem′o·rate
com·mem′o·ra′-
tion
com·mem′o·ra′-
tive
com·mence′
com·mence′ment
com·menc′ing
com·mend′
com·mend′a·ble
com′men·da′tion
com·mend′a·to′ry
com·men′su·ra-
bil′i·ty
com·men′su·ra-
ble
com·men′su·rate
com·men′su-
rate·ly
com′ment
com′men·tar′y
com′men·ta′tor
com′merce
com·mer′cial
com·mer′cial·ize
com·mer′cial-
ized
com·min′gle
com′mi·nu′tion
com·mis′er·ate
com·mis′er·a′-
tion
com′mis·sar′i·at
com′mis·sar′y
com·mis′sion
com·mis′sion-
aire′
com·mis′sion·er
com·mit′
com·mit′ment
com·mit′ted
com·mit′tee
com·mit′ting
com·mode′
com·mo′di·ous
com·mod′i·ties
com·mod′i·ty
com′mo·dore′
com′mon
com′mon·al·ty
com′mon·er
com′mon·place′
common sense, *n.*
com′mon–sense′, *adj.*
com′mon·wealth′
com·mo′tion
com′mu·nal
com′mune, *n.*
com·mu′ni·ca·ble

com·mu'ni·cant
com·mu'ni·cate
com·mu'ni·cat'-
ing
com·mu'ni·ca'-
tion
com·mu'ni·ca'-
tive
com·mu'ni·ca'tor
com·mun'ion
com·mu'ni·qué'
com'mu·nism
com'mu·nist
com·mu'ni·ties
com·mu'ni·ty
com'mu·ta'tion
com'mu·ta'tor
com·mute'
com·mut'er
com·pact', *v.*
and *adj.*
com'pact, *n.*
com·pan'ion
com·pan'ion·a·ble
com·pan'ion·ship
com·pan'ion-
way'
com'pa·nies
com'pa·ny
com'pa·ra·ble
com·par'a·tive
com·pare'
com·par'ing
com·par'i·son
com·part'ment
com'pass
com·pas'sion
com·pas'sion·ate
com·pat'i·bil'i·ty
com·pat'i·ble
com·pa'tri·ot
com·peer'
com·pel'
com·pelled'
com·pel'ling
com·pen'di·ous
com·pen'di·um
com'pen·sate
com'pen·sa'tion
com'pen·sa'tive
com·pen'sa·to'ry
com·pete'
com'pe·tence
com'pe·ten·cy
com'pe·tent
com·pet'ing
com'pe·ti'tion
com·pet'i·tive
com·pet'i·tor
com'pi·la'tion
com·pile'
com·pil'er
com·pla'cence
com·pla'cen·cy
com·pla'cent
com·plain'
com·plain'ant
com·plaint'
com·plai'sant
com'ple·ment
(full quantity.
cf. *compliment.*)
com'ple·men'tal
com'ple·men'ta-
ry
com·plete'
com·ple'tion
com·plex', *adj.*
com'plex, *n.*
com·plex'ion
com·plex'ioned
com·plex'i·ty
com·pli'ance
com·pli'ant
com'pli·cate
com'pli·ca'tion
com·plic'i·ty
com·plied'
com'pli·ment
(flatter. cf.
complement.)
com'pli·men'-
ta·ry
com·ply'
com·ply'ing
com·po'nent
com·port'
com·port'ment
com·pose'

com·posed′
com·pos′er
com·pos′ite
com·pos′ite·ly
com′po·si′tion
com·pos′i·tor
com′post
com·po′sure
com′pound, *n.*
com·pound′, *v.*
com′pre·hend′
com′pre·hen′si-
ble
com′pre·hen′-
sion
com′pre·hen′-
sive
com′press, *n.*
com·press′, *v.*
com·pressed′
com·press′i·ble
com·pres′sion
com·pres′sor
com·prise′
com′pro·mise
Comp·tom′e·ter
comp·trol′ler
com·pul′sion
com·pul′so·ry
com·punc′tion
com·put′a·ble
com′pu·ta′tion
com·pute′
com·put′ing
com′rade
con·cat′e·na′tion
con′cave
con·cav′i·ty
con·ceal′
conceal′ment
con·cede′
con·ced′ed
con·ced′ing
con·ceit′
con·ceit′ed
con·ceiv′a·ble
con·ceive′
con′cen·trate
con′cen·trat·ing
con′cen·tra′tion
con′cen·tra′tor
con·cen′tric
con′cept
con·cep′tion
con·cern′
con′cert, *n.*
con·cert′, *v.*
con′cer·ti′na
con·cer′to
con·ces′sion
con·ces′sion·aire′
conch
con′ci·erge
con·cil′i·ate
con·cil′i·a′tion
con·cil′i·a·to′ry
con·cise′
con′clave
con·clude′
con·clud′ing
con·clu′sion
con·clu′sive
con·coct′
con·coc′tion
con·com′i·tant
con′cord
con·cord′ance
con·cor′dat
con′course
con′crete
con′crete·ly
con′cu·bine
con·cur′
con·curred′
con·cur′rence
con·cur′rent
con·cur′ring
con·cus′sion
con·demn′
con′dem·na′tion
con·dem′na·to′ry
con·demned′
con·demn′ing
con′den·sa′tion
con·dense′
con·dens′er

con·dens′ing
con′de·scend′
con′de·scend′-
ing·ly
con′de·scen′sion
con·dign′
con′di·ment
con·di′tion
con·di′tion·al
con·di′tioned
con·dole′
con·do′lence
con′do·na′tion
con·done′
con′dor
con·duce′
con·du′cive
con′duct, *n.*
con·duct′, *v.*
con·duc′tion
con·duc′tor
con′duit
cone′–shaped′
con·fec′tion
con·fec′tion·er
con·fec′tion·er′y
con·fed′er·a·cy
con·fed′er·ate
con·fed′er·a′tion
con·fer′
con′fer·ee′
con′fer·ence

con·ferred′
con·fer′ring
con·fess′
con·fess′ed·ly
con·fes′sion
con·fes′sion·al
con·fes′sor
con·fet′ti
con′fi·dant′
(friend)
con·fide′
con·fid′ed
con′fi·dence
con′fi·dent
(sure)
con′fi·den′tial
con·fid′ing
con·fig′u·ra′tion
con′fine, *n.*
con·fine′, *v.*
con·fine′ment
con·fin′ing
con·firm′
con′fir·ma′tion
con′fis·cate
con′fis·cat·ing
con′fis·ca′tion
con·fis′ca·to′ry
con′fla·gra′tion
con′flict, *n.*
con·flict′, *v.*
con·flic′tion

con′flu·ence
con·form′
con·form′a·ble
con′for·ma′tion
con·form′ist
con·form′i·ty
con·found′
con·found′ed·ly
con′fra·ter′ni·ty
con·front′
con′fron·ta′tion
Con·fu′cian
con·fuse′
con·fus′ed·ly
con·fus′ing
con·fu′sion
con′fu·ta′tion
con·fute′
con·geal′
con′ge·ner
con·gen′ial
con·ge′ni·al′i·ty
con·gen′i·tal
con′ger eel
con·gest′
con·ges′tion
con·glom′er·ate
con·glom′er·a′-
tion
con·grat′u·late
con·grat′u·la′-
tion

con·grat′u·la-
to′ry
con′gre·gate
con′gre·ga′tion
con′gre·ga′tion-
al
con′gress
con·gres′sion·al
con′gress·man
con·gru′i·ty
con′gru·ous
con′ic
con′i·cal
co′ni·fer
co·nif′er·ous
con·jec′tur·al
con·jec′ture
con′ju·gal
con′ju·gate
con′ju·ga′tion
con·junc′tion
con′junc·ti′va
con·junc′ture
con·jure′
con′jur·er
con·nect′
con·nect′ed·ly
con·nec′tion
con·nec′tive
con·niv′ance
con·nive′
con′nois·seur′

con′no·ta′tion
con·not′a·tive
con·note′
con·nu′bi·al
con′quer
con′quered
con′quer·ing
con′quer·or
con′quest
con′san·guin′-
e·ous
con′san·guin′i·ty
con′science
con′science·less
con′sci·en′tious
con′scious
con′scious·ness
con′script
con·scrip′tion
con′se·crate
con′se·cra′tion
con·sec′u·tive
con·sen′sus
con·sent′
con′se·quence
con′se·quent
con′se·quen′tial
con′se·quent·ly
con′ser·va′tion
con·serv′a·tism
con·serv′a·tive
con·serv′a·to′ry

con·serve′
con·serv′ing
con·sid′er
con·sid′er·a·ble
con·sid′er·ate
con·sid′er·a′tion
con·sign′
con′sign·ee′
con·sign′ment
con·sign′or
con·sist′
con·sist′en·cy
con·sist′ent
con·sis′to·ry
con′so·la′tion
con·sol′a·to′ry
con·sole′
con·sol′i·date
con·sol′i·da′tion
con·sol′ing
con′som·mé′
con′so·nance
con′so·nant
con′so·nan′tal
con′sort, *n.*
con·sort′, *v.*
con·spec′tus
con·spic′u·ous
con·spir′a·cy
con·spir′a·tor
con·spire′
con·spir′ing

con′sta·ble
con·stab′u·lar′y
con′stan·cy
con′stant
con′stel·la′tion
con′ster·na′tion
con′sti·pa′tion
con·stit′u·en·cy
con·stit′u·ent
con′sti·tute
con′sti·tu′tion
con′sti·tu′tion·al
con′sti·tu′tion-
al′i·ty
con′sti·tu′tion-
al·ly
con·strain′
con·strained′
con·straint′
con·strict′
con·stric′tion
con·stric′tor
con·struct′
con·struc′tion
con·struc′tive
con·strue′
con·strued′
con·stru′ing
con′sul
con′su·lar
con′su·late
con·sult′
con·sult′ant
con′sul·ta′tion
con·sume′
con·sum′ed·ly
con·sum′ing
con·sum′mate,
adj.
con′sum·mate, *v.*
con′sum·ma′tion
con·sump′tion
con·sump′tive
con′tact
con·ta′gion
con·ta′gious
con·tain′er
con·tam′i·nate
con·tam′i·na′tion
con′tem·plate
con′tem·plat·ing
con′tem·pla′tion
con·tem′pla·tive
con·tem′po·ra′-
ne·ous
con·tem′po·rar′y
con·tempt′
con·tempt′i·ble
con·temp′tu·ous
con·tend′
con·tent′, *adj.*
con′tent, *n.*
con·ten′tion
con·ten′tious
con·tent′ment
con′test, *n.*
con·test′, *v.*
con·test′ant
con′tes·ta′tion
con′text
con·tex′tu·al
con·tex′ture
con′ti·gu′i·ty
con·tig′u·ous
con′ti·nence
con′ti·nent
con′ti·nen′tal
con·tin′gen·cy
con·tin′gent
con·tin′u·al
con·tin′u·ance
con·tin′u·a′tion
con·tin′ue
con·tin′u·ing
con′ti·nu′i·ty
con·tin′u·ous
con·tort′
con·tor′tion
con·tor′tion·ist
con′tour
con′tra·band
con′tra·bass′
con′tract, *n.*
con·tract′, *v.*
con·tract′ed
con·trac′tion

con·trac′tor
con′tra·dict′
con′tra·dic′tion
con′tra·dic′to-
ri·ly
con′tra·dic′to·ry
con′tra·dis·tinc′-
tion
con′tra·in′di·cant
con′tra·in′di·cate
con·tral′to
con′tra·pun′tal
con′tra·ri·ness
con′tra·ri·wise′
con′tra·ry
con·trast′
con′tra·vene′
con′tra·ven′tion
con′tre·danse′
con′tre·temps′
con·trib′ute
con′tri·bu′tion
con·trib′u·tor
con·trib′u·to′ry
con′trite
con·tri′tion
con·triv′ance
con·trive′
con·triv′ing
con·trol′
con·trolled′
con·trol′ler
con·trol′ling
con′tro·ver′sial
con′tro·ver′sy
con′tro·vert
con′tu·ma′cious
con′tu·ma·cy
con′tu·me′li·ous
con′tu·me′ly
con·tuse′
con·tu′sion
co·nun′drum
con′va·lesce′
con′va·les′cence
con′va·les′cent
con′va·lesc′ing
con·vec′tion
con·vene′
con·ven′ience
con·ven′ient
con′vent
con·ven′ti·cle
con·ven′tion
con·ven′tion·al
con·ven′tion·al′-
i·ty
con·ven′tu·al
con·verge′
con·ver′gence
con·verg′ing
con′ver·sant
con′ver·sa′tion
con′ver·sa′tion·al
con′ver·sa′tion-
al·ist
con′verse, *n.*
con·verse′, *v.*
con·vers′ing
con·ver′sion
con′vert, *n.*
con·vert′, *v.*
con·vert′i·ble
con′vex
con·vex′i·ty
con·vey′
con·vey′ance
con·vey′ing
con′vict, *n.*
con·vict′, *v.*
con·vic′tion
con·vince′
con·vinc′ing·ly
con·viv′i·al
con·viv′i·al′i·ty
con′vo·ca′tion
con·voke′
con′vo·lu′tion
con·vol′vu·lus
con′voy, *n.*
con·voy′, *v.*
con·voyed′
con·voy′ing
con·vulse′
con·vul′sion
con·vul′sive

cook′er·y
cool′er
cool′ie
(laborer)
cool′ly
(coldly)
coon′skin′
coop′er
coop′er·age
co–op′er·ate
co–op′er·a′tion
co–op′er·a′tive
co–opt′
co–or′di·nate
Co·per′ni·can
co′pi·ous
cop′per
cop′per·as
cop′per–col′ored
cop′per·head′
cop′per·plate′
cop′per·smith′
cop′per·ware′
cop′pice
cop′ra
cop′u·la′tive
cop′y
cop′y·book′
cop′y·hold′er
cop′y·ing
cop′y·ist
cop′y·right′

co′quet·ry
co·quette′
cor′al
cor′al·line
cord
(string. cf. *chord.*)
cord′age
cor′dial
cor·dial′i·ty
cor′don
Cor′do·van
cor′du·roy
co′re·spond′ent
(legal term. cf. *correspondent.*)
Co·rin′thi·an
cork′–lined′
cork′screw′
cork′wood′
cor′mo·rant
corn bread
corn′cob′
cor′ner
cor′ner·stone′
cor′ner·wise′
cor′net
cor·net′tist
corn′field′
cor′nice
corn pone
corn′stalk′
corn′starch′

cor′nu·co′pi·a
co·rol′la
cor′ol·lar′y
co·ro′na
cor′o·nach
cor′o·na′tion
cor′o·ner
cor′o·net
cor′po·ral
cor′po·rate
cor′po·ra′tion
cor·po′re·al
corps
corpse
cor′pu·lence
cor′pu·lent
cor′pus
cor′pus·cle
cor·ral′
cor·rect′
cor·rec′tion
cor·rec′tive
cor·rec′tor
cor′re·late
cor′re·la′tion
cor·rel′a·tive
cor′re·spond′
cor′re·spond′-
ence
cor′re·spond′ent
(writer of letters. cf. *corespondent.*)

cor′ri·dor
cor·rob′o·rate
cor·rob′o·ra′tion
cor·rob′o·ra′tive
cor·rode′
cor·ro′sive
cor′ru·gate
cor′ru·ga′tion
cor·rupt′
cor·rupt′i·ble
cor·rup′tion
cor·sage′
cor′sair
corse′let
cor′set
cor·tege′
co·run′dum
cor′us·cate
cor′us·ca′tion
cor′vée′
cor·vette′
co·ry′za
cos·met′ic
cos′mic
cos·mog′o·ny
cos·mol′o·gy
cos′mo·pol′i·tan
cos·mop′o·lite
cos′mos
Cos′sack
cos′tume, *n.*
cos·tume′, *v.*
cos·tum′er
co′te·rie
cot′tage
cot′ton
cot′ton·tail′
cot′ton·wood′
cou′gar
cou·lomb′
coun′cil
(assembly)
coun′cil·man
coun′ci·lor
coun′sel
(advice)
coun′se·lor
coun′te·nance
coun′ter·act′
coun′ter·bal′-
ance, *n.*
coun′ter·bal′-
ance, *v.*
coun′ter·claim′
coun′ter·clock′-
wise′
coun′ter·feit
coun′ter·feit′er
coun′ter·foil′
coun′ter·ir′ri·tant
coun′ter·mand′
coun′ter·pane′
coun′ter·part′
coun′ter·point′
coun′ter·sign′
count′ess
coun′ties
count′ing·house′
coun′tries
coun′try
coun′try·man
coun′try·side′
coun′ty
coup′ d′é′tat′
cou′pé′
cou′ple
cou′pler
cou′plet
cou′pling
cou′pon
cour′age
cou·ra′geous
cour′i·er
course
(way. cf. *coarse.*)
cour′te·ous
cour′te·san
cour′te·sy
court′house′
cour′ti·er
court′–mar′tial
court′room
court′ship
court′yard′
cous′in
cous′in–ger′man

cov'e·nant
Cov'en·try
cov'er
cov'er·age
cov'ered
cov'er·let
cov'ert
cov'er·ture
cov'et·ous
cov'ey
cow'ard
cow'ard·ice
cow barn
cow'bell'
cow'bird'
cow'boy'
cow'catch'er
cow'herd'
cow'hide'
co–work'er
cow'path
cow'pox'
cow'shed
cow'slip
cox'comb'
cox'swain
coy'ly
coy'ote
crab apple
crab grass
crack'er
crack'le

cra'dle
craft'i·ly
crafts'man
cram
crammed
cram'ming
cran'ber'ry
cra'ni·al
cra'ni·um
crank'i·ness
crank'y
cran'ny
cra'ter
cra·vat'
cra'ven
Cra'ven·ette'
crav'ing
cray'fish'
cray'on
cra'zi·ly
cra'zi·ness
cra'zy
creak
(sound)
cream–col'ored
cream'er·y
cre·ate'
cre·a'tion
cre·a'tive
cre·a'tor
crea'ture
cre'dence

cre·den'tial
cred'i·bil'i·ty
cred'i·ble
cred'it
cred'it·a·ble
cred'i·tor
cre'do
cre'dos
cre·du'li·ty
cred'u·lous
creek
(water)
cre'mate
cre·ma'tion
cre'ma·to'ry
Cre·mo'na
cre'o·sote
crepe
cre·pus'cu·lar
cre·scen'do
cre·scen'dos
cres'cent
crest'fall'en
Cre'tan
cre·tonne'
cre·vasse'
crev'ice
crib'bage
crib'work'
crick'et
cried
cri'er

Cri·me'an
crim'i·nal
crim'i·nal'i·ty
crim'i·nal·ly
crim'i·nol'o·gy
crim'son
cringe
cring'ing
crin'kle
crin'o·line
crip'ple
crip'pled
crip'pling
cri'ses, *pl.*
cri'sis
criss'cross'
cri·te'ri·on
crit'ic
crit'i·cal
crit'i·cism
crit'i·cize
cri·tique'
Cro·a'tian
cro·chet'
crock'er·y
croc'o·dile
cro'cus
Croe'sus
croon'er
cro·quet'
cro·quette'

cro'sier
cross'bar'
cross'bow'
cross'cut'
cross'–ex·am'ine
cross'–grained'
cross'ing
cross'o'ver
cross'–ques'tion
cross reference
cross'road'
cross sec'-
tion, *n.*
cross–sec'-
tion, *adj.*
cross'trees'
cross'walk'
cross'wise'
crotch'et
crotch'et·y
crou'pi·er
crou·ton'
crow'bar'
cru'cial
cru'ci·ble
cru'ci·fied
cru'ci·fix
cru'ci·fix'ion
cru'ci·form
cru'ci·fy
cru'di·ty

cru'el
cru'el·ly
cru'el·ty
cru'et
cruis'er
crul'ler
crum'ble
crum'bling
crum'pet
crum'ple
crum'pling
crunch'ing
crup'per
cru·sade'
crus·ta'ceous
crux
cry
(cried, cries)
cry'ing
crypt
cryp'tic
cryp'to·gram
crys'tal
crys'tal·line
crys'tal·li·za'tion
crys'tal·lize
cu'bic
cu'bi·cal
cu'bi·cle
cu'bit
cuck'old

cuck′oo
cu′cum·ber
cud′dle
cudg′el
cui·rass′
cui·sine′
cu′li·nar′y
cul′mi·nate
cul′mi·na′tion
cul′pa·bil′i·ty
cul′pa·ble
cul′prit
cul′ti·vate
cul′ti·va′tion
cul′ti·va′tor
cul′tur·al
cul′ture
cul′vert
cum′ber·some
cum′brous
cu′mu·la′tive
cu′mu·lus
cu·ne′i·form
cun′ning·ly
cup′bear′er
cup′board
cu′pel
cup′ful
cu·pid′i·ty
cu′po·la
cup′–shaped′

cur′a·ble
cu′ra·çao′
cu′rate
cur′a·tive
cu·ra′tor
curb′stone′
cur′dle
cu·rette′
cur′few
cu′ri·o
cu′ri·os
cu′ri·os′i·ty
cu′ri·ous
curl′i·cue
curl′i·ness
cur′rant
(berry)
cur′rent
(prevalent)
cur·ric′u·lum
cur′ried
cur′ry
cur′ry·comb′
cur′sive
cur′so·ry
cur·tail′
cur′tain
cur′va·ture
curve
curv′ing
cush′ion

cus′pi·dor
cus′tard
cus·to′di·an
cus′to·dy
cus′tom
cus′tom·ar′y
cus′tom·er
cus′tom·house′
cut′a·way′
cu′ti·cle
cut′lass
cut′ler
cut′let
cut′off′
cut′out′
cut′purse′
cut′–rate′
cut′throat′
cut′tle·fish′
cut′wa′ter
cut′worm′
cy′an·am′ide
cy·an′ic
cy′an·ide
cy·an′o·gen
cy′a·no′sis
cy′cle
cy′cloid
cy′clone
cy′clo·pe′di·a
Cy′clops

cy′clo·ra′ma
cyg′net
cyl′in·der
cy·lin′dri·cal
cym′bal
(musical. cf. *symbol.*)
cyn′ic
cyn′i·cal
cyn′i·cism
cy′no·sure
cy′press
cyst
cyst′ic
cyst′oid
czar
czar′e·vitch
cza·ri′na
Czech

D

dab′ble
da ca′po
dachs′hund′
da·coit′
da′cron
dac′tyl
Daed′a·lus
daf′fo·dil
dag′ger
da·guerre′o·type
dahl′ia
dai′lies
dai′ly
dain′ties
dain′ti·ly
dain′ti·ness
dain′ty
dair′ies
dair′y
da′is
dai′sies
dai′sy
dal′li·ance
Dal·ma′tian
dam′age
dam′a·scene′
dam′ask
dammed
(blocked)
dam′ming
dam′na·ble
dam·na′tion
damned
(cursed)
damn′ing
Dam′o·cles
damp′en
damp′er
dam′sel
dance
danc′ing
dan′de·li′on
dan′druff
dan′ger
dan′ger·ous
dan′gle
Dan′ish
dan′seuse′
dare′dev′il
dark′en
dark horse
dark′ness
dark′room′
dar′ling
Dar·win′i·an
dash′board′
das′tard·ly
da′ta, *pl.*
(sing.: *datum*)
date

dat′ed
dat′ing
da′tum
(plural: *data*)
daugh′ter
daugh′ter–in–law′
daunt′less·ly
dau′phin
dav′it
daw′dle
day′book′
day′break′
day coach
day′dream′
day letter
day′light′
day′star′
day′time′
daz′zle
dea′con
dead′en
dead′eye′
dead′fall′
dead′head′
dead′light′
deadline
dead′li·ness
dead′lock′
deaf′–mute′
dearth
death′bed′
death′blow′
death′less
death′like′
death′ly
death mask
death's′–head′
death warrant
death′watch′
de·ba′cle
de·base′
de·bat′a·ble
de·bate′
de·bauch′
de·bauch′er·y
de·ben′ture
de·bil′i·tate
de·bil′i·ty
deb′it
deb′o·nair′
de·bris′
debt′or
de·but′
dec′ade
de·ca′dence
de·ca′dent
dec′a·gon
de·cal′co·ma′ni·a
Dec′a·logue
de·camp′
de·cant′
de·cant′er
de·cath′lon
de·cay′
de·cayed′
de·cease′
de·ce′dent
de·ceit′ful
de·ceive′
de·cem′vir
de′cen·cy
de′cent
de·cen′tral·ize
de·cep′tion
de·cep′tive
de·cide′
de·cid′ed
de·cid′u·ous
dec′i·mal
dec′i·mate
de·ci′pher
de·ci′sion
de·ci′sive
de·claim′
dec′la·ma′tion
de·clam′a·to′ry
dec′la·ra′tion
de·clar′a·tive
de·clare′
de·clen′sion
dec′li·na′tion
de·cline′
de·cliv′i·ty
de·coc′tion
dé·col′le·té

de′com·pose′
de′com·po·si′tion
dec′o·rate
dec′o·ra′tion
dec′o·ra′tive
dec′o·ra′tor
dec′o·rous
de·co′rum
de·coy′
de·coyed′
de·coy′ing
de·crease′
de·cree′
de·cree′ing
de·crep′it
de′cre·scen′do
de·cry′
ded′i·cate
ded′i·ca′tion
de·duce′
de·duc′i·ble
de·duc′ing
de·duct′
de·duc′tion
de·duc′tive
deep′en
deer hide
deer′hound′
deer′meat
deer′skin′
de·face′
de·fac′ing

de fac′to
de·fal′cate
de′fal·ca′tion
def′a·ma′tion
de·fam′a·to′ry
de·fame′
de·fault′er
de·feat′
de·fect′
de·fec′tion
de·fec′tive
de·fence′
de·fend′
de·fend′ant
de·fense′
de·fen′si·ble
de·fen′sive
de·fer′
def′er·ence
def′er·en′tial (respectful. cf. *differential.*)
de·ferred′
de·fer′ring
de·fi′ance
de·fi′ant
de·fi′cien·cy
de·fi′cient
def′i·cit
de·fied′
de·file′
de·file′ment

de·fin′a·ble
de·fine′
def′i·nite
def′i·ni′tion
de·fin′i·tive
de·flate′
de·flect′
de·flec′tion
de·form′
de′for·ma′tion
de·form′i·ty
de·fraud′
de·fray′
de·frayed′
de·fray′ing
de·funct′
de·fy′
de·fy′ing
de·gen′er·a·cy
de·gen′er·ate
de′gen·er·a′tion
deg′ra·da′tion
de·grade′
de·gree′
de·hy′drate
deign
de′ist
de′i·ties
de′i·ty
de·ject′ed
de·jec′tion
de ju′re

Del′a·ware
le·lay′
le·layed′
le-lay′ing
le·lec′ta·ble
le′lec·ta′tion
lel′e·gate
lel′e·ga′tion
le·lete′
lel′e·te′ri·ous
le·le′tion
lelft′ware′
le·lib′er·ate
e·lib′er·a′tion
e·lib′er·a′tive
lel′i·ca·cies
lel′i·ca·cy
lel′i·cate
lel′i·ca·tes′sen
e·li′cious
e·light′
e·light′ful
e·lin′e·ate
e·lin′e·a′tion
e·lin′e·a′tor
e·lin′quen·cy
e·lin′quent
el′i·quesce′
el′i·ques′cent
e·lir′i·ous
e·lir′i·um
e·liv′er
de·liv′er·ance
de·liv′er·ies
de·liv′er·y
de·lude′
del′uge
de·lu′sion
de luxe′
delve
delv′ing
de·mag′net·ize
dem′a·gogue
de·mand′
de′mar·ca′tion
de·mean′
de·mean′or
de·ment′ed
de·men′ti·a
de·mer′it
de·mesne′
dem′i·god′
dem′i·john
dem′i·lune′
dem′i·monde
de·mise′
dem′i·tasse′
de·mo′bi·lize
de·moc′ra·cy
dem′o·crat
dem′o·crat′ic
de·mol′ish
dem′o·li′tion
de′mon
de·mon′e·ti·za′-
tion
de·mon′e·tize
de·mon′ic
de·mon′stra·ble
dem′on·strate
dem′on·stra′tion
de·mon′stra·tive
dem′on·stra′tor
de·mor′al·ize
demount′a·ble
de·mur′
(delay)
de·mure′
(modest)
de·mur′rage
de·murred′
de·mur′rer
de·mur′ring
de·na′ture
de·ni′al
de·nied′
de·nies′
den′im
den′i·zen
de·nom′i·na′tion
de·nom′i·na′tor
de·note′
de·noue′ment
de·nounce′
de·nounc′ing
den′si·ty

den'tal
den'ti·frice
den'tist
den'tist·ry
de·nude'
de·nun'ci·a'tion
de·nun'ci·a·to'ry
de·ny'
de·o'dor·ant
de·o'dor·ize
de·part'
de·part'ment
de'part·men'tal
de·par'ture
de·pend'a·ble
de·pend'en·cy
de·pend'ent
de·pict'
de·pic'tion
de·pil'a·to'ry
de·plete'
de·ple'tion
de·plor'a·ble
de·plore'
de·ploy'
de·po'nent
de·pop'u·late
de·port'
de'por·ta'tion
de·port'ment
de·pose'
de·pos'it
de·pos'i·tar'y
dep'o·si'tion
de·pos'i·tor
de·pos'i·to'ry
de'pot
dep'ra·va'tion
(corruption)
de·prave'
de·prav'i·ty
dep're·cate
dep're·ca'tion
dep're·ca·to'ry
de·pre'ci·ate
de·pre'ci·a'tion
dep're·da'tion
de·press'
de·pressed'
de·pres'sion
dep'ri·va'tion
(loss)
de·prive'
dep'u·ta'tion
de·pute'
dep'u·ties
dep'u·tize
dep'u·ty
de·rail'
de·range'
de·range'ment
der'e·lict
der'e·lic'tion
de·ride'
de·ri'sion
de·ri'sive
de·ri'so·ry
der'i·va'tion
de·riv'a·tive
de·rive'
der'ma·tol'o·gy
de·rog'a·to'ry
der'rick
der'vish
des'cant, *n.*
des·cant', *v.*
de·scend'
de·scend'ant
de·scent'
de·scrib'a·ble
de·scribe'
de·scrip'tion
de·scrip'tive
des'e·crate
des'ert, *n*
(dry country.
cf. *dessert.*)
de·sert', *v.*
(leave)
de·ser'tion
de·serve'
de·serv'ed·ly
de·serv'ing
des'ic·cate
des'ic·ca'tion
des'ic·ca'tor

de·sid'er·a'ta, *pl.*
de·sid'er·a'tum
de·sign'
les'ig·nate
les'ig·na'tion
le·sign'ed·ly
le·sign'er
le·sir'a·bil'i·ty
le·sir'a·ble
le·sire'
le·sir'ous
le·sist'
Des Moines, Iowa
les'o·late
les'o·la'tion
le·spair'
les'per·a'do
les'per·a'dos
les'per·ate
les'per·a'tion
les'pi·ca·ble
le·spise'
le·spite'
le·spoil'
le·spond'
le·spond'en·cy
le·spond'ent
les'pot
es·pot'ic
es·pot'i·cal
es'pot·ism

des·sert'
(food. cf. *desert.*)
des'ti·na'tion
des'tine
des'ti·nies
des'ti·ny
des'ti·tute
des'ti·tu'tion
de·stroy'
de·struct'i·ble
de·struc'tion
de·struc'tive
des'ue·tude
des'ul·to'ry
de·tach'
de·tach'ment
de·tail'
de·tain'
de·tect'
de·tec'tion
de·tec'tive
de·tec'tor
de·ten'tion
de·ter'
de·ter'gent
de·te'ri·o·rate
de·te'ri·o·ra'tion
de·ter'mi·na·ble
de·ter'mi·nant
de·ter'mi·nate
de·ter'mi·na'tion
de·ter'mine

de·ter'min·ism
de·terred'
de·ter'rent
de·ter'ring
de·test'
de·test'a·ble
de'tes·ta'tion
de·throne'
det'i·nue
det'o·nate
det'o·na'tion
det'o·na'tor
de·tract'
de·trac'tion
det'ri·ment
det'ri·men'tal
Deu'ter·on'o·my
dev'as·tate
dev'as·ta'tion
de·vel'op
de·vel'oped
de·vel'op·ing
de·vel'op·ment
de'vi·ate
de'vi·a'tion
de·vice', *n.*
dev'il·fish'
dev'il·ish
dev'il·ment
de'vi·ous
de·vise', *v.*
de·void'

de·volve′
de·volv′ing
de·vote′
dev′o·tee′
de·vo′tion
de·vo′tion·al
de·vour′
de·vout′
dew′ber′ry
dew′drop′
dew′lap′
dew point
dew′y
dex′ter
dex·ter′i·ty
dex′ter·ous
dex′trose
dhow
di′a·be′tes
di′a·bet′ic
di·a′ble·rie
di′a·bol′i·cal
di·ab′o·lism
di′a·crit′i·cal
di′a·dem
di·aer′e·sis
di′ag·nose′
di′ag·no′sis
di′ag·nos′tic
di′ag·nos·ti′cian
di·ag′o·nal
di′a·gram
di′a·gram·mat′ic
di′al
di′a·lect
di′a·lec′tic
di′aled
di′al·ing
di′a·logue
di·am′e·ter
di′a·met′ric
di′a·mond
di′a·pa′son
di′a·per
di·aph′a·nous
di′a·phragm
di′ar·rhe′a
di′a·ries
di′a·ry
di′a·ton′ic
di′a·tribe
di·chot′o·my
dic′ta, *pl.*
Dic′ta·phone
dic′tate
dic·ta′tion
dic·ta′tor
dic′ta·to′ri·al
dic′tion
dic′tion·ar′ies
dic′tion·ar′y
dic′tum
(plural: *dicta*)
di·dac′tic
die cut′ter
died
(perished. cf. *dyed.*)
di′e·lec′tric
die′mak′er
die′sel
di′et
di′e·tar′y
di′e·tet′ic
di′e·tet′ics
dif′fer
dif′fer·ence
dif′fer·ent
dif′fer·en′tial
(change. cf. *deferential.*)
dif′fer·en′ti·ate
dif′fer·en′ti·a′-
tion
dif′fi·cult
dif′fi·cul·ties
dif′fi·cul·ty
dif′fi·dence
dif′fi·dent
dif·frac′tion
dif·fuse′
dif·fu′sion
di′gest, *n.*
di·gest′, *v.*
di·gest′i·ble
di·ges′tion

di·ges′tive
dig′it
dig′i·ta′lis
dig′ni·fied
dig′ni·fy
dig′ni·fy·ing
dig′ni·tar·ies
dig′ni·tar′y
dig′ni·ties
dig′ni·ty
di·gress′
di·gres′sion
di·lap′i·date
di·lap′i·dat′ed
di·lap′i·da′tion
dil′a·ta′tion
di·late′
di·la′tion
dil′a·to′ry
di·lem′ma
dil′et·tan′te
dil′i·gence
dil′i·gent
di·lute′
di·lu′tion
di·men′sion
di·min′ish
di·min′u·en′do
dim′i·nu′tion
di·min′u·tive
dim′i·ty
dim′ness

dim′ple
din′er
din′ghy
(boat)
din′gy
(dull)
din′ner
din′ner bell
din′ner dance
din′ner hour
din′ner ta′ble
din′ner·time′
din′ner·ware′
din′ing room
di′no·saur
di·oc′e·san
di′o·cese
diph·the′ri·a
diph′thong
di·plo′ma
di·plo′ma·cy
dip′lo·mat
dip′lo·mat′ic
dip′per
dip′so·ma′ni·a
di·rect′
di·rec′tion
di·rect′ly
di·rec′tor
di·rec′to·rate
di·rec′to·ry
dire′ful

dirge
dir′i·gi·ble
dirt′i·ly
dirt′i·ness
dirt′y
dis′a·bil′i·ty
dis·a′ble
dis′a·buse′
dis′ad·van′tage
dis·ad′van·ta′-
geous
dis′af·fect′ed
dis′af·fec′tion
dis′a·gree′
dis′a·gree′a·ble
dis′a·gree′ment
dis′al·low′
dis′ap·pear′
dis′ap·pear′ance
dis′ap·point′
dis′ap·point′ment
dis′ap·pro·ba′tion
dis′ap·prov′al
dis′ap·prove′
dis·ar′ma·ment
dis′ar·range′
dis′ar·tic′u·late
dis′as·so′ci·ate
dis·as′ter
dis·as′trous
dis′a·vow′
dis′a·vow′al

dis·band′
dis·bar′
dis·bar′ring
dis′be·lief′
dis′be·lieve′
dis′be·liev′er
dis·burse′
dis·burse′ment
dis·burs′ing
dis·card′
dis·cern′
dis·cern′i·ble
dis·cern′ment
dis·charge′
dis·ci′ple
dis′ci·pli·nar′i·an
dis′ci·pli·nar′y
dis′ci·pline
dis·claim′
dis·claim′er
dis·close′
dis·clo′sure
dis·cob′o·lus
dis·cog′ra·phy
dis·col′or
dis·col′or·a′tion
dis·com′fit
(balk)
dis·com′fi·ture
dis·com′fort
(uneasiness)
dis′com·pose′
dis′com·po′sure
dis′con·cert′
dis′con·nect′
dis·con′so·late
dis′con·tent′
dis′con·tent′ment
dis′con·tin′u·ance
dis′con·tin′ue
dis′con·tin′u·ous
dis′cord, *n.*
dis·cord′, *v.*
dis·cord′ance
dis·cord′ant
dis′count
dis·cour′age
dis·cour′age-
ment
dis·course′
dis·cour′te·ous
dis·cour′te·sy
dis·cov′er
dis·cov′er·er
dis·cov′er·ies
dis·cov′er·y
dis·cred′it
dis·cred′it·a·ble
dis·creet′
(prudent)
dis·crep′an·cy
dis·crete′
(separate)
dis·cre′tion
dis·cre′tion·ar′y
dis·crim′i·nate
dis·crim′i·na′tion
dis·cur′sive
dis′cus
(athletic term)
dis·cuss′
(talk about)
dis·cus′sion
dis·dain′
dis·dain′ful
dis·ease′
dis·em′bar·ka′-
tion
dis′em·bar′rass
dis′en·chant′-
ment
dis′en·gage′
dis′en·tan′gle
dis′es·teem′
dis·fa′vor
dis·fig′ure
dis·fig′ure·ment
dis·fran′chise
dis·gorge′
dis·grace′
dis·grace′ful
dis·grun′tle
dis·guise′
dis·gust′
dis′ha·bille′
dish′cloth′

dis·heart′en
di·shev′el
dish mop
dis·hon′est
dis·hon′or
dis·hon′or·a·ble
dish′pan
dish rack
dish tow′el
dish′wash′er
dish′wa′ter
dis′il·lu′sion
dis·in′cli·na′tion
dis′in·fect′
dis′in·fect′ant
dis′in·fec′tion
dis′in·gen′u·ous
dis′in·her′it
dis·in′te·grate
dis·in′te·gra′tion
dis·in′ter·est·ed
disjoin′
dis′junc′tion
dis·junc′tive
dis·like′
dis′lo·cate
dis′lo·ca′tion
dis·lodge′
dis·loy′al
dis·loy′al·ty
dis′mal
dis·man′tle

dis·man′tling
dis·mast′
dis·may′
dis·mem′ber
dis·miss′
dis·miss′al
dis·mount′
dis′o·be′di·ence
dis′o·be′di·ent
dis′o·bey′
dis′o·beyed′
dis′o·blige′
dis′o·blig′ing
dis·or′der
dis·or′dered
dis·or′der·ly
dis·or′gan·i·za′-
tion
dis·or′gan·ize
dis·own′
dis·par′age
dis·par′age·ment
dis′pa·rate
dis·par′i·ty
dis·pas′sion·ate
dis·patch′
dis·pel′
dis·pelled′
dis·pel′ling
dis·pen′sa·ry
dis′pen·sa′tion
dis·pense′

dis·per′sal
dis·per′sion
dis·pir′it
dis·place′
dis·place′ment
dis·play′
dis·please′
dis·pleas′ure
dis·port′
dis·pos′al
dis·pose′
dis′po·si′tion
dis′pos·sess′
dis·proof′
dis′pro·por′tion
dis′pro·por′tion-
ate
dis·prove′
dis′pu·ta·ble
dis′pu·tant
dis′pu·ta′tion
dis′pu·ta′tious
dis·pute′
dis·qual′i·fi·ca′-
tion
dis·qual′i·fied
dis·qual′i·fy
dis′qui·si′tion
dis′re·gard′
dis′re·pair′
dis·rep′u·ta·ble
dis′re·pute′

dis′re·spect′
dis′re·spect′ful
dis·robe′
dis·rupt′
dis′sat·is·fac′tion
dis·sat′is·fied
dis·sect′
dis·sec′tion
dis·sem′ble
dis·sem′i·nate
dis·sen′sion
dis·sent′
dis·sent′er
dis·sen′tient
dis′ser·ta′tion
dis·serv′ice
dis′si·dence
dis′si·dent
dis·sim′i·lar
dis·sim′i·lar′i·ty
dis·sim′i·la′tion
dis·sim′u·late
dis′si·pate
dis′si·pat′ed
dis′si·pa′tion
dis·so′ci·ate
dis·so′ci·a′tion
dis·sol′u·ble
dis′so·lute
dis′so·lu′tion
dis·solve′
dis·solv′ing
dis′so·nance
dis′so·nant
dis·suade′
dis·sua′sion
dis′taff
dis′tance
dis′tant
dis·taste′
dis·taste′ful
dis·tem′per
dis·tend′
dis·ten′tion
dis′tich
dis·till′
dis′til·late
dis′til·la′tion
dis·till′er
dis·till′er·y
dis·tinct′
dis·tinc′tion
dis·tinc′tive
dis·tinct′ly
dis·tinct′ness
dis·tin′guish
dis·tort′
dis·tor′tion
dis·tract′
dis·trac′tion
dis·traught′
dis·tress′
dis·trib′ute
dis′tri·bu′tion
dis·trib′u·tor
dis′trict
dis·trust′
dis·trust′ful
dis·turb′
dis·turb′ance
dis·un′ion
dis·use′
dit′to
di·ur′nal
di′va
di′va·gate
di′van
di·verge′
di·ver′gence
di·ver′gent
di′vers
(several)
di·verse′
(different)
di·ver′si·fi·ca′tion
di·ver′si·fy
di·ver′sion
di·ver′si·ty
di·vert′
di·vest′
di·vide′
div′i·dend
div′i·na′tion
di·vine′
di·vin′i·ty
di·vis′i·bil′i·ty

di·vi′sion
di·vorce′
div′ot
di·vulge′
diz′zi·ly
diz′zi·ness
doc′ile
do·cil′i·ty
dock′et
dock fore′man
dock hand
dock′house
dock′man
dock′mas′ter
dock′rent
dock′side
dock′yard′
doc′tor
doc′tor·ate
doc′tri·naire′
doc′tri·nal
doc′trine
doc′u·ment
doc′u·men′ta·ry
doc′u·men·ta′tion
doe′skin′
dog′ber′ry
dog′bite′
dog′cart′
dog′catch′er
dog col′lar
dog days

doge
dog′fight′
dog′fish′
dog′ged
dog′ger·el
dog′ging
dog′house′
dog Lat′in
dog′ma
dog·mat′ic
dog·mat′i·cal
dog′ma·tism
dog′ma·tize
dog rose
dog′trot′
dog′watch′
dog′wood′
doi′lies
doi′ly
dol′drums
dole′ful
dol′lar
dol′man (cloak)
dol′men (monument)
do′lor
dol′or·ous
dol′phin
do·main′
domes′day′
do·mes′tic

do·mes′ti·cate
do′mes·tic′i·ty
dom′i·cile
dom′i·nant
dom′i·nate
dom′i·na′tion
dom′i·neer′ing
Do·min′i·can
dom′i·nie
do·min′ion
dom′i·no
dom′i·noes
do′nate
do·na′tion
don′jon
don′key
do′nor
don't
dooms′day′
door′nail′
door′plate′
door′sill′
door′step′
door′way′
door′yard′
dor′mant
dor′mer
dor′mi·to′ries
dor′mi·to′ry
dor′mouse′
dor′sal
dos′age

dot′age
do′tard
dou′ble
dou′blet
dou·bloon′
doubt′ful
doubt′less
dough′boy′
dough′nut′
dove′tail′
dow′a·ger
dow′dy
dow′el
dow′er
down′cast′
down′fall′
down′heart′ed
down′hill′
down′pour′
down′right′
down′stairs′, *adv.*
down′stairs′, *n.*
down′throw′
down′trod′den
down′ward
down′y
dow′ries
dow′ry
dox·ol′o·gy
doz′en
drach′ma

Dra·co′ni·an
draft
drafts′man
drag
dragged
drag′ging
drag′net′
drag′o·man
drag′on
drag′on·et
drag′on·fly′
dra·goon′
drag′rope′
drain′age
drain cock
drain′er
drainpipe
drain pump
drain valve
dra·mat′ic
dram′a·tist
dram′a·tize
dram′a·tur′gy
dra′per·y
dras′tic
draw′back′
draw′bar′
draw′bridge′
draw′ee′
draw′er
dray′age
dray′man

dread′ful
dread′nought′
dream′i·ly
dream′i·ness
dream′land′
drear′i·ly
drear′y
dress′er
dress′ing room
dress′mak′er
dri′er
drift′wood′
drill
drilled
drill′ing
drill′mas′ter
drill′stock′
drink′a·ble
drip
dripped
drip′ping
driv′el
drive′way′
driz′zle
droll′er·y
drom′e·dar′y
drop
dropped
drop′ping
drop′sy
drought
drow′sy

drudg'er·y
drug
drug clerk
drugged
drug'ging
drug'gist
drug'store'
drum
drummed
drum'ming
drum'stick'
drunk'ard
drunk'en
dry
(*dried, dries*)
dry'ad
dry'ly
dry'ness
dry'–shod'
lu·bi'e·ty
lu'bi·ous
lu'cal
luc'at
luch'ess
luch'y
luc'tile
ludg'eon
lue bill
lu'el
lu'el·ist
lu·en'na
lu·et'

du'gong
dug'out'
duke'dom
dul'cet
dul'ci·mer
dull'ard
dull'ness
dul'ly
dumb'bell'
dumb'–wait'er
dum'my
dump'ling
dun'ga·ree'
dun'geon
dun'nage
du'o·dec'i·mal
du'o·dec'i·mo
du'o·de'nal
du'o·de'num
du'plex
du'pli·cate
du'pli·ca'tion
du'pli·ca'tor
du·plic'i·ty
du'ra·bil'i·ty
du'ra·ble
dur'ance
du·ra'tion
dur'bar
du'ress
dur'ing
dusk'y

dust'bin'
dust brush
dust cap
dust'cloth'
dust cover
dust heap
dust'man'
dust'pan'
dust'proof'
dust'–tight'
du'te·ous
du'ti·a·ble
du'ties
du'ti·ful
du'ty
dwarf'ish
dwell'ing
dwin'dle
dyed
(colored. cf. *died.*)
dye'ing
dye'stuff'
dy·nam'ic
dy'na·mite
dy'na·mo
dy'na·mom'e·ter
dy'na·mos
dy'nast
dy'nas·ty
dys'en·ter'y
dys·pep'sia
dys·pep'tic

E

ea′ger
ea′gle
ea′gle–eyed′
ea′gre
ear′drop′
ear′drum′
earl′dom
ear′li·er
ear′li·est
ear′ly
ear′mark′
ear′nest
ear′ring′
ear′shot′
earth′born′
earth′en·ware′
earth′li·ness
earth′ly
earth′quake′
earth′ward
earth′work′
earth′worm′
ear′wax′
ear′wig′
ease′ment
eas′i·er
eas′i·est
eas′i·ly
East′er
east′ern
east′ward
eas′y·go′ing
eat′a·ble
ebb
ebbed
ebb′ing
eb′on·y
e·bul′li·ent
eb′ul·li′tion
ec·cen′tric
ec′cen·tric′i·ty
ec′chy·mo′sis
ec·cle′si·as′ti·cal
ech′e·lon
ech′o
ech′oes
é·clair′
ec·lec′tic
e·clipse′
e′co·nom′ic
e′co·nom′i·cal
e·con′o·mies
e·con′o·mist
e·con′o·my
ec′sta·sies
ec′sta·sy
ec·stat′ic
ec′u·men′i·cal
ec′ze·ma
ed′died
ed′dies
ed′dy
ed′dying
edge′ways′
edg′ing
ed′i·ble
e′dict
ed′i·fi·ca′tion
ed′i·fice
ed′i·fied
ed′i·fies
ed′i·fy
Ed′in·burg, Texas
Ed′in·burgh, Scotland
ed′it
e·di′tion
ed′i·tor
ed′i·to′ri·al
ed′u·cate
ed′u·ca′tion
ed′u·ca′tion·al
ed′u·ca′tor
ef·face′
ef·face′ment
ef·fect′

ef·fec′tive
ef·fec′tu·al
ef·fec′tu·ate
ef·fem′i·nate
ef′fer·vesce′
ef′fer·ves′cence
ef′fer·ves′cent
ef·fete′
ef′fi·ca′cious
ef′fi·ca·cy
ef·fi′cien·cy
ef·fi′cient
ef′fi·gy
ef′flo·res′cent
ef·flu′vi·um
ef′fort
ef·fron′ter·y
ef·ful′gence
ef·fu′sion
ef·fu′sive
egg′head′
egg′nog′
egg′plant′
egg′–shaped′
e′go
e′go·ism
e′go·ist
e′go·tism
e′go·tist
e·gre′gious
e′gress
ei′der
ei′ther
e·jac′u·late
e·jac′u·la′tion
e·jac′u·la·to′ry
e·ject′
e·jec′tion
e·lab′o·rate
e·lab′o·ra′tion
e·lapse′
e·las′tic
e·las′tic′i·ty
e·lat′ed
e·la′tion
el′bow
el′bow·room′
eld′er
el′der·ber′ry
eld′est
e·lect′
e·lec′tion
e·lec′tion·eer′
e·lec′tive
e·lec′tor
e·lec′tor·al
e·lec′tor·ate
e·lec′tric
e·lec′tri·cal
e·lec′tri′cian
e·lec′tric′i·ty
e·lec′tri·fi·ca′tion
e·lec′tri·fied
e·lec′tri·fy
e·lec′tro
e·lec′tro·cute
e·lec′trode
e·lec′trol′y·sis
e·lec′tro·lyte
e·lec′tro·mag′net
e·lec′tron
e·lec′tro·plate′
e·lec′tros
e·lec′tro·scope
e·lec′tro·type
e·lec′tu·ar′y
el′ee·mos′y·nar′y
el′e·gance
el′e·gant
el′e·gi′ac
el′e·gy
el′e·ment
el′e·men′tal
el′e·men′ta·ry
el′e·phant
el′e·phan·ti′a·sis
el′e·phan′tine
el′e·vate
el′e·va′tor
e·lic′it
e·lide′
el′i·gi·bil′i·ty
el′i·gi·ble
e·lim′i·nate
e·lim′i·na′tion
e·li′sion

e·lite′
e·lix′ir
E·liz′a·be′than
el·lipse′
el·lip′sis
el·lip′tic
el·lip′ti·cal
el′o·cu′tion
el′o·cu′tion·ist
e·lon′gate
e·lon′ga′tion
e·lope′
el′o·quence
el′o·quent
else′where
e·lu′ci·date
e·lu′ci·da′tion
e·lude′
(escape. cf. *allude.*)
e·lu′sive
e·ma′ci·ate
e·ma′ci·a′tion
em′a·nate
em′a·na′tion
e·man′ci·pate
e·man′ci·pa′tion
e·man′ci·pa′tor
e·mas′cu·late
em·balm′
em·bank′ment
em·bar′go
em·bar·goes
em·bar′rass
em·bar′rassed
em·bar′rass·es
em·bar′rass·ing
em·bar′rass·ment
em′bas·sies
em′bas·sy
em·bel′lish
em·bez′zle
em·bit′ter
em·bla′zon
em′blem
em′blem·at′ic
em·bod′i·ment
em·bod′y
em·bold′en
em′bon′point′
em·boss′
em·bossed′
em·boss′ing
em′bou·chure′
em·brace′
em·bra′sure
em·broi′der·y
em·broil′
em′bry·o
em′bry·os
em′bry·on′ic
e·mend′
e′men·da′tion
em′er·ald
e·merge′
e·mer′gen·cies
e·mer′gen·cy
e·merg′ing
e·mer′i·tus
e·met′ic
em′i·grant
em′i·grate
em′i·gra′tion
é′mi′gré′
em′i·nence
em′i·nent
e·mir′
em′is·sar′ies
em′is·sar′y
e·mis′sion
e·mit′
e·mit′ted
e·mit′ting
e·mol′li·ent
e·mol′u·ment
e·mo′tion
e·mo′tion·al
em′per·or
em′pha·ses, *pl.*
em′pha·sis
em′pha·size
em·phat′ic
em′pire
em·pir′ic
em·pir′i·cal
em·ploy′
em·ploy′ee

em·ploy'er
em·ploy'ment
em·po'ri·um
em·pow'er
em'press
emp'tied
emp'ties
emp'ty
emp'ty–head'ed
emp'ty·heart'ed
emp'ty·ing
em'py·e'ma
em'py·re'an
e'mu
em'u·late
em'u·la'tion
em'u·lous
e·mul'si·fy
e·mul'sion
en·a'ble
en·act'
en·act'ment
en·am'el
en·am'el·er
en·am'el·ware'
en·am'or
en·camp'ment
en·caus'tic
en'ceinte'
en·chant'er
en·chant'ing
en·chant'ment

en·chant'ress
en·cir'cle
en'clave
en·clit'ic
en·close'
en·clos'ing
en·clo'sure
en·co'mi·as'tic
en·co'mi·um
en·com'pass
en'core, *n.*
en·core', *v.*
en·coun'ter
en·cour'age
en·cour'age·ment
en·cour'ag·ing
en·croach'
en·croach'ment
en·cum'ber
en·cum'brance
en·cy'cli·cal
en·cy'clo·pe'di·a
en·dan'ger
en·dear'
en·dear'ment
en·deav'or
en·dem'ic
end'ing
en'dive
end'less
end'long'
end man

end'most
en·dorse'
en·dorse'ment
en·dow'
en·dow'ment
en·dur'a·ble
en·dur'ance
en·dure'
en·dur'ing
end'ways'
en'e·ma
en'e·mies
en'e·my
en'er·get'ic
en'er·gies
en'er·gize
en'er·giz'er
en'er·gy
en'er·vate
en'er·va'tion
en·face'
en·fee'ble
en·fet'ter
en·fold'
en·force'
en·force'a·ble
en·force'ment
en·forc'er
en·fran'chise
en·fran'chise-
ment
en·gage'

en·gaged′
en·gage′ment
en·gag′ing
en·gen′der
en′gine
en′gi·neer′
en′gi·neer′ing
en′gine room
Eng′lish
Eng′lish·man
Eng′lish·wom′an
en·graft′
en·grain′
en·grave′
en·grav′er
en·grav′ing
en·gross′
en·gross′ing
en·gross′ment
en·gulf′
en·hance′
en·hance′ment
e·nig′ma
e′nig·mat′ic
en·join′
en·joy′
en·joy′a·ble
en·joy′ment
en·lace′
en·large′
en·large′ment
en·light′en
en·light′en·ment
en·list′
en·list′ment
en·liv′en
en′mi·ties
en′mi·ty
en′nui
e·nor′mi·ty
e·nor′mous
e·nough′
en·rage′
en·rap′ture
en·rav′ish
en·rich′
en·rich′ment
en·robe′
en·roll′
en·rolled′
en·roll′ing
en·roll′ment
en route′
en·sconce′
en·shrine′
en·shroud′
en′sign
en′sign·cy
en·slave′
en·slave′ment
en·slav′er
en·snare′
en·sue′
en·sure′
en·tab′la·ture
en·tail′
en·tail′ment
en·tan′gle
en·tan′gle·ment
en′ter
en′ter·prise
en′ter·pris′ing
en′ter·tain′
en′ter·tain′er
en′ter·tain′ing
en′ter·tain′ment
en·thrall′
en·throne′
en·thuse′
en·thu′si·asm
en·thu′si·ast
en·thu′si·as′tic
en·thu′si·as′ti-
cal·ly
en·tice′
en·tice′ment
en·tire′
en·tire′ty
en′ti·ties
en·ti′tle
en′ti·ty
en·tomb′
en·tomb′ment
en′trails
en·train′
en′trance, *n.*

en·trance′, *v.*
en′trance·way′
en′trant
en·trap′
en·treat′
en·treat′ies
en·treat′y
en′tre·mets
en′tre·pre·neur′
en′tries
en′try
en′try·way′
en·twine′
e·nu′mer·ate
e·nu′mer·a′tion
e·nu′mer·a′tive
e·nu′mer·a′tor
e·nun′ci·ate
e·nun′ci·a′tion
e·nun′ci·a′tive
e·nun′ci·a′tor
en·vel′op, *v.*
en′ve·lope, *n.*
en·vel′oped
en·vel′op·ing
en·vel′op·ment
en·ven′om
en′vi·a·ble
en′vied
en′vies
en′vi·ous
en·vi′ron
en·vi′ron·ment
en·vis′age
en′voy
en′vy
en′zyme
e′o·lith
e′o·lith′ic
ep′au·let
e·phem′er·a
e·phem′er·al
ep′ic
ep′i·cal
ep′i·cure
ep′i·cu·re′an
ep′i·dem′ic
ep′i·der′mal
ep′i·der′mic
ep′i·der′mis
ep′i·gram
ep′i·graph
ep′i·graph′ic
ep′i·lep′sy
ep′i·lep′tic
ep′i·logue
e·pis′co·pal
e·pis′co·pa′li·an
ep′i·sode
ep′i·sod′ic
ep′i·sod′i·cal
ep′i·spas′tic
e·pis′tle
e·pis′to·lar′y
ep′i·taph
ep′i·thet
e·pit′o·me
e·pit′o·mize
ep′och
ep′och·al
Ep′som salts
eq′ua·bil′i·ty
eq′ua·ble
e′qual
e′qualed
e′qual·ing
e·qual′i·ty
e′qual·ize
e′qual·iz′er
e′qual·ly
e′qua·nim′i·ty
e·qua′tion
e·qua′tor
e′qua·to′ri·al
e·ques′tri·an
e′qui·an′gu·lar
e′qui·dis′tance
e′qui·dis′tant
e′qui·lat′er·al
e′qui·lib′ri·um
e′qui·noc′tial
e·quip′
e·quip′ment
e·quipped′
e·quip′ping
eq′ui·ta·ble

eq′ui·ty
e·quiv′a·lence
e·quiv′a·lent
e·quiv′o·cal
e·quiv′o·cate
e·quiv′o·ca′tion
e·quiv′o·ca′tor
e′ra
e·rad′i·ca·ble
e·rad′i·cate
e·rad′i·ca′tion
e·rad′i·ca′tive
e·ras′a·ble
e·rase′
e·ras′er
e·ra′sure
Er′e·bus
e·rect′
e·rec′tile
e·rec′tion
e·rect′ly
e·rect′ness
er′go
er′mine
e·ro′sion
e·ro′sive
e·rot′ic
er′rand
er′rant
er′rant·ry
er·ra′ta, *pl.*
er·rat′ic
er·ra′tum, *sing.*
err′ing·ly
er·ro′ne·ous
er′ror
er′ror–proof′
erst′while′
e·ruct′
e′ruc·ta′tion
er′u·dite
er′u·di′tion
e·rupt′
e·rup′tion
e·rup′tive
er′y·sip′e·las
es′ca·lade′
es′ca·la′tor
es′ca·pade′
es·cape′
es·cape′ment
es·cheat′
es·chew′
es·chew′al
es′cort, *n.*
es·cort′, *v.*
es·cutch′eon
Es′ki·mo
es′o·ter′ic
es·pe′cial
Es′pe·ran′to
es′pi·o·nage
es′pla·nade′
es·pous′al
es·pouse′
es′prit′
es·py′
es·quire′
es′say, *n.*
es·say′, *v.*
es′say·ist
es′sence
es·sen′tial
es·sen′ti·al′i·ty
es·tab′lish
es·tab′lish·ment
es·tate′
es·teem′
es′ti·ma·ble
es′ti·mate
es′ti·ma′tion
es·top′
es·topped′
es·top′pel
es·top′ping
es·trange′
es·trange′ment
es′tu·ar′y
et cet′er·a
etch′ing
e·ter′nal
e·ter′ni·ty
e′ther
e·the′re·al
e·the′re·al·ize
e′ther·i·za′tion

e′ther·ize
eth′i·cal
eth′ics
E′thi·o′pi·an
eth′nic
eth′ni·cal
eth′yl
eth′yl·ene
et′i·quette
et′y·mo·log′i·cal
et′y·mol′o·gy
eu′chre
Eu′clid
Eu·clid′e·an
eu′lo·gies
eu′lo·gist
eu′lo·gis′tic
eu′lo·gize
eu′lo·gy
eu′phe·mism
eu′phe·mis′tic
eu′phe·mize
eu·pho′ni·ous
eu′pho·ny
Eu′ro·pe′an
e·vac′u·ate
e·vac′u·a′tion
e·vade′
e·val′u·ate
e·val′u·a′tion
e′van·gel′ic
e′van·gel′i·cal

e·van′ge·lism
e·van′ge·list
e·van′ge·lis′tic
e·van′ge·lize
e·vap′o·ra·ble
e·vap′o·rate
e·vap′o·ra′tion
e·vap′o·ra′tive
e·va′sion
e·va′sive
e·vec′tion
e′ven
e′ven·fall′
e′ven·hand′ed
eve′ning
e′ven·ly
e′ven·ness
e′ven·song′
e·vent′
e·vent′ful
e′ven·tide′
e·ven′tu·al
e·ven′tu·al′i·ty
e·ven′tu·al·ly
e·ven′tu·ate
ev′er
ev′er·glade
ev′er·green′
ev′er·last′ing
ev′er·more′
e·vert′
ev′er·y

ev′er·y·bod′y
ev′er·y·day′
ev′er·y·thing′
ev′er·y·where′
e·vict′
e·vic′tion
ev′i·dence
ev′i·dent
ev′i·den′tial
e′vil·ly
e′vil·ness
e·vince′
e·vis′cer·ate
ev′o·ca·ble
ev′o·ca′tion
e·voc′a·tive
ev′o·ca′tor
e·voke′
ev′o·lu′tion
ev′o·lu′tion·ar′y
e·volve′
e·volve′ment
e·vul′sion
ex·ac′er·bate
ex·ac′er·ba′tion
ex·act′
ex·act′ing
ex·act′i·tude
ex·act′ly
ex·act′ness
ex·ag′ger·ate
ex·ag′ger·a′tion

ex·ag'ger·a'tor
ex·alt'
ex'al·ta'tion
ex·alt'ed
ex·am'i·na'tion
ex·am'ine
ex·am'ple
ex·as'per·ate
ex·as'per·a'tion
Ex·cal'i·bur
ex'ca·vate
ex'ca·va'tion
ex'ca·va'tor
ex·ceed'
ex·ceed'ing
ex·cel'
ex·celled
ex'cel·lence
ex'cel·len·cy
ex'cel·lent
ex·cel'ling
ex·cel'si·or
ex·cept'
ex·cept'ing
ex·cep'tion
ex·cep'tion·a·ble
ex·cep'tion·al
ex'cerpt, *n.*
ex·cerpt', *v.*
ex·cess'
ex·ces'sive
ex·change'
ex·cheq'uer
ex·cis'a·ble
ex·cise'
ex·ci'sion
ex·cit'a·bil'i·ty
ex·cit'a·ble
ex'ci·ta'tion
ex·cite'
ex·cite'ment
ex·cit'ing
ex·claim'
ex'cla·ma'tion
ex·clam'a·to'ry
ex·clude'
ex·clu'sion
ex·clu'sive
ex'com·mu'ni-
cate
ex'com·mu'ni-
ca'tion
ex·co'ri·ate
ex·crete'
ex·cre'tion
ex·cru'ci·ate
ex·cru'ci·a'tion
ex'cul·pate
ex'cul·pa'tion
ex·cul'pa·to'ry
ex·cur'sion
ex·cur'sive
ex·cus'a·ble
ex·cuse', *n.*
ex·cuse', *v.*
ex·cus'ing
ex'e·crate
ex'e·cra'tion
ex'e·cute
ex'e·cu'tion
ex'e·cu'tion·er
ex·ec'u·tive
ex·ec'u·tor
ex·ec'u·to'ri·al
ex·ec'u·to'ry
ex·ec'u·trix, *fem.*
ex'e·ge'sis
ex·em'plar
ex·em'pla·ry
ex·em'pli·fi·ca'-
tion
ex·em'pli·fy
ex·empt'
ex·emp'tion
ex'er·cise
(exertion)
ex·ert'
(exercise. cf.
exsert.)
ex·er'tion
ex'e·unt
ex·hal'ant
ex'ha·la'tion
ex·hale'
ex·haust'
ex·haust'ed

ex·haust′er
ex·haust′i·ble
ex·haus′tion
ex·haus′tive
ex·hib′it
ex′hi·bi′tion
ex′hi·bi′tion·er
ex·hib′i·tive
ex·hib′i·tor
ex·hib′i·to′ry
ex·hil′a·rant
ex·hil′a·rate
ex·hil′a·ra′tion
ex·hil′a·ra′tive
ex·hort′
ex′hor·ta′tion
ex′hu·ma′tion
ex·hume′
ex′i·gen·cies
ex′i·gen·cy
ex′ile
ex·ist′
ex·ist′ence
ex·ist′ent
ex′it
ex′o·dus
ex·on′er·ate
ex·on′er·a′tion
ex·on′er·a′tive
ex′o·ra·ble
ex·or′bi·tan·cy
ex·or′bi·tant

ex′or·cise
(expel)
ex′o·ter′ic
ex·ot′ic
ex·pand′
ex·panse′
ex·pan′si·ble
ex·pan′sion
ex·pan′sive
ex par′te
ex·pa′ti·ate
ex·pa′tri·ate
ex·pa′tri·a′tion
ex·pect′
ex·pect′an·cy
ex·pect′ant
ex′pec·ta′tion
ex·pec′to·rant
ex·pec′to·rate
ex·pec′to·ra′tion
ex·pe′di·en·cy
ex·pe′di·ent
ex·pe′di·ent·ly
ex′pedite
ex′pe·di′tion
ex′pe·di′tion·ar′y
ex′pe·di′tious
ex·pel′
ex·pelled′
ex·pel′ling
ex·pend′
ex·pend′i·ture

ex·pense′
ex·pen′sive
ex·pe′ri·ence
ex·pe′ri·enced
ex·per′i·ment
ex·per′i·men′tal
ex·per′i·men·ta′-
tion
ex·pert′, *adj.*
ex′pert, *n.*
ex·pert′ly
ex·pert′ness
ex′pi·a·ble
ex′pi·ate
ex′pi·a′tion
ex′pi·a·to′ry
ex′pi·ra′tion
ex·pire′
ex·plain′
ex·plain′a·ble
ex′pla·na′tion
ex·plan′a·to′ry
ex′ple·tive
ex′pli·ca·ble
ex·plic′it
ex·plode′
ex′ploit, *n.*
ex·ploit′, *v.*
ex′ploi·ta′tion
ex′plo·ra′tion
ex·plor′a·to′ry
ex·plore′

ex·plor′er
ex·plo′sion
ex·plo′sive
ex·po′nent
ex′port, *n.*
ex·port′, *v.*
ex·port′a·ble
ex′por·ta′tion
ex·port′er
ex′po·sé′, *n.*
ex·pose′, *v.*
ex·posed′
ex·pos′er
ex′po·si′tion
ex·pos′i·tive
ex·pos′i·to′ry
ex post fac′to
ex·pos′tu·late
ex·pos′tu·la′tion
ex·po′sure
ex·pound′
ex·press′
ex·press′age
ex·press′i·ble
ex·press′ing
ex·pres′sion
ex·pres′sive
ex·press′ly
ex·press′man
ex·pul′sion
ex·pul′sive
ex·punge′

ex′pur·gate
ex′pur·ga′tion
ex·pur′ga·to′ry
ex′qui·site
ex·sert′
(protrude. cf. *exert.*)
ex·sert′ed
ex·ser′tion
ex′tant
ex·tem′po·ra′ne-ous
ex·tem′po·rar′y
ex·tem′po·re
ex·tem′po·rize
ex·tend′
ex·ten′si·ble
ex·ten′sion
ex·ten′sive
ex·tent′
ex·ten′u·ate
ex·ten′u·a′tion
ex·te′ri·or
ex·ter′mi·nate
ex·ter′mi·na′tion
ex·ter′mi·na′tive
ex·ter′mi·na′tor
ex·ter′mi·na·to′ry
ex·ter′nal
ex·ter′nal·ize
ex·ter′nal·ly
ex·tinct′

ex·tinc′tion
ex·tinc′tive
ex·tin′guish
ex·tin′guish·a-ble
ex′tir·pate
ex·tol′
ex·tolled′
ex·tol′ling
ex·tort′
ex·tor′tion
ex′tra
ex′tract, *n.*
ex·tract′, *v.*
ex·tract′a·ble
ex·trac′tion
ex·trac′tive
ex·trac′tor
ex′tra·dite
ex′tra·di′tion
ex·tra′ne·ous
ex·traor′di·nar′-i·ly
ex·traor′di·nar′y
ex·trav′a·gance
ex·trav′a·gant
ex·trav′a·gan′za
ex·trav′a·sa′tion
ex·treme′
ex·trem′ist
ex·trem′i·ty
ex′tri·ca·ble

ex′tri·cate
ex′tri·ca′tion
ex·trin′sic
ex·trude′
ex·trud′ing
ex·tru′sion
ex·u′ber·ance
ex·u′ber·an·cy
ex·u′ber·ant
ex·u′ber·ate
ex′u·da′tion
ex·ude′
ex·ult′
ex′ul·ta′tion
eye′ball′
eye′bright′
eye′brow′
eye′cup′
eyed
eye′glass′
eye′hole′
eye′lash′
eye′less
eye′let
eye′lid′
eye′piece′
eye′shade′
eye′sight′
eye′sore′
eye′spot′
eye′stone′
eye′strain′
eye′string′
eye′tooth′
eye′wash′
eye′wa′ter
eye′wink′
eye′wit′ness
ey′ing

F

fa′ble
fa′bled
fab′ric
fab′ri·cate
fab′ri·ca′tion
fab′u·lous
fa·çade′
face′–hard′en
fac′er
fac′et
fa·ce′tious
fa′cial
fac′ile
fa·cil′i·tate
fa·cil′i·ties
fa·cil′i·ty
fac′ing
fac·sim′i·le
fac′tion
fac′tion·al
fac′tious
fac·ti′tious
fac′tor
fac·to′ri·al
fac′tor·ies
fac′tor·ize
fac′to·ry
fac′tu·al
fac′ul·ta′tive
fac′ul·ties
fac′ul·ty
fad
fade
fag′ot
fag′ot·ing
Fahr′en·heit
fail′ing
fail′ure
faint′heart′ed
faint′ish
faint′ly
faint′ness

fair′ies
fair′ly
fair′–mind′ed
fair′ness
fair′–sized′
fair′–spo′ken
fair′way′
fair′y
fair′y·hood
fair′y·land′
faith′ful
faith′less
fak′er
fa·kir′
fal′con
fal′la·cies
fal·la′cious
fal′la·cy
fall′en
fal′li·bil′i·ty
fal′li·ble
fall′ing
fal′low
false′heart′ed
false′hood
false′ly
false′ness
fal·set′to
false′work′
fal′si·fi·ca′tion
fal′si·fied
fal′si·fi′er
fal′si·fy
fal′si·fy·ing
fal′si·ty
fal′ter
fa·mil′iar
fa·mil′i·ar′i·ty
fa·mil′iar·ize
fa·mil′iar·ly
fam′i·lies
fam′i·ly
fam′ine
fam′ish
fa′mous
fa·nat′ic
fa·nat′i·cal
fa·nat′i·cism
fan′ci·er
fan′cies
fan′ci·ful
fan′cy
fan′cy–free′
fan′cy·work′
fan′fare
fanned
fan′ning
fan′tail′
fan·tas′tic
fan·tas′ti·cal
far′a·way′
farce
far′ci·cal
fare′well′
far′fetched′
fa·ri′na
farm′er
farm′house′
farm′ing
farm′stead
farm′yard′
far′–off′
far′row
far′see′ing
far′sight′ed
far′ther
far′ther·most
far′thest
far′thing
fas′ci·nate
fas′ci·na′tion
fas′ci·na′tor
fash′ion
fash′ion·a·ble
fas′ten
fas′ten·ing
fas·tid′i·ous
fas·tig′i·ate
fas·tig′i·at′ed
fast′ness
fa′tal
fa′tal·ist
fa′tal·is′tic
fa·tal′i·ty
fa′tal·ly
fat′ed

fate′ful
fa′ther
fa′ther·hood
fa′ther–in–law′
fa′ther·land′
fa′ther·less
fa′ther·like′
fa′ther·ly
fath′om
fath′om·a·ble
fath′om·less
fa·tigue′
fat′ness
fat′tish
fat′ty
fa·tu′i·tous
fa·tu′i·ty
fat′u·ous
fau′cet
fault′i·ly
fault′i·ness
fault′less
fault′y
faux′ pas′
fa′vor
fa′vor·a·ble
fa′vored
fa′vor·er
fa′vor·ite
fa′vor·it·ism
faze
fe′al·ty
fear′ful
fear′less
fear′some
fea′si·bil′i·ty
fea′si·ble
feath′er
feath′er·brain′
feath′ered
feath′er·edge′
feath′er·head′
feath′er–veined′
feath′er·weight′
feath′er·y
fea′ture
fea′tured
fea′ture·less
feb′ri·fuge
Feb′ru·ar′y
fe·cun′di·ty
fed′er·al
fed′er·al·ist
fed′er·al·ize
fed′er·ate
fed′er·a′tion
fee′ble
fee′ble·heart′ed
fee′ble–mind′ed
feed′bin′
feed′er
feed pipe
feed′stuff′
feed valve
feel′er
feel′ing
feel′ing·ly
feign
feigned
feint
fe·lic′i·tate
fe·lic′i·ta′tion
fe·lic′i·tous
fe·lic′i·ty
fe′line
fell′ness
fel′low
fel′low·ship
fel′on
fe·lo′ni·ous
fel′o·ny
felt′ing
fe′male
fem′i·nine
fem′i·nin′i·ty
fe′mur
fence
fence′less
fenc′er
fenc′ing
fend′er
fe·ra′cious
fer′ment, *n.*
fer·ment′, *v.*
fer·ment′a·ble
fer′men·ta′tion

fern′er·y
fe·ro′cious
fe·roc′i·ty
fer′ret
fer′ried
fer′ries
Fer′ris wheel′
fer′rous
fer′rule
(metal ring)
fer′ry
fer′ry·boat′
fer′ry·ing
fer′tile
fer·til′i·ty
fer′ti·li·za′tion
fer′ti·lize
fer′ti·liz′er
fer′ule
(rod)
fer′vent
fer′vid
fer′vor
fes′ti·val
fes′tive
fes·tiv′i·ty
fes·toon′
fetch′ing
fete
fe′tish
feu′dal
feu′dal·ism
feu′dal·ize
feu′dal·ly
feu′da·to′ry
feud′ist
fe′ver
fe′ver·ish
fe′ver·weed′
fi′an·cé′, *masc.*
fi′an·cée′, *fem.*
fi·as′co
fi′at
fi′ber
fi′brous
fib′u·la
fick′le
fic′tion
fic′tion·al
fic·ti′tious
fid′dle
fid′dler
fid′dle·stick′
fi·del′i·ty
fidg′et
fidg′et·y
fi·du′ci·ar′y
field day
field′er
field glass
field′piece′
field′work′er
fiend
fiend′ish
fierce
fi′er·y
fies′ta
fif′teen′
fif′teenth′
fif′ti·eth
fif′ty
fig′ment
fig′ur·a·tive
fig′ure
fig′ured
fig′ure·head′
fil′a·ment
fil′a·ture
fil′bert
fil′i·al
fil′i·bus′ter
fil′i·gree
fil′ing
Fil′i·pi′no
fill′er
fil′let
fill′ing
fil′ter
(strainer)
filth′y
fi′nal
fi·na′le
fi′nal·ist
fi·nal′i·ty
fi′nal·ly
fi·nance′

i·nan′cial
in′an·cier′
ind′er
ind′ing
ine′ly
ine′ness
in′er·y
ine′spun′
i·nesse′
in′ger
in′i·cal
i′nis
in′ish
in′ished
in′ish·er
i′nite
ire ant
ire′arm′
ire′bird′
ire′box′
ire′brand′
ire′brick′
ire′bug′
ire′crack′er
ire′dog′
ire′–eat′er
ire′fly′
ire′man
ire′place′
ire′plug′
ire′pow′er
ire′proof′

fire′side′
fire′stone′
fire tow′er
fire′trap′
fire wall
fire′wa′ter
fire′wood′
fire′works′
fir′ing
fir′kin
firm′er
firm′ly
firm′ness
first′–born′
first′–class′
first′hand′
first′–rate′
first water
fis′cal
fish′er
fish′er·man
fish′er·y
fish′hook′
fish′i·ly
fish′i·ness
fish′ing
fish′tail′
fish′y
fis′sion
fis′sure
fist′ic
fit′ful

fit′ness
fit′ted
fit′ting
five′fold′
fix′a·ble
fix′ate
fix·a′tion
fix′a·tive
fix′ing
fix′ture
fiz′zle
flab′by
flag′el·late
flag′el·la′tion
flag′ging
flag′man
flag′on
fla′grance
fla′grant
flag′ship′
flag′staff′
flag′stone′
flair
flak′y
flam·boy′ant
flame′proof
fla·min′go
fla·min′gos
flan′nel
flap′jack′
flapped
flap′per

flap'ping
flare'–up'
flash'board'
flash'i·ly
flash'i·ness
flash'ing
flash'light'
flash'y
flat'–foot'ed
flat'i'ron
flat'ten
flat'ter
flat'ter·er
flat'ter·y
flat'ware'
flaunt
fla'vor
fla'vor·ing
flax'seed'
flax'y
flea'bite'
flea'–bit'ten
flec'tion
fledg'ling
flee'ing
Flem'ish
flesh'i·ness
flesh'ly
flew
flex'i·bil'i·ty
flex'i·ble
flick'er

flight
flight'i·ness
flight'less
flim'si·ly
flim'si·ness
flim'sy
flin'der
flint'i·er
flint'y
flip'pan·cy
flip'pant
flipped
flip'ping
flir·ta'tion
flir·ta'tious
flit'ter
float'ing
floc'cu·lent
flood'gate'
flood'light'
flood'proof
floor'ing
floor'walk'er
flop'py
flo'ral
Flor'en·tine
flo·res'cence
flo·res'cent
flor'id
flor'in
flo·ta'tion
flo·til'la

flot'sam
flounce
flounc'ing
floun'der
flour'ish
flour'y
flow'er
flow'er·pot'
flow'er·y
flown
fluc'tu·ate
fluc'tu·a'tion
flu'en·cy
flu'ent
fluff'y
flu'id
flu'o·res'cent
flu'o·ro·scope
flur'ries
flur'ry
flus'ter·a'tion
flut'er
flut'ter
flut'ter·y
fly'catch'er
fly'er
fly'ing
fly'leaf'
fly'speck'
fly'trap'
fly'wheel'
foam'y

fo′cal
fo′cal·ize
fo′cus
fod′der
foe′man
fo′gy
fold′er
fold′ing
fo′li·age
fo′li·ate
fo′li·at′ed
fo′li·a′tion
fo′li·o
folk′lore′
fol′low
fol′low·er
fol′low·ing
fol′low–up′
fol′ly
fo·ment′
fo′men·ta′tion
fon′dant
fon′dle
fon′dler
fond′ly
fond′ness
food′stuff′
fool′er·y
fool′har′dy
fool′ing
fool′ish
fool′proof′
fools′cap′
foot′ball′
foot bath
foot′board′
foot′–can′dle
foot′hill′
foot′hold′
foot′ing
foot′less
foot′lights′
foot′–loose′
foot′man
foot′mark′
foot′note′
foot′path′
foot′print′
foot′room
foot rule
foot′sore′
foot′step′
foot′stool′
foot′walk′
foot′wear′
foot′work′
foot′worn′
for′age
for′ay
for·bade′
for·bear′
for·bear′ance
for·bid′
for·bid′den
for·bid′der
for·bid′ding
for·bore′
forced
force′ful
for′ceps
for′ci·ble
forc′ing
fore′arm′, *n.*
fore·arm′, *v.*
fore·bode′
fore·bod′ing
fore·cast′, *v.*
fore′cast′, *n.*
fore·cast′er
fore′cas·tle
fore·close′
fore·clo′sure
fore′fa′ther
fore′fin′ger
fore′foot′
fore′front′
fore·go′
fore·go′ing
fore·gone′
fore′ground′
fore′hand′
fore′hand′ed
fore′head
for′eign
for′eign·er
fore·judge′

fore·knowl′edge
fore′man
fore′mast′
fore′most
fore′name′
fore′noon′
fo·ren′sic
fore′or·dain′
fore part
fore·run′
fore·run′ner
fore·see′
fore·see′ing
fore·shad′ow
fore′sight′
for′est
fore·stall′
for′est·a′tion
for′est·er
for′est·ry
fore·tell′
fore′thought′
for·ev′er
fore′word′
for′feit
for′fei·ture
for·gave′
forg′er
for′ger·y
for·get′
for·get′ful
for·get′–me–not′
for·get′ta·ble
for·get′ting
for·give′
for·give′ness
for·giv′ing
for·go′
for·got′
for·lorn′
for′mal
for·mal′i·ty
for′mal·ize
for′mal·ly
for′mat
for·ma′tion
form′a·tive
form′er, *n.*
for′mer, *adj.*
for′mer·ly
for′mi·da·ble
form′less
for′mu·la
for′mu·late
for′mu·la′tion
for·sake′
for·sooth′
for·syth′i·a
forth′com′ing
forth′right′
forth′with′
for′ti·eth
for′ti·fi·ca′tion
for′ti·fied
for′ti·fi′er
for′ti·fy
for·tis′si·mo
for′ti·tude
fort′night
for′tress
for·tu′i·tous
for·tu′i·ty
for′tu·nate
for′tune
for′tune·tell′er
for′ty
fo′rum
for′ward
for′ward·er
for′ward·ly
for′ward·ness
for′wards
fos′sil
fos′ter
foul
(bad. cf. *fowl.*)
foul′ness
foun·da′tion
found′er *n.*
foun′der, *v.*
found′ling
found′ries
found′ry
foun′tain
foun′tain·head′
four′score′

four′some
four′teen′
four′teenth′
fowl
(poultry. cf. *foul.*)
fox′i·ness
fox′tail′
fox terrier
fox trot
foy′er
fra′cas
frac′tion
frac′tion·al
frac′ture
frag′ile
fra·gil′i·ty
frag′ment
frag′men·tar′y
fra′grance
fra′grant
frail′ties
frail′ty
fram′er
frame′–up′
frame′work′
fram′ing
franc
fran′chise
Fran·cis′can
frank′in·cense
frank′ly
frank′ness
fran′tic
fra·ter′nal
fra·ter′ni·ty
frat′er·nize
Frau
fraud′u·lence
fraud′u·lent
Fräu′lein
freak′ish
freck′le
free′board′
free′born′
freed′man
free′dom
free′hand′
free′ly
free′man
free′way
freeze
(from cold. cf. *frieze.*)
freight′er
fren′zy
fre′quen·cy
fre′quent, *adj.*
fre·quent′, *v.*
fre′quent·ly
fres′co
fres′coes
fresh′en
fresh′ly
fresh′ness
fresh′–wa′ter
fret′ful
fret′work′
fri′ar
fric′tion
fric′tion·al
Fri′day
friend′less
friend′li·ness
friend′ly
friend′ship
frieze
(ornament. cf. *freeze.*)
frig′ate
fright
fright′en
fright′ened
fright′ful
frig′id
fri·gid′i·ty
frit′ter
fri·vol′i·ty
friv′o·lous
frol′ic·some
front′age
fron′tal
fron·tier′
fron·tiers′man
fron′tis·piece
front′less
frost′bite′

frost′i·ness
frost′ing
frost′proof′
froze
fro′zen
fru′gal
fru·gal′i·ty
fru′gal·ly
fru′gal·ness
fruit′er
fruit′ful
fru·i′tion
fruit′less
frus′trate
frus·tra′tion
fu′el
fu′gi·tive
ful′crum
ful·fill′
ful·fill′ing
ful·fill′ment
full′ness
full′–sized′
ful′ly
ful′mi·nate

ful′some
fum′ble
fu′mi·gate
fu′mi·ga′tion
fu′mi·ga′tor
func′tion
func′tion·al
func′tion·ar′y
fun′da·men′tal
fu′ner·al
fu·ne′re·al
fun′gi·ble
fun′gous, *adj.*
fun′gus, *n.*
fun′gus–proof′
fun′nel
fun′ny
fur
fur′be·low
fur′bish
fu′ri·ous
fur′long
fur′lough
fur′nace
fur′nish

fur′ni·ture
fu′ror
fur′ri·er
fur′row
fur′ry
(with fur)
fur′ther
fur′ther·ance
fur′ther·more′
fur′ther·most
fur′thest
fur′tive
fu′ry
(rage)
furze
fu′se·lage
fu′si·bil′i·ty
fu′si·ble
fu′sion
fuss′i·ly
fuss′y
fu′tile
fu·til′i·ty
fu′ture
fu·tu′ri·ty

G

ga′ble
Gael′ic

gai′e·ty
gain′er

gain′ful
gait

gai′ter
gal′ax·y
gal′lant
gal′lant·ly
gal′lant·ry
gal′ler·ies
gal′ler·y
gal′ley
gal′leys
gal′lon
gal′lop
gal′lop·ing
gal′loped
gal′lows
gall′stone′
gal·van′ic
gal′va·ni·za′tion
gal′va·nize
gam′bit
gam′ble
(to bet)
gam′bler
gam′bling
gam′bol
(to play)
game′ness
game′ster
gan′gli·on
gang′plank′
gan′grene
gang′ster
gang′way′
gant′let
ga·rage′
gar′bage
gar′den
gar′den·er
gar·de′ni·a
Gar′di·ner,
Maine
Gard′ner, Mass.
gar′gle
gar′goyle
gar′land
gar′lic
gar′ment
gar′ner
gar′net
gar′nish
gar′nish·ee′
gar′nish·er
gar′nish·ment
gar′ri·son
gar·ru′li·ty
gar′ru·lous
gar′ter
gas′house′
gas′ket
gas′light′
gas mask
gas′o·line
gas station
gas′tight′
gas′tric
gas′tro·nom′ic
gas·tron′o·my
gas′works′
gate′way′
gath′er
gath′er·ing
gauge
gaug′er
gaunt′let
gauze
gav′el
gay′ly
gay′ness
ga·zelle′
ga·zette′
gear′ing
gel′a·tin
ge·lat′i·nate
ge·lat′i·nize
ge·lat′i·nous
gen·darme′
gen′e·al′o·gy
gen′er·al
gen′er·al·is′si·mo
gen′er·al′i·ty
gen′er·al·i·za′-
tion
gen′er·al·ize
gen′er·al·ly
gen′er·al·ship′
gen′er·ate
gen′er·a′tion

gen′er·a′tive
gen′er·a′tor
ge·ner′ic
gen′er·os′i·ty
gen′er·ous
gen′e·sis
gen′ial
ge′ni·al′i·ty
gen′ial·ly
gen′i·tal
gen′i·tive
gen′ius
gen·teel′
gen′tile
gen·til′i·ty
gen′tle
gen′tle·man
gen′tle·ness
gen′tly
gen′try
gen′u·flect
gen′u·flec′tion
gen′u·ine
ge′nus
ge·og′ra·pher
ge′o·graph′ic
ge′o·graph′i·cal
ge·og′ra·phy
ge′o·log′ic
ge′o·log′i·cal
ge·ol′o·gist
ge·ol′o·gy
ge·om′e·ter
ge′o·met′ric
ge′o·met′ri·cal
ge·om′e·try
ge·ra′ni·um
Ger′man
ger·mane′
ger′mi·cide
ger′mi·nate
ger′mi·na′tion
germ′proof′
ger′und
ges′tate
ges·ta′tion
ges·tic′u·late
ges·tic′u·la′tion
ges·tic′u·la·to′ry
ges′ture
ghast′li·ness
ghast′ly
ghet′to
ghost′like′
ghost′ly
gi′ant
gib′ber·ish
gib′let
Gi·bral′tar
gid′di·ly
gid′di·ness
gid′dy
gi·gan′tic
gig′gle
gilt′–edged′
gim′let
gin′ger
gin′ger·bread′
gin′ger·ly
gin′ger·snap′
ging′ham
gink′go
gi·raffe′
gird′er
gir′dle
girl′hood
girl′ish
giv′en
giv′er
giz′zard
gla′cial
gla′cial·ly
gla′cier
glad′den
glad′i·a′tor
glad′i·a·to′ri·al
glad′i·o′lus
glad′ly
glad′ness
glam′or·ous
glam′our
glance
glanc′ing
glan′du·lar
glan′du·lous
glar′ing

glass′ful
glass′i·ness
glass′ware′
glass′y
gla′zier
gleam′y
glean′ing
glee′ful
glid′er
glid′ing
glim′mer
glim′mer·ing
glimpse
limps′ing
glis′ten
lit′ter
lit′ter·y
loam′ing
lob′u·lar
lock′en·spiel′
loom′i·ly
loom′i·ness
loom′ing
loom′y
lo′ri·fi·ca′tion
lo′ri·fi′er
lo′ri·fy
lo′ri·ous
lo′ry
los′sa·ry
loss′i·ly
loss′i·ness

gloss′y
glow′er
glow′worm′
glu′cose
glue
glu′ing
glum′ly
glum′ness
glu′ten
glu′ti·nous
glut′ton
glut′ton·ous
glut′ton·y
glyc′er·in
gnarl
gnarled
gnash
gnat
gnaw
gnaw′ing
gneiss
gnome
gno′mon
goat′skin′
gob′ble
gob′bler
gob′let
gob′lin
go′cart′
god′child′
god′daugh′ter
god′dess

god′fa′ther
god′head
Go·di′va
god′less
god′like′
god′ly
god′moth′er
god′par′ent
god′send′
god′ship
god′son′
God′speed′
gog′gle
go′ing
goi′ter
gold brick
gold′en
gold′en·rod′
gold′fish′
gold′i·locks′
gold′smith′
gold stick
Go·li′ath
gon′do·la
gon′do·lier′
good′–by′
good′ly
good′ness
good′–tem′pered
good will
goose′ber′ry
goose flesh

goose'foot'
goose'herd'
goose'neck'
go'pher
gor'geous
gorg'er
go·ril'la
gos'pel
gos'sip
gos'sip·ing
Goth'am
Goth'ic
gou'lash
gourd
gour'mand
gout
gov'ern
gov'ern·a·ble
gov'ern·ess
gov'ern·ment
gov'ern·men'tal
gov'er·nor
gov'er·nor–
gen'er·al
gov'er·nor·ship'
grab'ble
grace'ful
grace'less
gra'cious
gra·da'tion
gra·da'tion·al
grad'u·al
grad'u·ate
grad'u·a'tion
graft'er
gram
gram'mar
gram·mar'i·an
gram·mat'i·cal
gram'o·phone
gran'a·ry
grand'aunt'
grand'child'
grand'daugh'-
ter
gran'deur
grand'fa'ther
gran·dil'o·quence
gran·dil'o·quent
gran'di·ose
gran·dio'so
grand'moth'er
grand'neph'ew
grand'niece'
grand'sire'
grand'son'
grand'stand
grand'un'cle
grang'er
gran'ite
gran'ite·ware'
gran'tee'
grant'or
gran'u·lar
gran'u·late
gran'u·la'tion
gran'u·la'tor
grape'fruit'
grape juice
grape'shot'
grape'skin
grape'vine'
graph'ic
graph'i·cal
graph'ite
grap'ple
grasp'ing
grass'hop'per
grass'y
grate'ful
grat'i·fi·ca'tion
grat'i·fied
grat'i·fi'er
grat'i·fy
grat'i·fy·ing
grat'ing
gra'tis
grat'i·tude
gra·tu'i·ties
gra·tu'i·tous
gra·tu'i·ty
gra·va'men
grave'clothes'
grav'el
grave'ness
grave'stone'

grave′yard′
grav′i·tate
grav′i·ta′tion
grav′i·ta′tive
grav′i·ty
gra′vy
gray′beard′
gray′ish
gray′ness
graz′er
graz′ing
greas′er
grease′wood′
greas′y
great′coat′
great gross
great′heart′ed
greed′i·ly
greed′y
green′back′
green′er·y
green′–eyed′
green′gage′
green′gro′cer
green′horn′
green′house′
green′ing
green′ish
green′room′
greet′ing
gre·gar′i·ous
Gre·go′ri·an

gre·nade′
gren′a·dier′
grey′hound′
grid′dle
grid′dle·cake′
grid′i′ron
griev′ance
griev′ous
grif′fon
grill′room′
gri·mace′
grim′ly
grim′ness
grin
grind′stone′
grinned
grin′ning
grip
(grasp)
grippe
(sickness)
grip′ping
(grasping)
gris′tle
grist′mill′
grit′ty
griz′zle
griz′zled
griz′zly
gro′cer·ies
gro′cer·y
grog′gy

gross′ly
gro·tesque′
ground crew
ground hog
ground′less
ground′work′
grov′el
grow′er
growl′er
grudge
grudg′ing
gru′el
grue′some
grum′ble
grump′y
guar′an·tee′
(plural: *guarantees*)
guar′an·tor
guar′an·ty
(plural: *guaranties*)
guard′house′
guard′i·an
guard′i·an·ship′
guard′room′
guards′man
gu′ber·na·to′ri·al
guer·ril′la
guess′work′
guest room
guid′a·ble
guid′ance
guil′lo·tine

guilt'i·ly
guilt'i·ness
guilt'less
guilt'y
guimpe
guin'ea
gui·tar'
gul'li·bil'i·ty
gul'li·ble
gul'lies
gul'ly
gum'drop'
gum'my
gun'boat'
gun'cot'ton

gun'fire'
gun'flint'
gun'lock'
gun'man
gun metal
gun'ner
gun'pow'der
gun room
gun'run'ner
gun'shot'
gun'wale
gup'py
gur'gle
gush'er
gus'to

Gut'ten·berg, N. J.
gut'ter
gut'tur·al
guz'zle
gym·na'si·ast
gym·na'si·um
gym'nast
gym·nas'tic
gym·nas'tics
gyp'sum
gyp'sy
gy'rate
gy·ra'tion
gy'ro·scope

H

ha'be·as cor'pus
hab'er·dash'er
hab'er·dash'er·y
ha·bil'i·tate
hab'it
hab'it·a·ble
hab'it·ant
hab'i·tat
hab'i·ta'tion
ha·bit'u·al
ha·bit'u·ate
hab'i·tude

ha·cien'da
hack'man
hack'ney
hack'neyed
hack saw
had'dock
Ha'des
hag'gard
hag'gle
hail'stone'
hail'storm'
hair'brush'

hair'dress'er
hair'i·ness
hair net
hair oil
hair'pin'
hair'split'ter
hair'split'ting
hair'spring'
hair ton'ic
hair'y
Hai'ti·an
half'back'

half'–breed'
half brother
half'heart'ed
half'–mast'
half'–moon'
half note
half'pen·ny
half step
half title
half'tone'
half'–truth'
half'way'
hal'i·but
hall'mark'
hal'low
Hal'low·een'
hal·lu'ci·nate
hal·lu'ci·na'tion
hal·lu'ci·na·to'ry
hall'way'
hal'ter
halves
Ham'burg
Ham'il·to'ni·an
ham'let
ham'mer
ham'mock
ham'per
ham'ster
ham'string'
Ham·tramck', Mich.
hand'bag'
hand'ball'
hand'book'
hand'cart'
hand'cuff'
hand'ed
hand'ful
hand'i·cap
hand'i·craft
hand'i·ly
hand'i·ness
hand'i·work'
hand'ker·chief
han'dle
handle bar
han'dling
hand'made', *adj.*
hand'maid', *n.*
hand'out'
hand'rail'
hand'saw'
hand'some
hand'spike'
hand'spring'
hand'–to–mouth'
hand'work'
hand'–worked'
hand'writ'ing
hand'y
handy man
hang'ar
hang'er
hang'ing
hang'man
hang'nail'
han'ker
hap'haz'ard
hap'less
hap'ly
hap'pen
hap'pen·ing
hap'pi·ly
hap'pi·ness
hap'py
Haps'burg
ha·rangue'
har'ass
har'ass·ing
har'bin·ger
har'bor
hard'–boiled'
hard'en
hard'–eyed'
hard'–faced'
hard'fist'ed
hard'head'
hard'head'ed
hard'heart'ed
har'di·hood
har'di·ly
har'di·ness
hard'–look'ing
hard'ly
hard'ness

hard'ship
hard'tack'
hard'ware'
hard'wood'
har'dy
hare'brained'
hare'lip'
ha'rem
Har'le·quin
har'le·quin·ade'
harm'ful
harm'less
har·mon'ic
har·mon'i·ca
har·mo'ni·ous
har'mo·ni·za'tion
har'mo·nize
har'mo·ny
har'ness
harp'ings
harp'ist
har·poon'
harp'si·chord
har'ri·er
har'row
har'vest
har'vest·er
has'ten
hast'i·ly
hast'i·ness
hast'y
hat'band'
hat'box'
hat'brush'
hatch'er
hatch'er·y
hatch'et
hatch'ing
hatch'way'
hate'ful
hat'er
hat'rack'
ha'tred
hat'stand'
hat'ter
haugh'ty
haul'age
Ha·van'a
have'lock
ha'ven
hav'er·sack
hav'oc
Ha·wai'ian
hawk'–eyed'
haw'ser
haw'thorn
hay fever
hay'rack'
hay'seed'
hay'stack'
hay'ward'
haz'ard
haz'ard·ous
ha'zel
ha'zi·ly
ha'zi·ness
haz'ing
ha'zy
head'ache'
head'band'
head'dress'
head'first'
head'i·ly
head'i·ness
head'ing
head'land'
head'less
head'light'
head'long
head'piece'
head'quar'ters
head'room'
head'spring'
head'strong
head'way'
head'work'
health'ful
health'i·ly
health'i·ness
health'y
hear'ing
heark'en
hear'say'
heart'ache'
heart'break'
heart'break'ing

heart′bro′ken
heart′burn′
heart′ed
heart′en
heart′felt′
hearth
hearth′stone′
heart′i·ly
heart′i·ness
heart′land′
heart′less
heart′–rend′ing
heart′scald′
heart′–shaped′
heart′sick′
heart′string′
heart′y
heat′er
hea′then
heath′er
heat′proof′
heav′en
heav′en·ly
heav′en·ward
heav′i·ly
heav′i·ness
heav′y
heav′y–du′ty
heav′y–eyed′
heav′y–fist′ed
heav′y–foot′ed
heav′y–hand′ed
heav′y·heart′ed
heav′y–set
heav′y·weight′
He·bra′ic
He′brew
hec′tic
hec′to·graph
hedge′hog′
heed′ful
heed′less
he·gem′o·ny
he·gi′ra
height
height′en
hei′nous
heir
heir′ess
heir′loom′
hel′i·cop′ter
he′li·o·graph′
he′li·um
hel′met
hel′met·ed
help′er
help′ful
help′less
help′mate′
Hel·ve′tian
he′ma·to′sis
hem′i·sphere
hem′i·spher′ic
hem′i·spher′i·cal
hem′lock
he′mo·glo′bin
he′mo·phil′i·a
hem′or·rhage
hem′or·rhoid
hemp′seed′
hem′stitch′
hence′forth′
hence′for′ward
hench′man
hen′peck′
he·pat′ic
he·pat′i·ca
hep′ta·gon
her′ald
he·ral′dic
her′ald·ry
herb′age
herb′al
Her·cu′le·an
Her′cu·les
herd′er
here′a·bout′
here·aft′er
he·red′i·tar′y
he·red′i·ty
here·in′
here′in·aft′er
here·in′be·fore′
her′e·sy
her′e·tic
he·ret′i·cal

here'to·fore'
here'up·on'
here·with'
her'i·ot
her'it·a·ble
her'it·age
Her'mes
her'mit
her'mit·age
her'ni·a
he'ro
he'roes
he·ro'ic
he·ro'i·cal
her'o·ism
her'on
her'ring
her'ring·bone'
her·self'
hes'i·tan·cy
hes'i·tant
hes'i·tate
hes'i·ta'tion
Hes·per'i·des
het'er·o·dox
het'er·o·ge·ne'i·ty
het'er·o·ge'ne·ous
hex'a·gon
hex·ag'o·nal
hex·an'gu·lar
hey'day'
hi·a'tus
Hi'a·wa'tha
hi'ber·nate
hi'ber·na'tion
hi·bis'cus
hic'cup
hick'o·ry
hid'den
hid'e·ous
hi'er·arch
hi'er·ar'chal
hi'er·arch'y
hi'er·at'ic
hi'er·o·glyph'ic
high'born'
high'bred'
high'–brow'
high chair
High Church
high'–flown'
high'hand'ed
high'–heeled'
high'land
high'land·er
high'–lev'el
high'–mind'ed
high'ness
high'–pres'sure
high'road'
high school
high sea
high'–sound'ing
high'–spir'it·ed
high'–strung'
high'–ten'sion
high'–test'
high–toned'
high'way'
high'way'man
hi·lar'i·ous
hi·lar'i·ty
hil'ding
hill'i·ness
hill'ock
hill'side'
hill'top'
hill'y
Hi·ma'la·yan
him·self'
hind'er, *adj.*
hin'der, *v.*
hin'drance
hind'sight'
hinge
hing'ing
hin'ter·land'
hip'bone'
hip'po·drome
hip'po·pot'a·mus
hire'ling
hiss'ing
his·to'ri·an
his·tor'ic
his·tor'i·cal
his'to·ries

is'to·ry
is'tri·on'ic
ith'er
ith'er·to'
oard'ing
oar'i·ness
oarse
oar'y
ob'ble
ob'by·horse'
ob'gob'lin
ob'nail'
o'bo
o'boes
ock'ey
og'gish
ogs'head
Ioh'en·zol'lern
oi' pol·loi'
oist'er
old'back'
old'er
old'fast'
old'ing
old'o'ver
old'up'
ole'proof
ole'y
ol'i·day
o'li·ness
Iol'land·er
ol'low

hol'o·graph
hol'ster
ho'ly
hom'age
home'bred'
home'less
home'like'
home'li·ness
home'ly
home'made'
home'mak'er
ho'me·o·path
ho'me·o·path'ic
ho'me·op'a·thy
home'own'er
home'–own'ing
Ho·mer'ic
home rule
home'sick'
home'spun'
home'stead
home town
home'ward
hom'i·cide
hom'i·lies
hom'i·ly
ho'mo·ge·ne'i·ty
ho'mo·ge'ne·ous
ho·mog'e·nous
ho·mol'o·gous
hom'o·nym
hon'est

hon'es·ty
hon'ey
hon'ey·bee'
hon'ey·comb'
hon'ey·dew'
hon'eyed
hon'ey·moon'
hon'ey·suck'le
hon'or
hon'or·a·ble
hon'o·rar'i·um
hon'or·ar'y
hood'ed
hood'lum
hoo'doo
hood'wink
hoof'print'
hook'up'
hook'worm'
hope'ful
hope'less
hop'per
hop'scotch'
Ho'rae
hore'hound'
ho·ri'zon
hor'i·zon'tal
hor'mone
hor'net
horn'pipe'
horn'y
hor'o·scope

hor'ri·ble
hor'rid
hor'ri·fy
hor'ror
horse'back'
horse'car'
horse'flesh'
horse'fly'
horse'hair'
horse'hide'
horse'laugh'
horse'leech'
horse'less
horse'man
horse opera
horse pistol
horse'play'
horse'pow'er
horse'–rad'ish
horse sense
horse'shoe'
horse'whip'
horse'wom'an
hor'ti·cul'tur·al
hor'ti·cul'ture
ho'sier
ho'sier·y
hos'pi·ta·ble
hos'pi·tal
hos'pi·tal'i·ty
hos'tage
hos'tel·ry
host'ess
hos'tile
hos·til'i·ty
hos'tler
hot'bed'
hot'box'
hot dog
ho·tel'
hot'foot'
hot'head'
hot'head'ed
hot'house'
hot'ly
hot'ness
hour'glass'
hour'ly
house'break'ing
house'coat'
house flag
house'fly'
house'ful
house'hold
house'hold'er
house'keep'er
house'line'
house'maid'
house'own'er
house'room'
house'warm'ing
house'wife'
house'work'
hous'ing
hov'el
hov'er
how·ev'er
howl'er
hub'bub
huck'le·ber'ry
huck'ster
hud'dle
huff'i·ly
huff'i·ness
huff'y
Hu'gue·not
hulk'ing
hul'la·ba·loo'
hu'man
hu·mane'
hu'man·ism
hu'man·ist
hu'man·is'tic
hu·man'i·tar'i·an
hu·man'i·tar'i-
an·ism
hu·man'i·ty
hu'man·ize
hu'man·kind'
hu'man·ly
hum'ble
hum'ble·ness
hum'bly
hum'bug'
hum'drum'
hu'mid
hu·mid'i·fy
hu·mid'i·ty
hu'mi·dor

ıu·mil′i·ate
ıu·mil′i·a′tion
ıu·mil′i·a·to′ry
ıu·mil′i·ty
ıummed
ıum′ming
ıum′ming·bird′
ıum′mock
ıu′mor
ıu′mor·ist
ıu′mor·ous
ıump′back′
ıunch′back′
ıun′dred
ıun′dred·fold′
ıun′dredth
ıun′dred·weight′
Hun·gar′i·an
ıun′ger
ıun′ger·ly
ıun′gri·er
ıun′gri·ly
ıun′gry
ıunt′er
Hun′ting·don, Pa.
Hun′ting·ton, Ind., N. Y., W. Va.
ıunts′man
ıur′dle
ıur′dy–gur′dy
ıur′ly–bur′ly

Hu′ron
hur·rah′
hur′ri·cane
hur′ried
hur′ry
hurt′ful
hus′band
hus′band·ry
hush money
husk′i·ly
husk′i·ness
husk′ing
husk′y
hus·sar′
hus′sy
hus′tle
huz·za′
hy′a·cinth
hy′brid
Hy′dra
hy·dran′ge·a
hy′drant
hy′drate
hy·drau′lic
hy′dro·car′bon
hy′dro·chlo′ric
hy′dro·chlo′ride
hy′dro·dy·nam′-ics
hy′dro·e·lec′tric
hy′dro·gen
hy·drol′y·sis
hy·drom′e·ter

hy′dro·phane
hy′dro·pho′bi·a
hy′dro·phone
hy′dro·plane
hy′dro·scope
hy′dro·stat′ic
hy′drous
hy·e′na
hy′giene
hy′gi·en′ic
hy′gro·scope
hy′gro·scop′ic
hy′men
hy′me·ne′al
hymn
hy·per′bo·la (curve)
hy·per′bo·le (exaggeration)
hy′per·crit′i·cal
hy′per·phys′i·cal
hy′phen
hy′phen·ate
hyp·no′sis
hyp·not′ic
hyp′no·tism
hyp′no·tist
hy′po·chon′dri·a
hy′po·chon′dri·ac
hy′po·chon·dri′-a·cal
hy·poc′ri·sy
hyp′o·crite

hyp′o·crit′i·cal
hy′po·der′mal
hy′po·der′mic
hy′po·der′mis
hy′po·gas′tric
hy·pot′e·nuse
hy·poth′e·car′y
hy·poth′e·cate
hy·poth′e·ses, *pl.*
hy·poth′e·sis
hy′po·thet′i·cal
hy′po·thet′i·cal·ly
hys′sop
hys·te′ri·a
hys·ter′i·cal
hys·ter′ics

I

i·am′bic
i·am′bus
I·be′ri·a
i′bex (goat)
i′bis (bird)
ice bag
ice′berg′
ice′boat′
ice′bound′
ice′box′
ice′ cream′
ice′man′
ice plant
i′ci·cle
i′ci·ly
i′ci·ness
ic′ing
i′con
i·con′ic
i·con′o·clast
i·de′al
i·de′al·ism
i·de′al·ist
i·de′al·is′tic
i·de′al·ize
i·de′al·ly
i·den′ti·cal
i·den′ti·fi·ca′tion
i·den′ti·fied
i·den′ti·fies
i·den′ti·fy
id′e·o·gram′
id′i·o·cy
id′i·om
id′i·o·mat′ic
id′i·o·syn′cra·sy
id′i·ot
id′i·ot′ic
i′dle
i′dle·ness
i′dly
i′dol
i·dol′a·trize
i·dol′a·trous
i·dol′a·try
i′dol·ism
i′dol·ize
i′dyl
i·dyl′lic
ig′loo
ig′nis fat′u·us
ig·nite′
ig·nit′i·ble
ig·ni′tion
ig·no′ble
ig′no·min′i·ous
ig′no·min·y
ig′no·ra′mus
ig′no·rance
ig′no·rant
ig·nore′

i·gua′na
il′i·ac
Il′i·ad
il′eum
(intestine)
il′i·um
(pelvic bone)
ilk
ill′–bred′
il·le′gal
il′le·gal′i·ty
il·leg′i·bil′i·ty
il·leg′i·ble
il′le·git′i·ma·cy
il′le·git′i·mate
ill′–fa′vored
il·lib′er·al
il·lic′it
il·lim′it·a·ble
Il′li·nois′
il·lit′er·a·cy
il·lit′er·ate
ill′ness
il·log′i·cal
ill′–starred′
ill′–tem′pered
ill′–treat′
il·lu′mi·nate
il·lu′mi·na′tion
il·lu′mi·na′tive
il·lu′mi·na′tor
il·lu′mine
il·lu′sion
il·lu′sive
il·lu′so·ry
il′lus·trate
il′lus·tra′tion
il·lus′tra·tive
il′lus·tra′tor
il·lus′tri·ous
im′age
im′age·ry
im·ag′i·na·ble
im·ag′i·nar′y
im·ag′i·na′tion
im·ag′i·na′tive
im·ag′ine
im′be·cile
im′be·cil′i·ty
im·bed′
im·bibe′
im·bib′er
im·bit′ter
im′bri·cate
im′bri·cat′ed
im′bri·ca′tion
im·bro′glio
im·bue′
im′i·ta·ble
im′i·tate
im′i·ta′tion
im′i·ta′tive
im′i·ta′tor
im·mac′u·late
im′ma·te′ri·al
im′ma·te′ri·al′i·ty
im′ma·ture′
im·meas′ur·a·ble
im·me′di·a·cy
im·me′di·ate
im·me′di·ate·ly
im′me·mo′ri·al
im·mense′
im·men′si·ty
im·merge′
im·merse′
im·mer′sion
im′mi·grant
im′mi·grate
im′mi·gra′tion
im′mi·nence
im′mi·nent
im·mo′bile
im·mo′bi·li·za′-
tion
im·mo′bi·lize
im·mod′er·ate
im·mod′er·a′tion
im·mod′est
im′mo·late
im′mo·la′tion
im·mor′al
im′mo·ral′i·ty
im·mor′tal
im′mor·tal′i·ty
im·mor′tal·ize

im·mov′a·bil′i·ty
im·mov′a·ble
im·mov′a·bly
im·mune′
im·mu′ni·ty
im′mu·nize
im·mure′
im·mu′ta·bil′i·ty
im·mu′ta·ble
im·pact′
im·pair′
im·pair′ment
im·pal′pa·ble
im·pan′el
im·par′i·ty
im·park′
im·part′
im·par′tial
im′par·ti·al′i·ty
im·part′i·ble
im·pass′a·bil′i·ty
im·pass′a·ble
im·passe′
im·pas′si·bil′i·ty
im·pas′si·ble
im·pas′sion
im·pas′sion·ate
im·pas′sioned
im·pas′sive
im·pa′tience
im·pa′tient
im·peach′
im·peach′a·ble
im·peach′ment
im·pec′ca·bil′i·ty
im·pec′ca·ble
im′pe·cu′ni·os′-
i·ty
im′pe·cu′ni·ous
im·ped′ance
im·pede′
im·pe′di·ent
im·ped′i·ment
im·ped′i·men′ta
im·pel′
im·pel′lent
im·pelled′
im·pel′ling
im·pend′
im·pend′ing
im·pen′e·tra·bil′-
i·ty
im·pen′e·tra·ble
im·per′a·tive
im·per′a·tive·ly
im′per·cep′ti·ble
im·per′fect
im′per·fec′tion
im·per′fect·ly
im·per′fect·ness
im·per′fo·rate
im·per′fo·rat′ed
im·per′fo·ra′tion
im·pe′ri·al
im·pe′ri·al·ism
im·pe′ri·al·ist
im·pe′ri·al·ly
im·per′il
im·pe′ri·ous
im·per′ish·a·ble
im·per′me·a·ble
im·per′son·al
im·per′son·ate
im·per′son·a′tion
im·per′son·a′tor
im·per′ti·nence
im·per′ti·nen·cy
im·per′ti·nent
im′per·turb′a-
bil′i·ty
im′per·turb′a-
ble
im′per·tur·ba′-
tion
im·per′vi·ous
im·pet′u·os′i·ty
im·pet′u·ous
im′pe·tus
im·pi′e·ty
im·pinge′
im′pi·ous
imp′ish
im·pla′ca·ble
im·plant′
im′ple·ment
im′pli·cate

im′pli·ca′tion
im′pli·ca′tive
im·plic′it
im·plied′
im·plore′
im·ply′
im′po·lite′
im·pol′i·tic
im·pon′der·a·ble
im·port′, *v.*
im′port, *n.*
im·port′a·ble
im·por′tance
im·por′tant
im′por·ta′tion
im·por′tu·na·cy
im·por′tu·nate
im′por·tune′
im′por·tu′ni·ty
im·pose′
im·pos′ing
im′po·si′tion
im·pos′si·bil′i·ty
im·pos′si·ble
im′post
im·pos′tor
im·pos′ture
im′po·tence
im′po·ten·cy
im′po·tent
im·pound′
im·pov′er·ish
im·prac′ti·ca-
bil′i·ty
im·prac′ti·ca·ble
im′pre·cate
im′pre·ca′tion
im′pre·ca·to′ry
im·preg′na·bil′-
i·ty
im·preg′na·ble
im·preg′nate
im′preg·na′tion
im′pre·sa′ri·o
im·press′, *v.*
im′press, *n.*
im·press′i·ble
im·pres′sion
im·pres′sion-
a·ble
im·pres′sive
im·pri′mis
im·print′, *v.*
im′print, *n.*
im·pris′on
im·pris′on·ment
im′prob·a·bil′i·ty
im·prob′a·ble
im·promp′tu
im·prop′er
im′pro·pri′e·ty
im·prov′a·ble
im·prove′
im·prove′ment
im·prov′er
im·prov′i·dence
im·prov′i·dent
im′pro·vi·sa′tion
im′pro·vise
im·pru′dence
im·pru′dent
im·pru′dent·ly
im′pu·dence
im′pu·dent
im·pugn′
im·pugn′a·ble
im′pulse
im·pul′sion
im·pul′sive
im·pu′ni·ty
im·pure′
im·pu′ri·ty
im·put′a·ble
im′pu·ta′tion
im·put′a·tive
im·pute′
in′a·bil′i·ty
in′ac·ces′si·bil′-
i·ty
in′ac·ces′si·ble
in·ac′cu·ra·cy
in·ac′cu·rate
in·ac′tion
in·ac′tive
in′ac·tiv′i·ty
in·ad′e·qua·cy

in·ad′e·quate
in′ad·mis′si·ble
in′ad·vert′ence
in′ad·vert′ent
in′ad·vis′a·ble
in·al′ien·a·ble
in·al′ter·a·ble
in·ane′
in·an′i·mate
in·an′i·ty
in′ap·peas′a·ble
in·ap′pli·ca·ble
in·ap′po·site
in′ap·pre′ci·a·ble
in′ap·pre′ci·a′-
tive
in′ap·pre·hen′si-
ble
in′ap·pro′pri·ate
in·apt′
in′ar·tic′u·late
in′ar·tis′tic
in′as·much′
in′at·ten′tion
in′at·ten′tive
in·au′di·ble
in·au′gu·ral
in·au′gu·rate
in·au′gu·ra′tion
in′aus·pi′cious
in′born′
in′bred′
in′burst′
in·cal′cu·la·ble
in′ca·les′cent
in′can·desce′
in′can·des′cence
in′can·des′cent
in′can·ta′tion
in′ca·pa·bil′i·ty
in·ca′pa·ble
in′ca·pa′cious
in′ca·pac′i·tate
in′ca·pac′i·ta′-
tion
in′ca·pac′i·ty
in·car′cer·ate
in·car′cer·a′tion
in·car′nate
in′car·na′tion
in·case′ment
in·cau′tious
in·cen′di·ar′y
in·cense′, *v.*
in′cense, *n.*
in·cen′tive
in·cep′tion
in·cep′tive
in·ces′sant
in·cho′ate
in′ci·dence
in′ci·dent
in′ci·den′tal
in′ci·den′tal·ly
in·cin′er·ate
in·cin′er·a′tion
in·cin′er·a′tor
in·cip′i·ent
in·cise′
in·ci′sion
in·ci′sive
in·ci′sor
in·ci′so·ry
in′ci·ta′tion
in·cite′
in·cite′ment
in′ci·vil′i·ty
in·clem′en·cy
in·clem′ent
in′cli·na′tion
in·cline′, *v.*
in′cline, *n.*
in·clined′
in·clin′ing
in·clude′
in·clud′ed
in·clu′sion
in·clu′sive
in′co·er′ci·ble
in·cog′ni·to
in′co·her′ence
in′co·her′ent
in′com·bus′ti·ble

in′come
in′com′ing
in′com·men′su-
ra·ble
in′com·men′su-
rate
in′com·mu′ni-
ca·ble
in·com′pa·ra·ble
in′com·pat′i·bil′-
i·ty
in′com·pat′i·ble
in·com′pe·tence
in·com′pe·tent
in′com·plete′
in′com·pre·hen′-
si·ble
in′com·press′i-
ble
in′com·put′a·ble
in′con·ceiv′a·ble
in′con·clu′sive
in′con·gru′i·ty
in·con′gru·ous
in·con′se·quent
in·con′se·quen′-
tial
in′con·sid′er·a-
ble
in′con·sid′er·ate
in′con·sist′en·cy
in′con·sist′ent
in′con·sol′a·ble
in′con·spic′u-
ous
in·con′stant
in′con·test′a·ble
in′con·tro·vert′-
i·ble
in′con·ven′ience
in′con·ven′ient
in′con·vert′i·ble
in·cor′po·rate
in·cor′po·ra′tion
in·cor′po·ra′tor
in′cor·po′re·al
in′cor·rect′
in·cor′ri·gi·bil′-
i·ty
in·cor′ri·gi·ble
in′cor·rupt′
in′cor·rupt′i·ble
in·creas′a·ble
in·crease′, *v.*
in′crease, *n.*
in·creas′ing·ly
in·cred′i·bil′i·ty
in·cred′i·ble
in′cre·du′li·ty
in·cred′u·lous
in′cre·ment
in·crim′i·nate
in·crim′i·na·to′ry
in′cu·bate
in′cu·ba′tion
in′cu·ba′tor
in′cu·bus
in·cul′cate
in′cul·ca′tion
in·cul′pate
in′cul·pa′tion
in·cul′pa·to′ry
in·cum′ben·cy
in·cum′bent
in·cur′
in·cur′a·ble
in·cu′ri·ous
in·curred′
in·cur′ring
in·cur′vate
in′cur·va′tion
in·debt′ed·ness
in·de′cen·cy
in·de′cent
in′de·ci′pher·a-
ble
in′de·ci′sion
in′de·ci′sive
in′de·clin′a·ble
in·dec′o·rous
in′de·co′rum
in·deed′
in′de·fat′i·ga·ble

in′de·fen′si·ble
in′de·fin′a·ble
in·def′i·nite
in·del′i·ble
in·del′i·ca·cy
in·del′i·cate
in·dem′ni·fi·ca′-
tion
in·dem′ni·fied
in·dem′ni·fies
in·dem′ni·fy
in·dem′ni·ty
in·dent′
in′den·ta′tion
in·dent′ed
in·den′tion
in·den′ture
in′de·pend′ence
in′de·pend′ent
in′de·scrib′a·ble
in′de·struct′i·ble
in′de·ter′mi·nate
in′de·ter′mi·na-
ble
in′de·ter′mi·na′-
tion
in′dex
(pl. *indexes* or *indices*)
in′dex·er
In′di·a
In′di·an

in′di·cate
in′di·ca′tion
in·dic′a·tive
in′di·ca′tor
in′di·ca·to′ry
in′di·ces, *pl.*
in·dict′
(charge with crime. cf. *indite.*)
in·dict′a·ble
in·dic′tion
in·dict′ment
In′dies
in·dif′fer·ence
in·dif′fer·ent
in·dif′fer·ent·ly
in′di·gence
in·dig′e·nous
in′di·gent
in′di·gest′i·ble
in′di·ges′tion
in·dig′nant
in′dig·na′tion
in·dig′ni·ty
in′di·go
in′di·rect′
in′di·rect′ly
in′di·rect′ness
in′dis·cern′i·ble
in′dis·creet′
in′dis·crete′
in′dis·cre′tion

in′dis·crim′i·nate
in′dis·crim′i-
na′tion
in′dis·pen′sa·ble
in′dis·posed′
in′dis·po·si′tion
in·dis′pu·ta·ble
in·dis′so·lu·ble
in′dis·tinct′
in′dis·tinc′tive
in′dis·tinct′ly
in′dis·tin′guish-
a·ble
in·dite′
(write. cf. *indict.*)
in′di·vert′i·ble
in′di·vid′u·al
in′di·vid′u·al·ism
in′di·vid′u·al·ist
in′di·vid′u·al′i·ty
in′di·vid′u·al·ize
in′di·vid′u·al·ly
in′di·vis′i·ble
In′do–Chi·nese′
in·doc′ile
in′do·lence
in′do·lent
in·dom′i·ta·ble
in′door′
in′doors′
in′drawn′

in·du′bi·ta·ble
in·duce′
in·duce′ment
in·duct′
in·duc′tile
in′duc·til′i·ty
in·duc′tion
in·duc′tive
in·duc′tor
in·dulge′
in·dul′gence
in·dul′gent
in′du·rate
in′du·ra′tion
in·dus′tri·al
in·dus′tri·al·ism
in·dus′tri·al·ist
in·dus′tri·al·ize
in′dus·tries
in·dus′tri·ous
in′dus·try
in·e′bri·ant
in·e′bri·ate
in·e′bri·a′tion
in′e·bri′e·ty
in·ed′i·ble
in·ef′fa·ble
in′ef·face′a·ble
in′ef·fec′tive
in′ef·fec′tu·al
in′ef·fi·ca′cious
in·ef′fi·ca·cy
in′ef·fi′cien·cy
in′ef·fi′cient
in·el′e·gance
in·el′e·gant
in·el′i·gi·bil′i·ty
in·el′i·gi·ble
in·el′o·quent
in′e·luc′ta·ble
in·ept′
in·ept′i·tude
in′e·qual′i·ty
in·eq′ui·ta·ble
in·eq′ui·ty
in′e·rad′i·ca·ble
in′e·ras′a·ble
in·er′rant
in·ert′
in·er′tia
in′es·sen′tial
in·es′ti·ma·ble
in·ev′i·ta·bil′i·ty
in·ev′i·ta·ble
in′ex·act′
in′ex·act′i·tude
in′ex·cus′a·ble
in′ex·haust′i·bil′i·ty
in′ex·haust′i·ble
in·ex′o·ra·ble
in′ex·pe′di·ent
in′ex·pen′sive
in′ex·pe′ri·ence
in′ex·pert′
in·ex′pi·a·ble
in′ex·plain′a·ble
in·ex′pli·ca·ble
in′ex·plic′it
in′ex·press′i·ble
in′ex·pres′sive
in′ex·pug′na·ble
in′ex·ten′si·ble
in′ex·tin′guish·a·ble
in·ex′tri·ca·ble
in·fal′li·bil′i·ty
in·fal′li·ble
in′fa·mous
in′fa·my
in′fan·cy
in′fant
in·fan′ta, *fem.*
in·fan′te, *masc.*
in′fan·tile
in′fan·try
in·fat′u·ate
in·fat′u·a′tion
in·fect′
in·fec′tion
in·fec′tious
in·fec′tive
in·fec′tor
in′fe·lic′i·tous
in′fe·lic′i·ty
in·fer′

in′fer·ence
in′fer·en′tial
in·fe′ri·or
in·fe′ri·or′i·ty
in·fer′nal
in·fer′no
in·ferred′
in·fer′ring
in·fest′
in′fes·ta′tion
in′fi·del
in′fi·del′i·ty
in′field′
in·fil′trate
in′fi·nite
in′fin·i·tes′i·mal
in·fin′i·tive
in·fin′i·ty
in·firm′
in·fir′ma·ry
in·fir′mi·ty
in·flame′
in·flam′ma·ble
in′flam·ma′tion
in·flam′ma·to′ry
in·flate′
in·flat′ed
in·fla′tion
in·flect′
in·flec′tion
in·flex′i·ble
in·flict′
in·flic′tion
in′flow′
in′flu·ence
in′flu·en′tial
in′flu·en′za
in′flux
in·form′
in·for′mal
in′for·mal′i·ty
in·form′ant
in′for·ma′tion
in·form′a·tive
in·form′er
in·frac′tion
in′fra·red′
in′fra·struc′ture
in·fre′quent
in·fringe′
in·fringe′ment
in·fu′ri·ate
in·fuse′
in·fu′sion
in·gen′ious
in′gé′nue′
in′ge·nu′i·ty
in·gen′u·ous
in·ges′tion
in·glo′ri·ous
in′got
in′grained′
in′grate
in·gra′ti·ate
in·grat′i·tude
in·gre′di·ent
in′gress
in′grown′
in·hab′it
in·hab′it·ant
in·hale′
in′har·mo′ni·ous
in·here′
in·her′ence
in·her′ent
in·her′it
in·her′it·ance
in·hib′it
in′hi·bi′tion
in·hos′pi·ta·ble
in·hu′man
in′hu·man′i·ty
in′hu·ma′tion
in·im′i·cal
in·im′i·ta·ble
in·iq′ui·tous
in·iq′ui·ty
in·i′tial
in·i′ti·ate
in·i′ti·a′tive
in·ject′
in·jec′tion
in·jec′tor
in′ju·di′cious
in·junc′tion
in′jure

in′ju·ries
in′jur·ing
in·ju′ri·ous
in′ju·ry
in·jus′tice
ink bot′tle
ink′ling
ink′stain
ink′stand′
ink′well′
in·laid′
in′land
in′lay′
in·let′, *v.*
in′let, *n.*
in′mate
in′most
in′nate
in′ning
inn′keep′er
in′no·cence
in′no·cent
in·noc′u·ous
in′no·vate
in′nu·en′do
in′nu·en′does
in·nu′mer·a·ble
in·oc′u·late
in·oc′u·la′tion
in′of·fen′sive
in·op′er·a·ble
in·op′por·tune′
in·or′di·nate
in′or·gan′ic
in′put′
in′quest
in·qui′e·tude
in·quire′
in·quir′ies
in·quir′ing
in·quir′y
in′qui·si′tion
in·quis′i·tive
in·quis′i·tor
in′road′
in′rush′
in·sane′
in·san′i·tar′y
in·san′i·ty
in·sa′ti·a·ble
in·scribe′
in·scrip′tion
in·scru′ta·ble
in′sect
in·sec′ti·cide
in′se·cure′
in′se·cur′i·ty
in·sen′sate
in·sen′si·ble
in·sen′si·tive
in·sep′a·ra·ble
in·sert′, *v.*
in′sert, *n.*
in·ser′tion
in′side′
in·sid′i·ous
in′sight′
in·sig′ne, *n. sing.*
in·sig′ni·a, *n. pl.*
in′sig·nif′i·cance
in′sig·nif′i·cant
in′sin·cere′
in·sin′u·ate
in·sin′u·a′tion
in·sip′id
in·sist′
in·sist′ence
in·sist′ent
in′sole′
in′so·lence
in′so·lent
in·sol′u·ble
in·sol′ven·cy
in·sol′vent
in·som′ni·a
in·sou′ci·ance
in·sou′ci·ant
in·spect′
in·spec′tion
in·spec′tor
in′spi·ra′tion
in·spire′
in′sta·bil′i·ty
in·stall′
in′stal·la′tion
in·stalled′

in·stall′ing
in·stall′ment
in′stance
in′stan·ta′ne·ous
in·stan′ter
in′stant·ly
in·stead′
in′step
in′sti·gate
in′sti·ga′tion
in′sti·ga′tor
in·still′
in·stilled′
in·still′ing
in·stinct′, *adj.*
in′stinct, *n.*
in·stinc′tive
in′sti·tute
in′sti·tu′tion
in′sti·tu′tion·al
in·struct′
in·struct′ed
in·struc′tion
in·struc′tion·al
in·struc′tive
in·struc′tor
in′stru·ment
in′stru·men′tal
in′sub·or′di·nate
in′sub·or′di·na′-
tion
in·suf′fer·a·ble
in′suf·fi′cient
in′su·lar
in′su·late
in′su·la′tion
in′su·la′tor
in·sult′, *v.*
in′sult, *n.*
in·su′per·a·ble
in′sup·port′a·ble
in′sup·press′i·ble
in·sur′a·ble
in·sur′ance
in·sure′
in·sur′gent
in′sur·rec′tion
in·tact′
in·tagl′io
in′take′
in·tan′gi·ble
in′te·ger
in′te·gral
in′te·grate
in′te·gra′tion
in·teg′ri·ty
in·teg′u·ment
in′tel·lect
in′tel·lec′tu·al
in·tel′li·gence
in·tel′li·gent
in·tel′li·gi·ble
in·tem′per·ance
in·tem′per·ate
in·tend′
in·tend′ant
in·tense′
in·ten′si·fied
in·ten′si·fies
in·ten′si·fy
in·ten′si·ty
in·ten′sive
in·tent′
in·ten′tion
in·ter′
in′ter·cede′
in′ter·ced′ing
in′ter·cept′
in′ter·ces′sion
in′ter·course
in′ter·dict, *n.*
in′ter·est
in′ter·est·ed
in′ter·fere′
in′ter·fer′ence
in′ter·fer′ing
in′ter·im
in·te′ri·or
in′ter·ject′
in′ter·jec′tion
in′ter·leave′
in′ter·lin′e·ar
in′ter·loc′u·tor
in′ter·loc′u·to′ry
in′ter·lop′er
in′ter·lude

in′ter·mar′riage
in′ter·me′di·ate
in·ter′ment
in·ter′mi·na·ble
in′ter·mis′sion
in′ter·mit′tent
in·ter′nal
in′ter·na′tion·al
in′ter·ne′cine
in·ter′po·late
in′ter·pose′
in·ter′pret
in·ter′pre·ta′tion
in·ter′pret·er
in·terred′
in′ter·reg′num
in·ter′ring
in·ter′ro·gate
in·ter′ro·ga′tion
in′ter·rog′a·tive
in′ter·rog′a·to′ry
in′ter·rupt′
in′ter·rup′tion
in′ter·sect′
in′ter·sperse′
in′ter·state′
in·ter′stice
in′ter·ur′ban
in′ter·val
in′ter·vene′
in′ter·ven′tion
in′ter·view
in′ter·view′er
in·tes′tate
in·tes′ti·nal
in·tes′tine
in′ti·ma·cy
in′ti·mate
in′ti·ma′tion
in·tim′i·date
in·tim′i·da′tion
in·tol′er·a·ble
in·tol′er·ance
in·tol′er·ant
in′to·na′tion
in·tone′
in·tox′i·cant
in·tox′i·cate
in·tox′i·ca′tion
in·trac′ta·ble
in′tra·mu′ral
in·tran′si·gent
in·tran′si·tive
in·trep′id
in′tre·pid′i·ty
in′tri·ca·cy
in′tri·cate
in·trigue′
in·trigued′
in·tri′guing
in·trin′sic
in′tro·duce′
in′tro·duc′tion
in′tro·duc′to·ry
in·tro′it
in′tro·spec′tion
in′tro·vert′, *v.*
in′tro·vert′, *n.*
in·trude′
in·tru′sion
in′tu·i′tion
in·tu′i·tive
in·twist′
in·unc′tion
in′un·date
in′un·da′tion
in·ure′
in·vade′
in·vad′ing
in·val′id, *adj.*
in′va·lid, *n.*
in·val′i·date
in·val′u·a·ble
in·var′i·a·ble
in·va′sion
in·vec′tive
in·veigh′
in·vei′gle
in·vent′
in·ven′tion
in·ven′tive
in·ven′tor
in′ven·to′ries
in′ven·to′ry
in·verse′
in·ver′sion

in·vert', *v.*
in'vert, *adj.*
in·vest'
in·ves'ti·gate
in·ves'ti·ga'tion
in·ves'ti·ga'tor
in·ves'ti·ture
in·vest'ment
in·vet'er·ate
in·vid'i·ous
in·vig'or·ate
in·vin'ci·ble
in·vi'o·la·ble
in·vi'o·late
in·vis'i·ble
in'vi·ta'tion
in·vite'
in·vit'ing
in'vo·ca'tion
in'voice
in'voic·ing
in·voke'
in·vok'ing
in·vol'un·tar'y
in·volve'
in·volv'ing
in·vul'ner·a·ble
in'ward
i'o·dine
i'on·ize

i·o'ta
i·ras'ci·ble
i'rate
ir'i·des'cence
ir'i·des'cent
i·rid'i·um
irk'some
i'ron·clad'
iron gray
i·ron'i·cal
i'ron·mas'ter
i'ron·side'
i'ron·ware'
i'ron·wood'
i'ron·work'
i'ro·ny
ir·ra'tion·al
ir·rec'on·cil'a·ble
ir're·deem'a·ble
ir're·duc'i·ble
ir·ref'ra·ga·ble
ir·ref'u·ta·ble
ir·reg'u·lar
ir·rel'e·vance
ir·rel'e·vant
ir're·li'gious
ir·rep'a·ra·ble
ir're·press'i·ble
ir're·proach'a-
ble

ir're·sist'i·ble
ir·res'o·lu·ble
ir·res'o·lute
ir·res'o·lu'tion
ir're·spec'tive
ir're·spon'si·ble
ir're·triev'a·ble
ir·rev'er·ent
ir're·vers'i·ble
ir·rev'o·ca·ble
ir'ri·gate
ir'ri·ga'tion
ir'ri·ta·ble
ir'ri·tant
ir'ri·tate
ir'ri·ta'tion
ir·rup'tion
is'chi·um
i'sin·glass'
is'land
i'so·late
i'so·la'tion
i·sos'ce·les
Is'ra·el
is'sue
isth'mus
i'tem·ize
i·tin'er·ant
i·tin'er·ar'y
i'vo·ry

J

ja'bot'
jack'al
jack'et
jack'knife'
jack'-o'-lan'tern
jack plane
jack pot
jack rabbit
jack'straw'
Jac'o·bin
jag'uar
jan'i·tor
ja·pan'
(varnish)
Jap'a·nese'
jar
jar'gon
jarred
jar'ring
jas'mine
jas'per
jaun'dice
jaunt'i·ly
jaunt'y
jave'lin
jaw'bone'
jeal'ous
Je·ho'vah
je·june'
je·ju'num
jel'lied
jel'ly·fish'
jeop'ard·ize
jeop'ard·y
jer'e·mi'ad
jerk'i·ly
jerk'y
Jes'u·it
jet'sam
jet'ties
jet'ti·son
jet'ty
jew'el
jew'eled
jew'el·er
jew'el·ry
jin'gle
jin'go
jin'goes
job
job'ber
job'bing
jock'ey
jock'eys
jo·cose'
joc'u·lar
joc'u·lar'i·ty
joc'und
John'ston, R. I.
Johns'town,
N. Y., Pa.
joint'ly
jok'er
jol'li·ty
jon'quil
jos'tle
jour'nal
jour'nal·ism
jour'nal·ist
jour'nal·ize
jour'ney
jour'neyed
jour'ney·man
jour'neys
jo'vi·al
joy'ful
joy'ous
ju'bi·lant
ju'bi·la'tion
ju'bi·lee
judg'ing
judg'ment
ju'di·ca·to'ry
ju'di·ca·ture
ju·di'cial
ju·di'ci·ar'y
ju·di'cious

Jug′ger·naut
jug′gle
jug′u·lar
juic′i·ly
juic′i·ness
ju·jit′su
juke′box′
ju′lep
jum′ble
junc′tion
junc′ture
ju′ni·per
ju·rid′i·cal
ju′ries
ju′ris·dic′tion
ju′ris·pru′dence
ju′rist
ju′ror
ju′ry
ju′ry·man
jus′tice
jus′ti·fi′a·ble
jus′ti·fi·ca′tion
jus′ti·fied
jus′ti·fy
jus′ti·fy′ing
just′ness
ju′ve·nile
jux′ta·po·si′tion

K

kai′ser
ka·lei′do·scope
kan′ga·roo′
ka′o·lin
kar′a·kul
kar′ma
ka′ty·did′
Kear′ney, Nebr.
Kear′ny, N. J.
keel′haul′
keel′son
keen′ness
keep′sake′
ken′nel
ker′nel
ker′o·sene′
ket′tle·drum′
key′board′
key′hole′
key′note′
key′stone′
kha′ki
khe·dive′
kid′nap
kid′naped
kid′nap′ing
kid′ney
kil′o·gram
kil′o·me′ter
kil′o·watt
kil′o·watt′–hour′
ki·mo′no
ki·mo′nos
kin′der·gar′ten
kind′heart′ed
kind′li·ness
kin′dling
kind′ness
kin′dred
ki·net′ic
king′dom
king′fish′
king′pin′
king′ship
kins′folk′
kin′ship
kins′man
ki·osk′
kis′met
kitch′en
kitch′en·ette′

kitch′en·ware
kit′ten
knap′sack′
knav′er·y
knead
knee′cap′
knee′–deep′
knee′–high′
knick′knack′
knife
knight′hood
knit
knit′ted
knit′ting
knives
knock′a·bout′
knock′down′
knock′out′
knot′hole′
knot′ting
knot′ty
know′a·ble
know′–how′
knowl′edge
knuck′le
Koh′–i·noor′
ku·lak′

L

la′bel
la′beled
la′bel·ing
la′bi·al
la′bor
lab′o·ra·to′ry
la′bor·er
la·bo′ri·ous
la·bur′num
lab′y·rinth
lac′er·ate
lac′er·a′tion
lace′work′
lach′ry·mal
lach′ry·mose
la·con′ic
lac′quer
la·crosse′
lac·ta′tion
la·cu′na
lad′der
la′dies
la·drone′
la′dy·bird′
la′dy·bug′
la′dy·fin′ger
la′dy–kill′er
la′dy·like′
la′dy·ship
la′dy's maid
la′dy's–slip′per
lag′gard
la·goon′
la′i·ty
lake′side′
lam′ben·cy
lam′bent
lamb′kin
lam′bre·quin
lamb′skin′
la·ment′
lam′en·ta·ble
lam′en·ta′tion
lam′i·nate
lamp′black′
lam·poon′
lam′prey
lamp′stand
lan′cet
lan′ci·nate
lan′dau
land′fall′
land′grave′
land′hold′er

landing craft
landing field
landing gear
landing strip
land'la'dy
land'locked'
land'lord'
land'lub'ber
land'mark'
land'own'er
land'–poor'
land'scape
land'slip'
lands'man
lan'guage
lan'guid
lan'guish
lan'guor
lan'tern
lan'yard
lap dog
la·pel'
lap'i·dar'y
lap'ping
lar'board
lar'ce·nous
lar'ce·ny
lar·ghet'to
lar'i·at
lark'spur
lar'va
(plural: *lar'vae*)

lar'yn·gi'tis
lar'ynx
las·civ'i·ous
las'si·tude
latch'key'
latch'string'
late'ness
la'tent
lat'er·al
lat'ish
lat'i·tude
lat'tice
lat'tice·work'
laud'a·ble
lau'da·num
laud'a·to'ry
laugh'a·ble
laugh'ing·stock'
laugh'ter
laun'der
laun'dress
laun'dries
laun'dry
lau're·ate
lau'rel
lav'a·to'ry
lav'en·der
lav'ish
law'–a·bid'ing
law'ful
law'giv'er
law'less

law'mak'er
law'mak'ing
law'suit'
law'yer
lax'a·tive
lax'i·ty
lay'man
lay'out'
lead'en
lead'er
lead'er·ship
leads'man
leaf'let
league
leak'age
leak'proof
lean
(thin. cf. *lien.*)
leap'frog'
lease'hold'
leath'er
leath'er·work'
leav'en
lec'tern
lec'ture
ledg'er
lee'ward
lee'way'
left'–hand'ed
leg'a·cies
leg'a·cy
le'gal

le·gal′i·ty
le′gal·ize
le′gal·ly
leg′ate
leg′a·tee′
le·ga′tion
le·ga′to
leg′end·ar′y
leg′er·de·main′
leg′ging
leg′horn
leg′i·bil′i·ty
leg′i·ble
le′gion
leg′is·late
leg′is·la′tion
leg′is·la′tive
leg′is·la′tor
leg′is·la′ture
le·git′i·ma·cy
le·git′i·mate
le·git′i·ma·tize
leg′man′
lei′sure
lem′on·ade′
le′mur
length
length′en
length′i·er
length′wise
length′y
le′ni·ence
le′ni·ent
len′i·ty
len·tic′u·lar
len′til
leop′ard
lep′ro·sy
lep′rous
le′sion
les·see′
less′en
(decrease)
less′er
les′son
(study)
le·thar′gic
leth′ar·gy
letter box
letter carrier
let′tered
let′ter gram
let′ter·head′
let′ter–per′fect
let′ter·press′
let′tuce
lev′ee
(embankment)
lev′el
lev′eled
le′ver·age
le·vi′a·than
lev′i·ta′tion
lev′i·ty
lev′y
(tax)
Lew′is·ton, Idaho, Maine
Lew′is·town, Mont., Pa.
lex′i·con
li′a·bil′i·ty
li′a·ble
li′ai′son′
li·ba′tion
li′bel
li′bel·ant
li′bel·ee′
li′bel·ing
li′bel·ous
lib′er·al
lib′er·al′i·ty
lib′er·al·ize
lib′er·al·ly
lib′er·ate
lib′er·a′tion
lib′er·a′tor
lib′er·tine
lib′er·ty
li·bid′i·nous
li·brar′i·an
li′brar′y
li·bret′tist
li·bret′to
li·bret′tos
li′cense

li′cens·ing
li·cen′tious
li′chen
lic′o·rice
li′en
(claim. cf. *lean.*)
lieu·ten′an·cy
lieu·ten′ant
life belt
life′blood′
life′boat′
life buoy
life guard
life′less
life′like′
life′line
life′long′
life net
life raft
life′sav′er
life′sav′ing
life′time′
lig′a·ment
li·ga′tion
lig′a·ture
light′en
light′er·age
light′–fin′gered
light′heart′ed
light′house′
light′ning
light′proof′
light′ship′
light′tight′
light′weight′
lig′ne·ous
lig′nite
lik′a·ble
like′li·hood
like′ness
like′wise′
li′lac
Lil′li·pu′tian
lim′ber
lime′kiln′
lime′light′
Lim′er·ick
lime′stone′
lime′wa′ter
lim′i·nal
lim′i·ta′tion
lim′it·less
lim′ou·sine′
lim′pet
lim′pid
lin′age
(printed lines)
linch′pin′
lin′e·age
(family)
lin′e·al
lin′e·a·ment
lin′e·ar
line′man
lin′ge·rie′
lin′guist
lin′i·ment
lin′ing
link′age
li·no′le·um
Lin′o·type
lin′seed′
lin′tel
li′on·ess
li′on·heart′ed
li·po′ma
liq′ue·fac′tion
liq′ue·fied
liq′ue·fy
liq′ue·fy′ing
li·ques′cent
li·queur′
liq′uid
liq′ui·date
liq′ui·da′tion
liq′uor
lis′ten
list′less
lit′er·a·cy
lit′er·al
(exact)
lit′er·al·ly
lit′er·ar′y
lit′er·ate
lit′er·a·ture
lith′i·a

lith'i·um
lith'o·graph
li·thog'ra·pher
li·thog'ra·phy
lit'i·gant
lit'i·gate
lit'i·ga'tion
li·ti'gious
lit'mus
lit'tle
lit'to·ral
(shore)
lit'ur·gy
liv'a·ble
live'li·hood
live'long'
liv'e·ry
liv'er·y·man
liv'ing room
liz'ard
loath'some
lob'by·ing
lob'ster
lo·cal'i·ty
lo'cal·ize
lo'cate
lo·ca'tion
lock'jaw'
lock'out'
lock'smith'
lock step
lock stitch
lock'up'
lo'co·mo'tion
lo'co·mo'tive
lo'cust
lo·cu'tion
lode'stone'
lodge'ment
lodg'ing
log'a·rithm
log'gia
log'ging
log'i·cal
lo·gi'cian
log'o·type
log'roll'ing
Lo'hen·grin
loll'ing
lol'li·pop
lone'li·ness
lone'some
long'boat'
long'bow'
lon·gev'i·ty
long'hand'
long'head'ed
long'horn'
lon'gi·tude
long'–lost'
long'shore'man
long'–suf'fer·ing
long'–wind'ed
look'ing glass
look'out'
loop'hole'
loose'ly
lo·qua'cious
lor'gnette'
lo'tion
lot'ter·y
lov'a·ble
love'less
love'li·ness
love'lorn'
love'ly
love'sick'
low'born'
low'boy'
low'bred'
low'–brow'
Low Church
low'–cut'
low'–heeled'
low'land
low'li·ness
low'–priced'
low'–rent'
lox
loy'al·ty
loz'enge
lu'bri·cant
lu'bri·cate
lu'bri·ca'tion
lu'cid
lu·cid'i·ty

luck′i·er
luck′i·est
luck′i·ly
luck′y
lu′cra·tive
lu′cu·bra′tion
lu′di·crous
lug′gage
lu·gu′bri·ous
luke′warm′
lull′a·by′
lum·ba′go
lum′bar
(nerve)
lum′ber
(wood)

lum′ber·yard′
lu′mi·nar′y
lu′mi·nous
lu′na·cy
lu′na·tic
lunch′eon
lunch′room′
lu·nette′
lurch
lus′cious
lus′ter
lus′ter·ware′
lust′ful
lust′i·ly
lus′trous

lust′y
Lu′ther·an
lux·u′ri·ant
lux·u′ri·ate
lux′u·ries
lux·u′ri·ous
lux′u·ry
ly·ce′um
ly′ing
lym·phat′ic
lynch
lynx
ly′on·naise′
lyr′ic
lyr′i·cal

M

ma·ca′bre
mac·ad′am
mac′a·ro′ni
mac′a·roon′
mac′er·ate
mac′er·a′tion
ma·chic′o·la′tion
mach′i·na′tion
ma·chine′
machine gun
ma·chin′er·y

machine shop
machine tool
ma·chin′ist
Mc′ In·tosh
(apple)
mack′er·el
mack′in·tosh
(raincoat)
ma′cron
ma′de·moi′selle′
mad′ri·gal

mag′a·zine′
ma·gen′ta
mag′got
mag′ic
ma·gi′cian
mag′is·te′ri·al
mag′is·tra·cy
mag′is·trate
mag′is·tra·ture
Mag′na Char′ta
mag′na·nim′i·ty

mag·nan′i·mous
mag′nate
mag·ne′sia
mag·ne′si·um
mag′net
mag·net′ic
mag′net·ism
mag′net·ite
mag′net·ize
mag·ne′to
mag·ne′tos
mag′ni·fi·ca′tion
mag·nif′i·cence
mag·nif′i·cent
mag·nif′i·co
mag′ni·fi′er
mag′ni·fy
mag′ni·fy′ing
mag·nil′o·quent
mag′ni·tude
mag·no′li·a
mag′num
mag′pie
mag′uey
Mag′yar
ma·ha′ra′ja
ma·hog′a·ny
maid′en
maid′en·hair′
maid′en·head
maid′en·ly
maid′serv′ant
mail′a·ble
mail′bag′
mail′box′
mail′er
mail′man′
main′land′
main′ly
main′mast′
main′sail′
main′spring′
main′stay′
main·tain′
main′te·nance
maize
(corn. cf. *maze.*)
ma·jes′tic
maj′es·ty
ma·jol′i·ca
ma′jor
ma′jor–do′mo
major general
ma·jor′i·ty
ma·jus′cule
make′–be·lieve′
make′fast′
make′shift′
make′–up′
make′weight′
mak′ing
ma·la′ceous
(apple family)
mal′a·chite
mal′ad·just′ment
mal′ad·min′is·ter
mal′ad·min′is-
tra′tion
mal′a·droit′
mal′a·dy
ma·laise′
mal′a·pert
mal′ap·ro·pos′
ma·lar′i·a
ma·lar′i·al
mal′as·sim′i·la′-
tion
Ma·lay′
mal′con·tent′
mal′e·dic′tion
mal′e·fac′tion
mal′e·fac′tor
ma·lef′ic
ma·lef′i·cence
ma·lef′i·cent
ma·lev′o·lence
ma·lev′o·lent
mal·fea′sance
mal′for·ma′tion
mal·formed′
mal′ice
ma·li′cious
(mischievous)
ma·lign′
ma·lig′nan·cy
ma·lig′nant

ma·lig′ni·ty
ma·lin′ger
ma·lin′ger·er
mal′lard
mal′le·a·bil′i·ty
mal′le·a·ble
mal′let
mal′low
malm′sey
mal′nu·tri′tion
mal·o′dor
mal·o′dor·ous
mal′po·si′tion
mal′prac′tice
Mal′tese′
Mal·thu′sian
malt′ose
mal·treat′
malt′ster
mal′ver·sa′tion
mam′mal
mam′mon
mam′moth
man′a·cle
man′age
man′age·a·ble
man′age·ment
man′ag·er
man′a·ge′ri·al
man′ag·ing
man′a·tee′
Man′chu′
man′ci·ple
man·da′mus
man′da·rin
man′da·tar′y (agent)
man′date
man′da·to′ry (compelling)
man′–day′
man′di·ble
man′do·lin
man′drel
man′du·cate
man′–eat′er
ma·nège′
ma·neu′ver
man′ful
man′ga·nese
man′gel–wur′zel
man′ger
man′gi·ly
man′gle
man′go
man′goes
man′grove
man′gy
man′han′dle
man′hole′
man′hood
man′–hour′
ma′ni·a
ma′ni·ac
ma·ni′a·cal
man′i·cure
man′i·fest
man′i·fes·ta′tion
man′i·fest·ly
man′i·fes′to
man′i·fes′toes
man′i·fold
man′i·fold′er
Ma·nil′a
man′i·ple
ma·nip′u·late
ma·nip′u·la′tion
ma·nip′u·la′tive
ma·nip′u·la′tor
ma·nip′u·la·to′ry
man′i·to
man′kind′
man′like′
man′ly
man′na
man′ne·quin
man′ner
man′ner·ism
man′nish
man′–of–war′
man′–of–war′ bird
ma·nom′e·ter
man′or
ma·no′ri·al
man′rope′

man'sard roof
man'serv'ant
man'sion
man'slaugh'ter
man'slay'er
man'stop'ping
man'sue·tude
man'teau
man'tel
(shelf)
man'tel·et
man'tel·piece'
man'tel·tree'
man·til'la
man'tle
(cloak)
man'u·al
man'u·fac'ture
man'u·fac'tur·er
man'u·mis'sion
man'u·mit'
ma·nure'
man'u·script
Manx
man'y
Ma'o·ri
ma'ple
mar'a·schi'no
ma·ras'mus
Ma·ra'tha
mar'a·thon
ma·raud'
mar'ble
mar'ble·ize
mar'bling
marc
mar'ca·site
mar·ces'cent
mar·che'sa
mar·che'se
mar'chion·ess
Mar·co'ni
mar·co'ni·gram
Mar'di gras'
mare's'–nest'
mare's'–tail'
mar'ga·rine
mar'ga·rite
mar'gin
mar'gin·al
mar'gi·na'li·a
mar'grave
mar'i·gold
mar'i·nade'
ma·rine'
mar'i·ner
mar'i·o·nette'
mar'i·tal
mar'i·time
mar'ket
mar'ket·a·ble
mar'ket·er
mar'ket·ing
market place
marks'man
mar'line·spike'
mar'ma·lade
mar'mo·set
mar'mot
ma·roon'
mar'que·try
mar·quee'
(canopy)
mar'quis
(nobleman)
mar·quise'
mar'riage
mar'riage·a·ble
mar'rons' gla'-
cés', *pl.*
mar'row
mar'row·bone'
mar'ry
Mar'seil·laise'
mar'shal
(officer)
marsh gas
marsh'i·ness
marsh'mal'low
marsh'y
mar'ten
(furbearing
animal)
mar'tial
(warlike)
mar'tial·ly

Mar′ti·an
mar′tin
(bird)
mar′ti·net′
Mar′tin·mas
mar′tyr
mar′tyr·dom
mar′tyr·ize
mar′tyr·o·log′i-
cal
mar′tyr·ol′o·gist
mar′tyr·ol′o·gy
mar′vel
mar′veled
mar′vel·ing
mar′vel·ous
Marx′i·an
Mar′y
mas′cle
mas′cot
mas′cu·line
mas′cu·lin′i·ty
mash′er
mash′ie
mask′er
ma′son
ma·son′ic
ma′son·ry
mas′quer·ade′
mas′sa·cre
mas·sage′
mas·sag′ing

mas·sag′ist
mas·sé′
mas·seur′, *m.*
mas·seuse′, *f.*
mas′si·cot
mas′sif
mass′i·ness
mas′sive
mass meeting
mass′y
mas′ta·ba
mas′ter
mas′ter–at–
arms′
mas′ter·dom
mas′ter·ful
mas′ter·ly
mas′ter·piece′
mas′ter·ship
mas′ter·work′
mas′ter·y
mast′head′
mas′ti·cate
mas′ti·ca′tion
mas′ti·ca·to′ry
mas′tiff
mas′to·don
mas′toid
mat′a·dor
match′board′
match′less
match′lock′

match′mak′er
match play
match′wood′
ma′té
mat′e·lote
ma·te′ri·al
(substance)
ma·te′ri·al·ism
ma·te′ri·al·ist
ma·te′ri·al·is′tic
ma·te′ri·al′i·ty
ma·te′ri·al·i·za′-
tion
ma·te′ri·al·ize
ma·te′ri·al·ly
ma·te′ri·a med′-
i·ca
ma·té′ri·el′
(equipment)
ma·ter′nal
ma·ter′ni·ty
math′e·mat′i·cal
math′e·ma·ti′cian
math′e·mat′ics
mat′i·nee′
ma′tri·arch
ma′tri·arch′ate
ma′tri·arch′y
mat′ri·ces, *pl.*
ma′tri·cide
ma·tric′u·lant
ma·tric′u·late

ma·tric′u·la′tion
mat′ri·mo′ni·al
mat′ri·mo′ny
ma′trix
ma′tron
ma′tron·age
ma′tron·ize
ma′tron·ly
mat′ter
mat′ter–of–fact′
Mat′thew
mat′ting
mat′tock
mat′toid
mat′tress
mat′u·rate
mat′u·ra′tion
ma·tur′a·tive
ma·ture′
ma·ture′ly
ma·ture′ness
ma·tu′ri·ty
ma·tu′ti·nal
matz′oth
maud′lin
maul′stick′
maun′der
mau′so·le′um
mauve
mav′er·ick
mawk′ish
max·il′la
max′il·lar′y
max′im
max′i·mal
max′i·mize
max′i·mum
may′be
May Day
May′flow′er
may′hap′
may′hem
may′on·naise′
may′or
may′or·al·ty
May′pole′
maze
(puzzle. cf. *maize.*)
ma′zer
ma′zi·ly
ma′zi·ness
ma·zur′ka
ma′zy
mead′ow
mea′ger
meal′time′
meal worm
meal′y·mouthed′
mean
me·an′der
mean′ing
mean′ly
mean′ness
meant
mean′time′
mean′while′
mea′sles
mea′sly
meas′ur·a·ble
meas′ure
meas′ured
meas′ure·less
meas′ure·ment
meas′ur·er
me·a′tus
Mec′ca
me·chan′ic
me·chan′i·cal
mech′a·ni′cian
me·chan′ics
mech′a·nism
mech′a·nist
med′al
med′al·ist
me·dal′lion
med′dle
med′dle·some
Me·de′a
me′di·a, *pl.*
me′di·al
me′di·an
me′di·ate
me′di·ate·ly
me′di·a′tion
me′di·a′tive
me′di·a·ti·za′tion

me′di·a·tize
me′di·a′tor
me′di·a·to′ry
med′i·ca·ble
med′i·cal
me·dic′a·ment
med′i·cate
med′i·ca′tion
med′i·ca′tive
med′i·ce′an
me·dic′i·na·ble
me·dic′i·nal
med′i·cine
medicine ball
medicine man
me′di·e′val
me′di·e′val·ism
me′di·e′val·ist
me′di·o′cre
me′di·oc′ri·ty
med′i·tate
med′i·ta′tion
med′i·ta′tive
med′i·ter·ra′-
ne·an
me′di·um
me′di·um·is′tic
med′lar
med′ley
Me·du′sa
meet′ing
meet′ing·house′
meet′ly
meg′a·phone
meg′a·scope
Meis′ter·sing′er
mel′an·cho′li·a
mel′an·cho′li·ac
mel′an·chol′ic
mel′an·chol′y
Mel′a·ne′sian
mé′lange′
mel′a·nin
mel′a·nism
mel′a·noid
mel′a·no′sis
mel′an·tha′ceous
Mel·chiz′e·dek
Mel′e·a′ger
me·lee′
me′li·a′ceous
mel′ic
mel′io·rate
mel′io·ra′tion
mel′io·ra′tive
mel′io·ra′tor
mel′io·rism
mel·ior′i·ty
mel·lif′er·ous
mel·lif′lu·ence
mel·lif′lu·ent
mel·lif′lu·ous
mel′low
me·lo′de·on
me·lod′ic
me·lo′di·ous
mel′o·dist
mel′o·dize
mel′o·dra′ma
mel′o·dra·mat′ic
mel′o·dram′a·tist
mel′o·dy
mel′on
Mel·pom′e·ne
melt′a·ble
mem′ber
mem′ber·ship
mem′brane
mem′bra·nous
me·men′to
me·men′tos
mem′oir
mem′o·ra·bil′i·ty
mem′o·ra·ble
mem′o·ran′da, *pl.*
mem′o·ran′dum
me·mo′ri·al
me·mo′ri·al·ist
me·mo′ri·al·ize
mem′o·ries
mem′o·rize
mem′o·riz′ing
mem′o·ry
men′ace
mé·nage′
me·nag′er·ie

men·da′cious
men·dac′i·ty
Men·de′li·an
mend′er
men′di·can·cy
men′di·cant
Men′e·la′us
me′ni·al
me·nin′ges
men′in·gi′tis
Men′non·ite
men′o·pause
men′ses
men′stru·al
men′stru·ate
men′stru·a′tion
men′sur·a·ble
men′su·ral
men′su·ra′tion
men′su·ra′tive
men′tal
men·tal′i·ty
men′tal·ly
men′thol
men′tion
men′tion·er
men′tor
men′u
Meph′i·stoph′e-
les
me·phi′tis
mer′can·tile
mer′can·til·ism
mer′ce·nar′y
mer′cer
mer′cer·ize
mer′chan·dise
mer′chant
mer′chant·a·ble
mer′chant·man
mer′cies
mer′ci·ful
mer′ci·less
mer·cu′ri·al
mer·cu′ri·al·ism
mer·cu′ri·al·ize
mer·cu′ric
mer·cu′rous
Mer′cu·ry
mer′cy
mere′ly
mer′e·tri′cious
mer·gan′ser
merge
mer′gence
merg′er
me·rid′i·an
me·rid′i·o·nal
me·ringue′
me·ri′no
mer′i·stem
mer′it
mer′i·to′ri·ous
mer′lin
mer′maid′
mer′ri·ly
mer′ri·ment
mer′ri·ness
mer′ry
mer′ry–an′drew
mer′ry–go–
round′
mer′ry·mak′ing
me′sa
mesh′work′
mesh′y
me′si·al
mes·mer′ic
mes′mer·ism
mes′mer·ize
mes′sage
mes′sen·ger
Mes·si′ah
Mes′si·an′ic
mes′sieurs
mess′mate′
mess′y
me·tab′o·lism
met′a·car′pus
met′al
met′al·ist
me·tal′lic
met′al·lif′er·ous
met′al·line
met′al·log′ra·phy
met′al·loid

met′al·lur′gic
met′al·lur′gy
met′al·ware
met′al·work′
met′a·mor′phic
met′a·mor′phism
met′a·mor′phose
met′a·mor′pho-
ses, *pl.*
met′a·mor′pho-
sis
met′a·phor
met′a·phor′i·cal
met′a·phrase
met′a·phys′i·cal
met′a·phy·si′cian
met′a·phys′ics
me·tas′ta·sis
met′a·tar′sal
met′a·tar′sus
me′te·or
me′te·or′ic
me′te·or·ite
me′te·or·o·graph′
me′te·or·oid′
me′te·or·o·log′-
i·cal
me′te·or·ol′o·gist
me′te·or·ol′o·gy
me′ter
meth′od
me·thod′i·cal

Meth′od·ism
Meth′od·ist
meth′od·ize
meth′od·ol′o·gy
Me·thu′se·lah
me·tic′u·los′i·ty
me·tic′u·lous
mé·tier′
me·ton′y·my
met′ric
met′ri·cal
me·tri′cian
me·trol′o·gy
met′ro·nome
me′tro·nym′ic
me·trop′o·lis
met′ro·pol′i·tan
met′tle
met′tle·some
Mex′i·can
mez′za·nine
mez′zo–so-
pra′no
mi·as′ma
Mi′chael
Mich′ael·mas
mi′crobe
mi·cro′bi·al
mi·cro′bic
mi·cro′bi·cide
mi·crom′e·ter

mi′cro·or′gan-
ism
mi′cro·phone
mi′cro·phon′ic
mi′cro·scope
mi′cro·scop′ic
mi′cro·scop′i-
cal·ly
mid′aft·er·noon′
Mi′das
mid′brain′
mid′day′
mid′dle
mid′dle–aged′
mid′dle·man′
mid′dle–sized′
mid′dle·weight′
mid′dling
midg′et
mid′i′ron
mid′land
mid′night′
mid′ship′man
mid′sum′mer
mid′way′
mid′week′
Mid′west′
mid′wife′
mid′win′ter
mid′year′
mien
might′i·ly

might′i·ness
might′y
mi′gnon·ette′
mi′grate
mi·gra′tion
mi′gra·to′ry
mi·ka′do
mi·la′dy
milch
mil′dew
mil′dew–proof
mild′ly
mild′ness
mile′age
mile′post′
mile′stone′
mil′i·tan·cy
mil′i·tant
mil′i·ta·rism
mil′i·ta·rist
mil′i·ta·ris′tic
mil′i·ta·rize
mil′i·tar′y
mil′i·tate
mi·li′tia
mi·li′tia·man
milk can
milk′er
milk′–fed′
milk′i·ness
milk leg
milk′–liv′ered
milk′maid′
milk′man′
milk punch
milk route
milk shake
milk snake
milk′sop′
milk sugar
milk tooth
milk train
milk′weed′
milk′y
mill′board′
mill′dam′
mil′le·nar′i·an
mil·len′ni·al
mil·len′ni·um
mill′er
mil′let
mil′li·gram
mil′li·me′ter
mil′li·ner
mil′li·ner′y
mill′ing
mil′lion
mil′lion·aire′
mil′lionth
mill′pond′
mill′stone′
mill wheel
mill′work′
mill′wright′
mi·lord′
Mil·ton′ic
Mim′e·o·graph′
mim′er
mi·me′sis
mi·met′ic
mim′ic
mim′icked
mim′ick·er
mim′ick·ing
mim′ic·ry
mi·mo′sa
mi·na′cious
min′a·ret′
min′a·to′ry
mince′meat′
mince pie
minc′er
minc′ing·ly
mind′er
mind′ful
mind reader
mind reading
min′er
(mine worker)
min′er·al
min′er·al·ize
min′er·al·og′i·cal
min′er·al′o·gist
min′er·al′o·gy
Mi·ner′va
min′gle

min′gler
min′gling
min′i·a·ture
min′i·mal
min′i·mi·za′tion
min′i·mize
min′i·mum
min′ing
min′ion
min′is·ter
min′is·te′ri·al
min′is·te′ri·al·ist
min′is·trant
min′is·tra′tion
min′is·tries
min′is·try
min′i·um
min′i·ver
min′ne·sing′er
min′now
mi′nor
(under age)
mi·nor′i·ty
Mi′nos
Min′o·taur
min′ster
min′strel
min′strel·sy
mint′age
min′u·end
min′u·et′
mi′nus
min′ute, *n.*
mi·nute′, *adj.*
min′ute gun
min′ute hand
min′ute·ly
(continually)
mi·nute′ly
(in detail)
min′ute·man′
mi·nute′ness
min′ute steak
mir′a·cle
mi·rac′u·lous
mi·rage′
mir′ror
mirth′ful
mirth′less
mir′y
mis′ad·ven′ture
mis′al·li′ance
mis′an·thrope
mis′an·throp′ic
mis·an′thro·py
mis′ap·pli·ca′tion
mis′ap·pre·hen′-
sion
mis′ap·pro′pri-
ate
mis′ar·range′
mis′be·got′ten
mis′be·have′
mis′be·lief′
mis·cal′cu·late
mis·car′riage
mis·car′ried
mis·car′ry
mis′ce·ge·na′tion
mis′cel·la′ne·a
mis′cel·la′ne·ous
mis′cel·la′ny
mis·chance′
mis′chief
mis′chief–
mak′er
mis′chie·vous
mis′con·cep′tion
mis′con·duct′, *v.*
mis·con′duct, *n.*
mis′con·struc′-
tion
mis′con·strue′
mis′cre·ance
mis′cre·ant
mis·cue′
mis·deal′
mis′de·mean′or
mis′di·rect′
mi′ser
mis′er·a·ble
Mis′e·re′re
mi′ser·li·ness
mi′ser·ly
mis′er·y
mis·fea′sance

mis·fire′
mis·fit′
mis·for′tune
mis·giv′ing
mis·gov′ern
mis·guide′
mis·hap′
mis′in·form′
mis′in·ter′pret
mis′in·ter′pre-
  ta′tion
mis·join′der
mis·judge′
mis·lay′
mis·lead′
mis·lead′ing
mis·man′age
mis·no′mer
mi·sog′a·mist
mi·sog′a·my
mi·sog′y·nous
mi·sog′y·ny
mi·sol′o·gy
mis·place′
mis·print′
mis′pro·nounce′
mis′quo·ta′tion
mis·read′
mis·reck′on
mis′rep·re·sent′
mis′rep·re·sen-
  ta′tion
mis·rule′
mis′sile
miss′ing
mis′sion
mis′sion·ar′y
Mis′sis·sip′pi·an
mis′sive
mis·spell′
mis·state′
mis·tak′a·ble
mis·take′
mis·tak′en
mist′i·ness
mis′tle·toe
mis·took′
mis′tral
mis·treat′
mis·treat′ment
mis′tress
mis·tri′al
mis·trust′
mist′y
mis′un·der·stand′
mis′un·der-
  stand′ing
mis′un·der·stood′
mis·us′age
mis·use′
mis·us′ing
mi′ter
mit′i·ga·ble
mit′i·gate
mit′i·ga′tion
mit′i·ga′tive
mit′i·ga′tor
mi′tis cast′ing
mi′trail·leuse′
mi′tral
mit′ten
mit′ti·mus
mix′er
mix′ture
miz′zen
miz′zen·mast′
miz′zle
mne·mon′ic
mne·mon′ics
Mo′ab·ite
mob′cap′
mo′bile
mo·bil′i·ty
mo′bi·li·za′tion
mo′bi·lize
mob·oc′ra·cy
mob′o·crat′ic
moc′ca·sin
mo′cha
mock′er
mock′er·y
mock′ing·bird′
mock′ing·ly
mod′al
mod′el
mod′eled

mod′el·ing
mod′er·ate
mod′er·a′tion
mod′er·a′tor
mod′ern
mod′ern·ism
mod′ern·ist
mo·der′ni·ty
mod′ern·ize
mod′ern·iz′ing
mod′ern·ly
mod′est
mod′es·ty
mod′i·cum
mod′i·fi′a·ble
mod′i·fi·ca′tion
mod′i·fi·ca′to·ry
mod′ifi′er
mod′i·fy
mod′i·fy′ing
mod′ish
mo·diste′
mod′u·lar
mod′u·late
mod′u·la′tion
mod′u·la′tor
mod′u·lus
mo′dus vi-
ven′di
mo′hair′
Mo·ham′med·an
Mo′hawk
Mo·hi′can
moi′e·ty
mois′ten
moist′ness
mois′ture
mois′ture·proof′
mo′lar
mo·las′ses
mold
mold′a·ble
mold′er
mold′i·ness
mold′ing
mold′y
mo·lec′u·lar
mol′e·cule
mole′hill′
mole′skin′
mo·lest′
mo′les·ta′tion
mol′li·fi·ca′tion
mol′li·fied
mol′li·fy
mol′li·fy′ing
mol′lusk
mol′ly·cod′dle
Mo′loch
mol′ten
mo·lyb′de·num
mo′ment
mo′men·tar′y
mo′ment·ly
mo·men′tous
mo·men′tum
mon′a·chal
mon′arch
mo·nar′chi·cal
mon′arch·ism
mon′arch·y
mon′as·te′ri·al
mon′as·ter′y
mo·nas′tic
mo·nas′ti·cism
mon′e·tar′y
mon′e·tize
mon′ey
mon′ey·bag′
mon′eyed
mon′ey–mak′ing
money order
mon′eys
mon′ey·wort′
mon′ger
Mon′gol
Mon·go′li·an
mon′grel
mo·ni′tion
mon′i·tor
mon′i·tor·ship′
mon′i·to′ry
mon′i·tress
monk′er·y
mon′key
mon′key·ish

mon′key·pot′
mon′key·shine′
mon′keys
monkey
wrench
monk′hood
monk′ish
mon′o·chro-
mat′ic
mon′o·chrome
mon′o·cle
mo·noc′ra·cy
mo·noc′u·lar
mo·nog′a·mist
mo·nog′a·mous
mo·nog′a·my
mon′o·gen′e·sis
mon′o·ge·net′ic
mon′o·gen′ic
mon′o·gram
mon′o·graph
mo·nog′y·ny
mo·nol′a·try
mon′o·lith
mon′o·log′ist
mon′o·logue
mon′o·ma′ni·a
mon′o·me·tal′lic
mon′o·met′al-
lism
Mo·non′ga·he′la
mon′o·plane
mon′o·ple′gi·a
mo·nop′o·list
mo·nop′o·lis′tic
mo·nop′o·li·za′-
tion
mo·nop′o·lize
mo·nop′o·ly
mon′o·rail′
mon′o·syl′la·ble
mon′o·tone
mo·not′o·nous
mo·not′o·ny
Mon′o·type
mon·ox′ide
mon′sei·gneur′
mon·sieur′
mon·si′gnor
mon·soon′
mon′ster
mon′strance
mon·stros′i·ty
mon′strous
mont·gol′fi·er
month′ly
mon′ti·cule
mon′u·ment
mon′u·men′tal
mood′i·ly
mood′i·ness
mood′y
moon′beam′
moon′–blind′
moon′calf′
moon′eye′
moon′fish′
moon′light′
moon′lit′
moon′rise′
moon′shine′
moon′shin′er
moon′shin′y
moon′stone′
moon′–struck′
moor′age
moor′ing
moor′ish
moot′er
mop′ping
mor′al
mo·rale′
mor′al·ism
mor′al·ist
mo·ral′i·ty
mor′al·i·za′tion
mor′al·ize
mor′al·ly
mor′als
mo·rass′
mor′a·to′ri·um
mor′a·to′ry
Mo·ra′vi·an
mor′bid
mor·bid′i·ty
mor·bif′ic

mor·da′cious
mor′dant
(dyeing term)
mor′dent
(musical term)
mo·reen′
mo·rel′lo
more·o′ver
Mor′gan·ton, N. C.
Mor′gan·town, W. Va.
mor′i·bund
Mor′mon
morn′ing
morn′ing–glo′ry
Mo·roc′can
mo·roc′co
mo′ron
mo·rose′
mo·rose′ness
Mor′pheus
mor′phine
Mor′ris chair
mor′row
mor′sel
mor′tal
mor·tal′i·ty
mor′tar
mor′tar·board′
mort′gage
mort′ga·gee′
mort′gag·ing
mort′ga·gor′
mor′ti·fi·ca′tion
mor′ti·fied
mor′ti·fy
mor′ti·fy′ing
mor′tise
mor′tu·ar′y
Mo·sa′ic
Mo′ses
mo′sey
Mos′lem
mos·qui′to
mos·qui′toes
moss′–grown′
moss′i·ness
most′ly
moth′–eat′en
moth′er
moth′er·hood
moth′er–in–law
moth′er·land′
moth′er·less
moth′er·li·ness
moth′er·ly
moth′er–of–pearl′
moth′proof′
mo·tif′
mo′tion
mo′tion·less
mo′ti·vate
mo′tive
mot′ley
mo′tor
mo′tor·boat′
mo′tor·bus′
mo′tor·car′
mo′tor·cy′cle
mo′torist
mo′tor·ize
mo′tor·man
mot′tle
mot′tled
mot′to
mot′toes
mount′a·ble
moun′tain
moun′tain·eer′
moun′tain·ous
moun′te·bank
mount′ed
mount′er
mount′ing
mourn′ful
mourn′ing
mouse′–ear′
mous′er
mouse′tail′
mouse′trap′
mous′y
mouth′ful
mouth′piece′
mov′a·bil′i·ty

mov′a·ble
mov′a·ble·ness
move′ment
mov′ie
mov′ies
mov′ing
mow′er
mow′ing ma-
chine′
moz·zet′ta
mu′cid
mu′ci·lage
mu′ci·lag′i·nous
muck rake
muck′rake′, *v.*
mu′cous, *adj.*
mu′cus, *n.*
mud′di·ly
mud′di·ness
mud′dle
mud′dy
mud′fish′
mud′guard′
mu·ez′zin
muf′fin
muf′fle
muf′fler
mug′ger
mug′gi·ness
mug′wump′
mu·lat′to
mu·lat′toes
mul′ber′ry
mulct
mu′li·eb′ri·ty
mul′ish
mull′er
mul′lion
mul·tan′gu·lar
mul′ti·far′ious
mul′ti·form
Mul′ti·graph
mul′ti·lat′er·al
mul′ti·mil′lion-
aire′
mul′ti·ped
mul′ti·plex
mul′ti·pli′a·ble
mul′ti·pli·cand′
mul′ti·pli·ca′tion
mul′ti·pli·ca′tive
mul′ti·plic′i·ty
mul′ti·pli′er
mul′ti·ply
mul′ti·ply′ing
mul′ti·tude
mul′ti·tu′di·nous
mum′mer·y
mum′mi·fy
mum′my
mun′dane
mun′go
mu·nic′i·pal
mu·nic′i·pal′i·ty
mu·nic′i·pal·ize
mu·nif′i·cence
mu·nif′i·cent
mu′ni·ment
mu·ni′tion
mu′ral
mur′der
mur′der·er
mur′der·ous
murk′y
mur′mur
mur′mur·ing
mur′mur·ous
mur′rhine
mus′ca·dine
mus′ca·tel′
mus′cle
mus′cle–bound′
mus′co·va′do
mus′cu·lar
mus′cu·lar′i·ty
muse′ful
mus′er
mu·se′um
mush′room
mush′y
mu′sic
mu′si·cal
mu′si·cale′
mu·si′cian
mu·si′cian·ly
mus′ing

musk deer
mus′ket
mus′ket·eer′
mus′ket·ry
musk′mel′on
musk ox
musk′rat′
musk′y
mus′lin
mus′sel
mus·tache′
mus′tang
mus′tard
mus′ter
mus′ti·ness
mus′ty
mu′ta·bil′i·ty
mu′ta·ble
mu′tate
mu·ta′tion
mu′ta·tive
mute′ness
mu′ti·late
mu′ti·la′tion
mu′ti·nied
mu′ti·nous
mu′ti·ny
mut′ism
mut′ter
mut′ton
mut′ton·chop′, *adj.*
mu′tu·al
mu′tu·al′i·ty
mu′tu·al·ly
muz′zle
muz′zle–load′ing
my·al′gi·a
my·o′pi·a
my·op′ic
myr′i·ad
myr′mi·don
myrrh
my·self′
mys′ter·ies
mys·te′ri·ous
mys′ter·y
mys′tic
mys′ti·cal
mys′ti·cism
mys′ti·fi·ca′tion
mys′ti·fied
mys′ti·fy
mys′ti·fy′ing
myth′i·cal
myth′i·cal·ly
myth′o·log′i·cal
my·thol′o·gy

N

na′cre
na′cre·ous
na′dir
nain′sook
na·ïve′
na·ïve′té′
na′ked
nam′a·ble
nam′by–pam′by
name′less
name′ly
nam′er
name′sake′
nan·keen′
na′per·y
naph′tha
nap′kin
na·po′le·on
Na·po′le·on′ic
nap′per
nap′ping

nar·cis′sus
nar′cot′ic
nar′co·tism
nar′co·tize
nar·rate′
nar·ra′tion
nar′ra·tive
nar·ra′tor
nar′row
nar′row·ly
nar′row–
mind′ed
nar′row·ness
na′sal
na·sal′i·ty
na′sal·ize
na′sal·ly
nas′cent
nas′ti·ly
nas′ti·ness
na·stur′tium
nas′ty
na′tal
na′tant
na·ta′tion
na′ta·to′ri·al
na′ta·to′ri·um
na′ta·to′ry
na′tion
na′tion·al
na′tion·al·ism
na′tion·al′i·ty
na′tion·al·ize
na′tion·al·iz′er
na′tion·al·ly
na′tive
na′tive·ly
na′tive·ness
na′tiv·ism
na·tiv′i·ty
nat′ty
nat′u·ral
nat′u·ral·ism
nat′u·ral·ist
nat′u·ral·is′tic
nat′u·ral·i·za′-
tion
nat′u·ral·ize
nat′u·ral·ly
nat′u·ral·ness
na′ture
naugh′ti·ly
naugh′ti·ness
naugh′ty
nau′se·a
nau′se·ate
nau′seous
nau′ti·cal
nau′ti·lus
na′val
na′vel
na·vic′u·lar
na′vies
nav′i·ga·ble
nav′i·gate
nav′i·ga′tion
nav′i·ga′tor
na′vy
navy yard
Naz′a·rene′
Ne′a·pol′i·tan
near′est
near′ly
near′ness
near′sight′ed
neat′herd′
neat′ly
neat′ness
neb′u·la
neb′u·lae, *pl.*
neb′u·lar
neb′u·lize
neb′u·los′i·ty
neb′u·lous
nec′es·sar′i·an
nec′es·sar′i·ly
nec′es·sar′y
ne·ces′si·tar′i·an
ne·ces′si·tar′i-
an·ism
ne·ces′si·tate
ne·ces′si·ties
ne·ces′si·tous
ne·ces′si·ty
neck′band′
neck′cloth′

neck′er·chief
neck′ing
neck′lace
neck′line′
neck′piece′
neck′tie′
neck′wear′
nec′ro·log′i·cal
ne·crol′o·gist
ne·crol′o·gy
nec′ro·man′cy
ne·crop′o·lis
ne·cro′sis
nec′tar
nec·tar′e·ous
nec′tar·ine′
need′ful
need′i·est
need′i·ness
nee′dle
nee′dle·fish′
nee′dle·ful
nee′dle–point′
need′less
nee′dle·wom′an
nee′dle·work′
need′y
ne'er′–do–well′
ne·far′i·ous
ne·ga′tion
neg′a·tive
neg′a·to′ry

neg·lect′
neg·lect′ful
neg′li·gee′
neg′li·gence
neg′li·gent
neg′li·gi·ble
ne·go′ti·a·bil′i·ty
ne·go′ti·a·ble
ne·go′ti·ate
ne·go′ti·a′tion
ne·go′ti·a′tor
Ne′gress
Ne′gro
Ne′groes
neigh′bor
neigh′bor·hood
neigh′bor·ing
neigh′bor·ly
nei′ther
nem′a·tode
Nem′e·sis
ne′o·lith′ic
ne·ol′o·gism
ne·ol′o·gist
ne·ol′o·gy
ne′o·phyte
ne′o·plasm
ne′o·ter′ic
neph′ew
ne·phol′o·gy
neph′o·scope
ne·phral′gi·a

ne·phri′tis
nep′o·tism
Nep′tune
Ne·ro′ni·an
nerve
nerve′less
nerv′ous
nerv′y
nes′ci·ence
nes′ci·ent
nest egg
nes′tle
nest′ling
Nes′tor
neth′er
neth′er·most
net′ting
net′tle
net′work′
neu′ral
neu·ral′gia
neu′ras·the′ni·a
neu·ri′tis
neu·rog′li·a
neu·rol′o·gist
neu·rol′o·gy
neu′ron
neu·ro′sis
neu·rot′ic
neu′ter
neu′tral
neu·tral′i·ty

neu'tral·i·za'tion
neu'tral·ize
neu'tral·ly
nev'er
nev'er·the·less'
New'ark, N. J.,
  N. Y., Ohio
new'born'
new'com'er
New Deal
new'el
new'fan'gled
new'–fash'ioned
New'found·land'
new'ly
new'mar'ket
new'–mown'
new'ness
news'boy'
news'cast'er
news'let'ter
news'man
news'mon'ger
news'pa'per
news'pa'per-
  man'
news'print'
news'reel'
news'room
news'stand'
news'y
new year

nib'ble
nib'lick
Nic'a·ra'guan
nice'ly
Ni·cene'
nice'ness
ni'ce·ty
niche
nick
nick'el
nick'el·if'er·ous
nick'el·o'de·on
nick'er
nick'name'
nic'o·tine
nic'o·tin·ism
nic'ti·tate
nid'i·fi·cate
nid'i·fi·ca'tion
niece
nig'gard
nig'gard ly
nig'gle
nig'gling
night'cap'
night clothes
night club
night'dress'
night'fall'
night'gown'
night'hawk'
night'in·gale

night key
night latch
night letter
night'long'
night'ly
night'mare'
night owl
night rider
night robe
night'shade'
night'shirt'
night'time'
night'walk'er
night watch
night'work'
ni·gres'cent
nig'ri·tude
ni'hil·ism
ni'hil·ist
ni'hil·is'tic
Ni'ke
nim'ble
nim'bus
Nim'rod
nin'com·poop
nine'fold'
nine'pence
nine'pin'
nine'teen'
nine'teenth'
nine'ti·eth
nine'ty

ninth
nip′per
nip′ping
nip′ple
Nip′pon·ese′
ni′trate
ni′tric
ni′tride
ni′tri·fi·ca′tion
ni′tri·fy
ni′trite
ni′tro·gen
ni′tro·gen–fix′-
ing
ni·trog′e·nous
ni′tro·glyc′er·in
ni′trous
Ni·zam′
No′ah
no·bil′i·ar′y
no·bil′i·ty
no′ble
no′ble·man
no′ble·wom′an
no′ble·ness
no′bly
no′bod·y
noc·tam′bu·lism
noc·tur′nal
noc′turne
nod′u·lar
nod′ule

noise′less
nois′i·ly
nois′i·ness
noi′some
nois′y
no′mad
no·mad′ic
no′mad·ism
nom′arch
nom′arch·y
no′men·cla′tor
no′men·cla′ture
nom′i·nal
nom′i·nal·ly
nom′i·nate
nom′i·na′tion
nom′i·na·tive
nom′i·na′tor
nom′i·nee′
non′ap·pear′ance
non′cha·lance
non′cha·lant
non·com′bat·ant
non′com·mis′-
sioned
non′com·mit′tal
non com′pos
men′tis
non′con·duc′tor
non′con·form′ist
non′con·form′-
i·ty

non′–co–op′er-
a′tion
non′de·script
non·en′ti·ty
non′ex·ist′ent
non·fea′sance
non′in·ter·ven′-
tion
non·join′der
non′me·tal′lic
non′pa·reil′
non′par·tic′i-
pat′ing
non·par′ti·san
non·res′i·dence
non·res′i·dent
non′sense
non·sen′si·cal
non′stop′
non′suit′
non′sup·port′
non·un′ion
noo′dle
noon′day′
noon′tide′
noon′time′
nor′mal
nor·mal′i·ty
nor′mal·ize
nor′mal·ly
Norse
Norse′man

north'east'
north'east'er
north'east'er·ly
north'east'ern
north'east'ward
north'er·ly
north'ern
north'ern·er
north'ern·most
north'land
north'ward
north'west'
north'west'er·ly
north'west'ern
Nor·we'gian
nose bag
nose'band'
nose'bleed'
nose dive
nose'gay'
nose'piece'
no·sol'o·gy
nos·tal'gi·a
nos'tril
nos'trum
no'ta·bil'i·ty
no'ta·ble
no'ta·ble·ness
no'ta·bly
no·tar'i·al
no'ta·ries
no'ta·rize
no'ta·ry
no·ta'tion
note'book'
note'less
note paper
note'wor'thy
noth'ing
noth'ing·ness
no'tice
no'tice·a·ble
no'ti·fi·ca'tion
no'ti·fied
no'ti·fy
no'ti·fy'ing
no'tion
no'tion·al
no'to·ri'e·ty
no·to'ri·ous
not'with·stand'-
ing
nour'ish
nour'ish·ment
no·va'tion
nov'el
nov'el·ette'
nov'el·ist
nov'el·is'tic
nov'el·ize
nov'el·ties
nov'el·ty
no·ve'na
nov'ice
No'vo·cain'
now'a·days'
no'way
no'ways
no'where
no'wise
nox'ious
noz'zle
nu'bi·lous
nu'cle·ar
nu'cle·ate
nu'cle·a'tion
nu'cle·us
nu'di·ty
nu'ga·to'ry
nug'get
nui'sance
nul'li·fi·ca'tion
nul'li·fied
nul'li·fi'er
nul'li·fy
nul'li·fy·ing
num'ber
num'ber·er
num'ber·less
numb'fish'
num'bles
numb'ly
numb'ness
nu'mer·a·ble
nu'mer·al
nu'mer·ate

nu′mer·a′tion
nu′mer·a′tor
nu·mer′i·cal
nu′mer·ous
nu′mis·mat′ic
nu′mis·mat′ics
nu·mis′ma·tist
num′skull′
nun′cu·pa′tive
nun′ner·y

nup′tial
nurse′maid′
nurs′er·y
nurs′er·y·man
nurs′ing
nurs′ling
nur′ture
nut′crack′er
nut′meg
nu′tri·ent

nu′tri·ment
nu·tri′tion
nu·tri′tious
nu′tri·tive
nut′shell′
nut′ter
nut′ty
nuz′zle
ny′lon
nymph

O

oa′kum
oar′fish′
oar′lock′
oars′man
oars′man·ship
o·a′ses, *pl.*
o·a′sis
oat′cake′
oat′meal′
ob′bli·ga′to
ob′du·ra·cy
ob′du·rate
o·be′di·ence
o·be′di·ent
o·bei′sance
ob′e·lisk
o·bese′

o·bes′i·ty
o·bey′
ob·fus′cate
ob′fus·ca′tion
o·bit′u·ar·ies
o·bit′u·ar′y
object′, *v.*
ob′ject, *n.*
ob·jec′tion
ob·jec′tion·a·ble
ob·jec′tive
ob·jec′tive·ly
ob·jec′tive·ness
ob′jec·tiv′i·ty
ob·jec′tor
ob′jur·gate
ob′jur·ga′tion

ob·la′tion
ob′la·to′ry
ob′li·gate
ob′li·ga′tion
ob·lig′a·to′ry
o·blige′
o·blig′er
o·blig′ing
ob·lique′
ob·liq′ui·ty
ob·lit′er·ate
ob·lit′er·a′tion
ob·liv′i·on
ob·liv′i·ous
ob′long
ob′lo·quy
ob·nox′ious

o'boe
o'bo·ist
ob·scene'
ob·scen'i·ty
ob·scur'ant
ob'scu·ra'tion
ob·scure'
ob·scure'ness
ob·scu'ri·ty
ob'se·quies
ob·se'qui·ous
ob'se·quy
ob·serv'a·ble
ob·serv'ance
ob·serv'ant
ob'ser·va'tion
ob'ser·va'tion·al
ob·serv'a·to'ry
ob·serve'
ob·serv'er
ob·sess'
ob·ses'sion
ob'so·les'cence
ob'so·lete
ob'sta·cle
ob·stet'ri·cal
ob'ste·tri'cian
ob·stet'rics
ob'sti·na·cy
ob'sti·nate
ob·strep'er·ous
ob·struct'
ob·struc'tion
ob·struc'tion·ist
ob·struc'tive
ob·tain'
ob·tain'a·ble
ob·trud'er
ob·tru'sion
ob·tru'sive
ob·tund'
ob'tu·rate
ob'tu·ra'tion
ob'tu·ra'tor
ob·tuse'
ob·verse', *adj.*
ob'verse, *n.*
ob·ver'sion
ob'vi·ate
ob'vi·a'tion
ob'vi·ous
ob'vo·lute
oc·ca'sion
oc·ca'sion·al
oc·ca'sion·al·ism
oc·ca'sion·al·ly
oc'ci·dent
oc'ci·den'tal
Oc'ci·den'tal·ism
oc'ci·den'tal·ize
oc·cip'ital
oc'ci·put
oc·clu'sion
oc·cult'
oc'cul·ta'tion
oc·cult'ism
oc·cult'ist
oc'cu·pan·cy
oc'cu·pant
oc'cupa'tion
oc'cu·pied
oc'cu·py
oc'cu·py'ing
oc·cur'
oc·curred'
oc·cur'rence
oc·cur'rent
oc·cur'ring
o'cean
o'ce·an'ic
o'·clock'
oc'ta·gon
oc·tag'o·nal
oc·tan'gu·lar
oc'tave
oc·ta'vo
oc·ta'vos
oc·ten'ni·al
oc'to·ge·nar'i·an
oc·tog'e·nar'y
oc'to·pus
oc'u·lar
oc'u·list
odd'i·ty
odd'ly
odd'ness

o′di·ous
o′di·um
o′do·graph
o′dor
o′dor·if′er·ous
o′dor·less
o′dor·ous
O·dys′seus
Od′ys·sey
of′fal
off′cast′
off′–chance′
off′–col′or
of·fend′
of·fend′er
of·fense′
of·fen′sive
of′fer
of′fer·ing
off′hand′
of′fice
of′fice·hold′er
of′fi·cer
of·fi′cial
of·fi′cial·ism
of·fi′cial·ly
of·fi′ci·ar′y
of·fi′ci·ate
of·fi′ci·a′tion
of·fi′ci·a′tor
of·fi′cious
off′ing
off′ish
off′print′
off′scour′ing
off′set′, *n.*
off′set′, *v.*
off′shoot′
off′shore′, *adj.*
off′shore′, *adv.*
off′spring′
of′ten
of′ten·times′
oft′times′
ohm
oil cake
oil′cloth′
oil′er
oil field
oil′i·ness
oil′man
oil painting
oil′skin′
oil slick
oil′stone′
oil well
oil′y
oint′ment
old′en
old′–fash′ioned
old′ish
old′–line
old′ness
Old Nick
old′ster
old′–tim′er
old′–world′, *adj.*
o′le·o·graph′
o′le·o·mar′ga·rine
ol·fac′tion
ol·fac′to·ry
ol′i·garch
ol′i·garch′y
ol′ive
O·lym′pi·ad
O·lym′pi·an
O·lym′pic
O·lym′pus
om′e·let
om′i·nous
o·mis′si·ble
o·mis′sion
o·mit′
o·mit′ted
o·mit′ting
om′ni·bus
om′ni·far′i·ous
om·nif′ic
om·nip′o·tence
om·nip′o·tent
om′ni·pres′ent
om·nis′cience
om·nis′cient
om·niv′o·rous
one′–armed′
one′–eyed′

one′–horse′
one′ness
on′er·ous
one·self′
one′–sid′ed
one′–step′
one′time′
on′ion
on′ion·skin′
on′look′er
on′ly
on′rush′
on′set′
on′slaught′
on′to
on·tog′e·ny
on′to·log′i·cal
on·tol′o·gy
o′nus
on′ward
oo′zy
o·pac′i·ty
o′pal·es′cent
o·paque′
o′pen
o′pen–and–shut′
o′pen·er
o′pen–eyed′
o′pen·hand′ed
o′pen·heart′ed
o′pen–hearth′
open house
o′pen·ing
o′pen·ly
o′pen·mouthed′
o′pen·ness
o′pen·work′
op′er·a
op′er·a·ble
op′er·ate
op′er·at′ic
op′er·a′tion
op′er·a′tive
op′er·a′tor
op′er·et′ta
op′er·ose
O·phel′ia
oph·thal′mo-
scope
o′pi·ate
o·pine′
o·pin′ion
o·pin′ion·at′ed
op·po′nent
op′por·tune′
op′por·tun′ism
op′por·tun′ist
op′por·tu′ni·ty
op·pos′a·ble
op·pose′
op′po·site
op′po·si′tion
op·press′
op·pres′sion
op·pres′sive
op·pres′sor
op·pro′bri·ous
op·pro′bri·um
op′ta·tive
op′ti·cal
op·ti′cian
op′tics
op′ti·mism
op′ti·mist
op′ti·mis′tic
op′tion
op′tion·al
op·tom′e·ter
op·tom′e·trist
op·tom′e·try
op′u·lence
op′u·lent
or′a·cle
o·rac′u·lar
o′ral
or′ange
or′ange·ade′
o·ra′tion
or′a·tor
or′a·tor′i·cal
or′a·to′ri·o
or′a·to′ry
or·bic′u·lar
or′bit
or′chard
or′ches·tra

or·ches′tral
or′ches·trate
or′ches·tra′tion
or′chid
or·dain′
or·de′al
or′der
or′der·li·ness
or′der·ly
or′di·nal
or′di·nance
or′di·nar′i·ly
or′di·nar′y
or′di·nate
or′di·na′tion
ord′nance
or′gan
or·gan′ic
or′gan·ism
or′gan·ist
or′gan·iz′a·ble
or′gan·i·za′tion
or′gan·ize
or′gy
o′ri·ent
o′ri·en′tal
o′ri·en′tal·ism
o′ri·en′tal·ize
o′ri·en·tate′
o′ri·en·ta′tion
or′i·fice
or′i·gin
o·rig′i·nal
o·rig′i·nal′i·ty
o·rig′i·nal·ly
o·rig′i·nate
o·rig′i·na′tion
o·rig′i·na′tive
o·rig′i·na′tor
o′ri·ole
O·ri′on
or′i·son
or′na·ment
or′na·men′tal
or′na·men·ta′tion
or·nate′
or′ni·thol′o·gy
o′ro·tund
or′phan
or′phan·age
or′phan·hood
Or′pheus
or′tho·dox
or·thog′ra·pher
or′tho·graph′ic
or′tho·graph′i·cal
or·thog′ra·phy
or′tho·pe′dic
os′cil·late
os′cil·la′tion
os′cil·la′tor
os′cil·la·to′ry
os′ci·tan·cy
os′cu·lant
os′cu·lar
os′cu·late
os′cu·la′tion
os′cu·la·to′ry
O·si′ris
os′mi·um
os·mo′sis
os′prey
os′si·fi·ca′tion
os′si·fy
os′su·ar′y
os·ten′si·ble
os·ten′sive
os·ten′sive·ly
os′ten·ta′tion
os′ten·ta′tious
os′te·o·path
os′te·o·path′ic
os′te·op′a·thist
os′te·op′a·thy
os′tra·cism
os′tra·cize
os′trich
oth′er
oth′er·wise′
Ot′ta·wa
Ot′to·man
our·selves′
oust′er
out′–and–out′
out·bal′ance
out·bid′

out′board′
out′break′
out′build′ing
out′burst′
out′cast′
out·class′
out′come′
out′crop′
out′cry′, *n.*
out·cry′, *v.*
out′curve′
out·do′
out′door′, *adj.*
out′doors′
out′er
out′er·most
out′field′
out′fit
out′fit′ter
out·flank′
out·gen′er·al
out·go′
out′go′ing
out·grow′
out′growth′
out′house′
out′ing
out′land′er
out·land′ish
out·last′
out′law′
out′law′ry
out·lay′, *v.*
out′lay′, *n.*
out′let
out′line′
out·live′
out′look′
out′ly′ing
out′ma·neu′ver
out′–of–door′
out′–of–the–
way′
out′pa′tient
out·play′
out·point′
out′post′
out·pour′, *v.*
out′pour′, *n.*
out′put′
out′rage
out·ra′geous
out·rank′
out·reach′, *v.*
out′reach′, *n.*
out′rid′er
out′right′, *adv.*
out′right′, *adj.*
out·root′
out′run′ner
out·sell′
out′set′
out′side′, *n.*
out′side′, *prep.*
out′sid′er
out·sit′
out′skirt′
out·smart′
out·soar′
out·speak′
out′spo′ken
out·spread′, *v.*
out′spread′, *n.*
out·stand′
out·stand′ing
out·stay′
out·stretch′
out′ward
out′ward·ly
out·wear′
out·weigh′
out·wit′
out′work′
out′worn′
o′val
o′val·ly
o′va·ry
o·va′tion
ov′en
ov′en·ware′
o′ver
o′ver–all′, *adj.*
o′ver·alls′
o′ver·arm′
o′ver·awe′
o′ver·bal′ance

o′ver·bear′
o′ver·board′
o′ver·build′
o′ver·bur′den
o′ver·cast′
o′ver·charge′, *v.*
o′ver·charge′, *n.*
o′ver·coat′
o′ver·come′
o′ver·do′
o′ver·draft′
o′ver·draw′
o′ver·due′
o′ver·flow′, *v.*
o′ver·flow′, *n.*
o′ver·grow′
o′ver·hand′, *adv.*
o′ver·hand′, *n.*
o′ver·hang′, *v.*
o′ver·hang′, *n.*
o′ver·haul′
o′ver·head′, *adv.*
o′ver·head′, *adj.*
o′ver·hear′
o′ver·land′
o′ver·look′
o′ver·lord′
o′ver·ly
o′ver·night′, *adv.*
o′ver·night′, *n.*
o′ver·pow′er
o′ver·pro·duc′-
tion
o′ver·reach′
o′ver·ride′
o′ver·rule′
o′ver·run′
o′ver·sea′
o′ver·shad′ow
o′ver·shoe′
o′ver·sight′
o′ver·sized′
o′ver·sleep′
o′ver·spread′
o′ver·stay′
o′ver·step′
o′vert
o′ver·take′
o′ver·throw′, *v.*
o′ver·throw′, *n.*
o′ver·time′, *v.*
o′ver·time′, *n.*
o′vert·ly
o′ver·tone′
o′ver·ture
o′ver·turn′, *v.*
o′ver·turn′, *n.*
o′ver·weigh′
o′ver·whelm′
o′ver·whelm′ing
o′ver·work′, *v.*
o′ver·work′, *n.*
owl′et
owl′ish
own′er
own′er·ship
ox·al′ic
ox′bow′
ox′eye′
Ox′ford
ox′heart′
ox′i·da′tion
ox′ide
ox′i·dize
ox′tail′
ox′tongue′
ox′y·gen
ox′y·gen·ate
oys′ter
oyster bed
oys′ter·man
oyster rake
oys′ter·root′
o′zone

P

pace′mak′er
pac′er
pach′y·san′dra
pa·cif′ic
pa·cif′i·cate
pac′i·fi·ca′tion
pa·cif′i·ca′tor
pa·cif′i·ca·to′ry
pac′i·fi′er
pac′i·fism
pac′i·fist
pac′i·fy
pac′i·fy·ing
pack′age
pack′er
pack′et
pack′ing
packing house
pack′man
pack rat
pack′sack′
pack′sad′dle
pack′thread′
pad′ding
pad′dle
pad′dle·fish′
pad′dler
pad′dock
pad′lock′
pa′dre
pa′gan
pa′gan·ish
pa′gan·ism
pa′gan·ize
pag′eant
pag′eant·ry
pag′i·nal
pag′i·na′tion
pa·go′da
pain′ful
pain′less
pains′tak′ing
paint′box′
paint′brush′
paint′er
paint′ing
paint work
pa·ja′ma
pa·la′bra
pal′ace
pal′at·a·ble
pal′a·tal
pal′a·tal·i·za′tion
pal′a·tal·ize
pal′ate
(roof of the mouth. cf. *palette, pallet.*)
pa·la′tial
pal′a·tine
pa·lav′er
pale′face′
pale′ness
pal′ette
(for paint. cf. *palate, pallet.*)
pal′frey
pal′ing
pal′i·sade′
Pal·la′di·an
pall′bear′er
pal′let
(couch. cf. *palate, palette.*)
pal′li·ate
pal′li·a′tion
pal′li·a′tive
pal′lid
pall′–mall′
pal′lor
palm′er
pal·met′to
palm′is·try
pal′pa·ble
pal′pate
pal′pi·tate
pal′pi·ta′tion
pal′sied

pal'sy
pal'try
pa·lu'dal
pam'per
pam·pe'ro
pam·pe'ros
pam'phlet
pan'a·ce'a
pa·nache'
Pan'–A·mer'i-
can
pan'cake'
pan'chro·mat'ic
pan'cre·as
pan'cre·a·tin
pan'de·mo'ni·um
Pan·do'ra
pan·dow'dy
pan'e·gyr'ic
pan'e·gyr'i·cal
pan'e·gyr'ist
pan'e·gy·rize
pan'el
pan'el·ing
pan'el·work'
pan'han'dle
pan'ic
pan'ic–strick'en
pan'o·ply
pan'o·ra'ma
pan'o·ram'ic
pan'sies
pan'sy
Pan·tag'ru·el
pan'ta·loon'
pan'the·ism
pan'the·ist
pan'the·is'ti·cal
pan·the'on
pan'ther
pant'ing·ly
pan'to·graph
pan'to·mime
pan'tries
pan'try
pa'pa·cy
pa'pal
pa'per
pa'per·back'
pa'per·board'
pa'per boy
paper chase
paper cutter
paper hanger
paper knife
pa'per–thin
pa'per·weight'
paper work
pap'e·terie
pa'pier–mâ·ché'
pa·poose'
pap'ri·ka
pa·py'rus
par'a·ble
pa·rab'o·la
par'a·bol'ic
pa·rab'o·lize
par'a·chute
pa·rade'
par'a·dise
par'a·dox
par'a·dox'i·cal
par'af·fin
par'a·gon
par'a·graph
par'al·lax
par'al·lel
par'al·lel'ing
par'al·lel·ism
par'al·lel'o·gram
pa·ral'y·sis
par'a·lyt'ic
par'a·lyze
par'a·mount
par'a·pet
par'a·pher·na'li·a
par'a·phrase
par'a·phras'er
par'a·phras'tic
pa·raph'y·sis
par'a·site
par'a·sit'ic
par'a·sit'i·cide
par'a·sol
par'a·troop·er
par'boil'

par′cel
par′cel·ing
parcel post
parch′ment
par′don
par′don·a·ble
par′don·er
par′e·gor′ic
par′ent
par′ent·age
pa·ren′tal
pa·ren′the·ses, *pl.*
pa·ren′the·sis
par′en·thet′i·cal
par′ent·hood
pa·re′sis
pa·ret′ic
pa·ri′e·tal
par′ing
par′ish
pa·rish′ion·er
Pa·ri′sian
par′i·ty
park′way′
par′lance
par′ley
par′lia·ment
par′lia·men·tar′-
i·an
par′lia·men′ta·ry
par′lor
parlor car

Par·nas′sus
pa·ro′chi·al
par′o·dy
pa·rol′
(oral)
pa·role′
(promise)
par′ox·ysm
par′ox·ys′mal
par·quet′
parse
Par′si·fal
par′si·mo′ni·ous
par′si·mo′ny
pars′ley
pars′nip
par′son
par′son·age
par·take′
par·tak′er
part′ed
par·terre′
Par′the·non
par′tial
par′ti·al′i·ty
par′tial·ly
par·tic′i·pant
par·tic′i·pate
par·tic′i·pa′tion
par·tic′i·pa′tor
par′ti·cip′i·al
par′ti·ci·ple

par′ti·cle
par·tic′u·lar
par·tic′u·lar′i·ty
par·tic′u·lar·ize
par·tic′u·lar·ly
par′ties
part′ing
par′ti·san
par′ti·san·ship′
par·ti′tion
part′ly
part′ner
part′ner·ship
par·took′
par′tridge
par′ty
par′ve·nu
par′vis
pas′chal
pass′a·ble
pas′sage
pas′sage·way′
pass′book′
pas·sé′
pas′sen·ger
pass′er
pass′er–by′
pas′si·ble
pass′ing
pas′sion
pas′sion·ate
pas·sion·less

pas'sive
pass'key'
pass'o'ver
pass'port
pass'word'
paste'board'
pas·tel'
past'er
pas'teur·i·za'tion
pas'teur·ize
pas'time'
pas'tor
pas'to·ral
pas'to·ral·ism
pas'to·ral·ist
pas'to·ral·ly
pas'tor·ate
pas'tor·ship
pas'tries
pas'try
pas'tur·a·ble
pas'tur·age
pas'ture
past'y
patch'er
patch test
patch'work'
patch'y
pa·tel'la
pat'ent
pat'ent·a·ble
pat'ent·ee'
pa·ter'nal
pa·ter'nal·ism
pa·ter'nal·ly
pa·ter'ni·ty
Pat'er·son, N. J.
pa·thet'ic
path'find'er
path'less
path'way'
path'o·log'ic
path'o·log'i·cal
pa·thol'o·gist
pa·thol'o·gy
pa'thos
path'way'
pa'tience
pa'tient
pa'ti·o
pa'tri·arch
pa'tri·ar'chal
pa'tri·arch'ate
pa'tri·arch'y
pa·tri'cian
pa·tri'ci·ate
pat'ri·mo'ny
pa'tri·ot
pa'tri·ot'ic
pa'tri·ot·ism
pa·trol'
pa·trolled'
pa·trol'ling
pa·trol'man
pa'tron
pa'tron·age
pa'tron·ize
pa·troon'
pat'ten
pat'ter
pat'tern
Pat'ter·son, N. Y.
pat'ty
pat'u·lous
pau'ci·ty
pau'per
pau'per·ism
pau'per·ize
pave'ment
pa·vil'ion
pav'ing
pav'o·nine
pawn'bro'ker
pawn'bro'king
pawn'er
pawn'shop'
pay'a·ble
pay'ee'
pay'er
pay'mas'ter
pay'ment
pay'roll
peace'a·ble
peace'ful
peace'mak'er

peace offering
peace pipe
peach'blow'
peach'y
pea'cock'
pea'hen'
pea jacket
pea'nut'
pearl'ash'
pearl'er
pearl'y
pear'–shaped'
peas'ant
peas'ant·ry
peb'ble
pec'ca·ble
pec'ca·dil'lo
pec'ca·dil'loes
pec'can·cy
pec'cant
peck'er
pec'to·ral
pec'u·late
pec'u·la'tion
pec'u·la'tor
pe·cul'iar
pe·cu'li·ar'i·ty
pe·cul'iar·ly
pe·cu'li·um
pe·cu'ni·ar'y
ped'a·gog'ic
ped'a·gog'i·cal
ped'a·gog'ics
ped'a·gogue
ped'a·go'gy
ped'al
ped'ant
pe·dan'tic
ped'ant·ry
ped'dle
ped'dler
ped'dler·y
ped'dling
ped'es·tal
pe·des'tri·an
pe·des'tri·an·ism
pe'di·at'rics
pe·dic'u·lar
ped'i·gree
ped'i·ment
pe·dom'e·ter
peep'er
peer'age
peer'ess
peer'less
pee'vish
Peg'a·sus
pe'jo·ra'tive
Pe'king·ese'
Pe·la'gi·an
pel'i·can
pel'let
pell'–mell'
pel·lu'cid
pelt'ry
pel'vis
pe'nal
pe'nal·i·za'tion
pe'nal·ize
pen'al·ties
pen'al·ty
pen'ance
pen'chant'
pen'cil
pen'ciled
pen'cil·er
pend'ant
pend'en·cy
pend'ent
pend'ing
pen·drag'on
pen'du·lous
pen'du·lum
pen'e·tra·bil'i·ty
pen'e·tra·ble
pen'e·trate
pen'e·tra'tion
pen'e·tra'tive
pen'guin
pen'hold'er
pen·in'su·la
pen·in'su·lar
pen'i·tence
pen'i·tent
pen'i·ten'tial
pen'i·ten'tia·ry

pen′i·tent·ly
pen′knife′
pen′man
pen′man·ship
pen name
pen′nant
pen′nies
pen′ni·less
Penn′syl·va′ni·an
pen′ny
pen′ny·weight′
pen′ny–wise′
pen′ny·worth′
pe′no·log′i·cal
pe·nol′o·gist
pe·nol′o·gy
pen point
pen′sile
pen′sion
pen′sion·ar′y
pen′sion·er
pen′sive
pen′stock′
pen′ta·cle
pen′ta·gon
pen·tag′o·nal
pen·tath′lon
Pen′te·cost
pent′house′
pe′nult
pe·nul′ti·mate
pe·nu′ri·ous

pen′u·ry
pen–writ′ten
pe′on
pe′on·age
pe′o·nies
pe′o·ny
peo′ple
pep′per
pep′per–and–salt′
pep′per·box′
pep′per·mint
pep′per·y
pep′sin
per′ad·ven′ture
per·am′bu·late
per·am′bu·la′tion
per·am′bu·la′tor
per·am′bu·la·to′ry
per an′num
per cap′i·ta
per·ceiv′a·ble
per·ceive′
per cent
per·cent′age
per′cept
per·cep′ti·ble
per·cep′tion
per·cep′tive
per·cep′tu·al
per·chance′

Per′che·ron
per·cip′i·ence
per·cip′i·en·cy
per·cip′i·ent
per′co·late
per′co·la′tion
per′co·la′tor
per·cuss′
per·cus′sion
per·cus′sive
per di′em
per·di′tion
per′e·gri·nate
per′e·gri·na′tion
per·emp′to·ri·ly
per·emp′to·ri·ness
per·emp′to·ry
per·en′ni·al
per′fect, *adj.*
per·fect′, *v.*
per·fect′i·ble
per·fec′tion
per·fec′tion·ism
per′fect·ly
per·fec′to
per·fec′tos
per·fid′i·ous
per′fi·dy
per′fo·rate
per′fo·rat′ed
per′fo·ra′tion

per′fo·ra′tive
per′fo·ra′tor
per·force′
per·form′
per·form′ance
per·form′er
per·fume′, *v.*
per′fume, *n.*
per·fum′er
per·fum′er·y
per·func′to·ry
per·fuse′
per·fu′sion
per·haps′
per′il
per′il·ous
per·im′e·ter
per′i·ne′al
per′i·ne′um
pe′ri·od
pe′ri·od′ic
pe′ri·od′i·cal
pe·riph′ra·sis
per′i·phras′tic
per′i·scope
per′i·scop′ic
per′i·scop′i·cal
per′ish
per′ish·a·ble
per′i·win′kle
per′jure
per′jur·er

per′ju·ry
perk′y
per′ma·nence
per′ma·nen·cy
per′ma·nent
per′me·a·bil′i·ty
per′me·a·ble
per′me·ance
per′me·ant
per′me·ate
per′me·a′tion
per′me·a′tive
per·mis′si·ble
per·mis′sion
per·mis′sive
per·mit′, *v.*
per′mit, *n.*
per·mit′ted
per·mit′ting
per′mu·ta′tion
per·mute′
per·ni′cious
per·nick′et·y
per′o·rate
per′o·ra′tion
per·ox′ide
per′pen·dic′u·lar
per′pe·trate
per′pe·tra′tion
per′pe·tra′tor
per·pet′u·al
per·pet′u·al·ly

per·pet′u·ate
per·pet′u·a′tion
per·pet′u·a′tor
per′pe·tu′i·ty
per·plex′
per·plexed′
per·plex′ed·ly
per·plex′ing
per·plex′i·ty
per′qui·site
per′ry
per′se·cute
per′se·cu′tion
per′se·cu′tor
per′se·cu′to·ry
Per′seus
per′se·ver′ance
per′se·vere′
Per′sian
per′si·flage
per·sim′mon
per·sist′
per·sist′ence
per·sist′en·cy
per·sist′ent
per′son
per′son·a·ble
per′son·age
per′son·al
per′son·al′i·ty
per′son·al·ize
per′son·al·ly

per·son′i·fi·ca′-
tion
per·son′i·fi′er
per·son′i·fy
per′son·nel′
per·spec′tive
per′spi·ca′cious
per′spi·cac′i·ty
per′spi·cu′i·ty
per·spic′u·ous
per′spi·ra′tion
per·spir′a·to′ry
per·spire′
per·suade′
per·sua′si·ble
per·sua′sion
per·sua′sive
per·tain′
per′ti·na′cious
per′ti·nac′i·ty
per′ti·nence
per′ti·nen·cy
per′ti·nent
per·turb′
per·turb′a·ble
per′tur·ba′tion
pe·rus′al
pe·ruse′
pe·rus′er
Pe·ru′vi·an
per·vade′
per·va′sion
per·va′sive
per·verse′
per·ver′sion
per·ver′si·ty
per·ver′sive
per·vert′, *v.*
per′vert, *n.*
per·vert′ed
per·vert′er
per·vert′i·ble
per′vi·ous
pes′si·mism
pes·si·mist
pes′si·mis′tic
pes′ter
pest′house′
pes·tif′er·ous
pes′ti·lence
pes′ti·lent
pes′ti·len′tial
pes′tle
pet′al
pet cock
pet′it
pe·tite′
pe·ti′tion
pe·ti′tion·ar′y
pe·ti′tion·er
pet′ri·fac′tion
pet′ri·fac′tive
pet′ri·fi·ca′tion
pet′ri·fied
pet′ri·fy
Pe′trine
pet′rol
pet′ro·la′tum
pe·tro′le·um
pet′ro·log′ic
pe·trol′o·gy
pet′rous
pet′ti·coat
pet′ti·fog
pet′ti·fog′ger·y
pet′ti·ly
pet′ti·ness
pet′ty
pet′u·lance
pet′u·lan·cy
pet′u·lant
pew′ter
pew′ter·er
pfen′nig
pha·lan′ges, *pl.*
pha′lanx
phan′tom
Phar′aoh
Phar′i·see
phar′ma·ceu′tist
phar′ma·cist
phar′ma·cy
pheas′ant
phe·nom′e·na, *pl.*
phe·nom′e·nal

phe·nom′e·nal-
ism
phe·nom′e·nol′o-
gy
phe·nom′e·non
phi′al
phi·lan′der
phi·lan′der·er
phil′an·throp′ic
phil′an·throp′i-
cal
phi·lan′thro·pist
phi·lan′thro·py
phi·lat′e·ly
phil′har·mon′ic
Phil′ip·pine
Phi·lis′tine
phil′o·log′i·cal
phi·lol′o·gist
phi·lol′o·gy
phi·los′o·pher
phil′o·soph′ic
phil′o·soph′i·cal
phi·los′o·phy
phil′ter
(drug)
phlegm
phleg·mat′ic
Phoe′be
Phoe·ni′cian
phoe′nix
pho·net′ic
pho′ne·ti′cian
pho′no·graph
pho′no·graph′ic
pho·nog′ra·phy
pho′no·type
pho′no·typ′ic
pho′no·typ′i·cal
pho′no·typ′y
phos′phate
phos′pho·resce′
phos′pho·res′-
cence
phos′pho·res′-
cent
phos·phor′ic
phos′pho·rous,
adj.
phos′pho·rus, *n.*
pho′to·cop′y
pho′to·en·grav′-
ing
pho′to·graph
pho·tog′ra·pher
pho′to·graph′ic
pho·tog′ra·phy
pho′to·gra·vure′
pho′to·lith′o-
graph
pho′to·play′
pho′to·stat
phra′se·ol′o·gy
phre·net′ic
phre·nol′o·gist
phre·nol′o·gy
phys′ic
phys′i·cal
phy·si′cian
phys′i·cist
phys′ics
phys′i·og′no·my
phys′i·og′ra·phy
phys′i·ol′o·gist
phys′i·ol′o·gy
phy·sique′
pi′a·nis′si·mo
pi·an′ist
pi·an′o
pi·an′os
pi·as′ter
pi·az′za
pi′ca
pic′a·dor
pic′a·resque′
pic′a·yune′
pic′ca·lil′li
pic′co·lo
pic′co·lo·ist
pick′a·nin′ny
pick′ax′
pick′er
pick′er·el
pick′et
pick′ing
pick′le

pick′lock′
pick′pock′et
pick′up′
pic′nic
pic′nick·er
pic′nick·ing
pic′to·graph
pic·tog′ra·phy
pic·to′ri·al
pic′ture
pic′tur·esque′
piece goods
piece′meal′
piec′er
piece rate
piece′work′
pie chart
pie′crust′
pie knife
pie′pan′
pie plate
pierc′er
pie tin
pi′e·ty
pif′fle
pi′geon
pi′geon·hole′
pi′geon–toed′
pi′geon·wing′
pig′fish′
pig′ger·y
pig′gish
pig′head′ed
pig iron
pig′ment
pig′men·tar′y
pig′men·ta′tion
pig′mies
pig′my
pig′pen′
pig′skin′
pig′stick′ing
pig′sty′
pig′tail′
pike′man
pike perch
pik′er
pike′staff′
pi·las′ter
pil′chard
pi′le·ous
pil′fer
pil′grim
pil′grim·age
pi·lif′er·ous
pil′ing
pil′lage
pil′lar
pil′lion
pil′lo·ry
pil′low
pil′low·case′
pi′lose
pi·los′i·ty
pi′lot
pi′lot′house′
pim′ple
pin′a·fore′
pince′–nez′
pinch′beck
pinch′er
pin′cush′ion
pine′ap′ple
pin′er·y
pin′feath′er
pin′fold′
Ping′–pong′
pin′head′
pin′hole′
pin′ion
pink′eye′
pink′root′
pin money
pin′na·cle
pi′noch′le
pin′tle
pin′–up′
pin′weed′
pin wheel
pi′o·neer′
pi′ous
pipe dream
pipe′line′
pipe organ
pip′er
pipe′stem′

pipe'stone'
pip'ing
pi'quan·cy
pi'quant
pique
pi'ra·cy
pi'rate
pi·rat'ic
pi·rat'i·cal
pis'ca·ry
pis'ca·tol'o·gy
pis'ca·to'ry
pis·ta'chi·o
pis'tol
pis'ton
pitch'er
pitch'fork'
pitch'stone'
pitch'y
pit'e·ous
pit'fall'
pith'i·ly
pith'i·ness
pith'y
pit'i·a·ble
pit'ied
pit'ies
pit'i·ful
pit'i·less
pit'man
pit saw
pit'tance
pit'ter–pat'ter
Pitts'burg,
Calif., Kansas
Pitts'burgh, Pa.
pi·tu'i·tar'y
pit'y
piv'ot
piv'ot·al
piz'zi·ca'to
pla'ca·bil'i·ty
pla'ca·ble
plac'ard, *n.*
pla·card', *v.*
pla'cate
pla'ca·to'ry
place kick
place'ment
plac'er
plac'id
pla·cid'i·ty
plac'ing
pla'gi·a·rism
pla'gi·a·rist
pla'gi·a·rize
pla'gi·a·ry
plague
pla'guy
plain'–laid'
plain'ly
plain'ness
plains'man
plain'tiff
plain'tive
plait
plan'et
plan'e·tar'i·um
plan'e·tar'y
plan'gent
plank'ing
plank'–sheer'
plan'ner
plan·ta'tion
plant'er
plaque
plas'ter
plas'ter·er
plas'tic
plas·tic'i·ty
plas'tid
pla·teau'
plate'ful
plate glass
plat'en
plat'er
plat'form'
plat'ing
plat'i·num
plat'i·tude
plat'i·tu'di·nize
plat'i·tu'di·nous
Pla·ton'ic
Pla'to·nism
pla·toon'
plat'ter

plau′dit
plau′si·bil′i·ty
plau′si·ble
play′back′
play′bill′
play′boy
play′er
play′fel′low
play′ful
play′ground′
play′house′
play′ing card
play′mate′
play′–off′
play′room
play′script′
play′thing′
play′time′
play′wright′
pla′za
plea
plead′a·ble
plead′er
plead′ing
plead′ing·ly
pleas′ant
pleas′ant·ry
pleas′ing
pleas′ur·a·ble
pleas′ure
pleat
plebe
ple·be′ian
pleb′i·scite
plec′trum
pledg′ee′
pledg′er
ple′na·ry
plen′i·po·ten′ti-ar′y
plen′i·tude
plen′te·ous
plen′ti·ful
plen′ty
pleth′o·ra
pleu′ri·sy
pli′a·bil′i·ty
pli′a·ble
pli′an·cy
pli′ant
pli′cate
pli·ca′tion
plod′der
plot′ter
plow
plow′boy′
plow′er
plow hand
plow′man
plow′share′
plug′board′
plug′–ug′ly
plum′age
plumb bob
plumb′er
plumb′ing
plumb line
plump′er
plump′ness
plun′der
plun′der·er
plung′er
plu′per′fect
plu′ral
plu′ral·ism
plu·ral′i·ty
plu′ral·ize
plu·toc′ra·cy
plu′to·crat
plu′to·crat′ic
Plu·ton′ic
pneu·mat′ic
pneu·mat′ics
pneu·mo′ni·a
pneu·mon′ic
poach′er
pock′et
pock′et·book′
pock′et·knife′
pocket money
pocket veto
pock′mark′
po′des·ta′
po′di·um
po′em
po′et

po′et·as′ter
po·et′ic
po·et′i·cal
po′et·ize
po′et·ry
poign′an·cy
poign′ant
poin·set′ti·a
point′–blank′, *adv.*
point′–blank′, *adj.*
point′–de·vice′
point′ed
point′er
point′less
poi′son
poison ivy
poi′son·ous
pok′er
po′lar
po·lar′i·ty
po′lar·i·za′tion
po′lar·ize
pole′ax′
pole′cat′
pole vault
po·lice′
po·lice′man
pol′i·cies
pol′i·clin′ic (dispensary)
pol′i·cy
pol′i·cy·hold′er
Pol′ish
pol′ish
pol′ish·er
po·lite′
po·lite′ness
pol′i·tic
po·lit′i·cal
po·lit′i·cal·ly
pol′i·ti′cian
pol′i·tics
pol′i·ty
pol′ka
polka dot
pol′lack
pol′li·wog
poll tax
pol·lute′
pol·lu′tion
po′lo
po′lo·naise′
pol′y·an′dry
pol′y·an′thus
pol′y·chro·mat′ic
pol′y·clin′ic (hospital)
po·lyg′a·mist
po·lyg′a·mous
po·lyg′a·my
pol′y·glot
pol′y·gon
pol′y·graph
pol′y·phon′ic
pol′y·syl·lab′ic
pol′y·syl′la·ble
pol′y·tech′nic
pom′mel
pom′pa·no
pom′pa·dour
Pom·pe′ian
pom·pos′i·ty
pomp′ous
pon′cho
pon′chos
pon′der
pon′der·a·ble
pon′der·os′i·ty
pon′der·ous
pon′iard
po′nies
pon′tiff
pon·tif′i·cal
pon·tif′i·cate
pon·toon′
po′ny
poo′dle
pool′room
poor′house′
poor′ly
poor′ness
poor′–spir′it·ed
pop′corn′
pope′dom

pop′er·y
pop′gun′
pop′lar
pop′pies
pop′py
pop′u·lace
pop′u·lar
pop′u·lar′i·ty
pop′u·lar·ize
pop′u·lar·ly
pop′u·late
pop′u·la′tion
pop′u·lous
por′ce·lain
por′cu·pine
pore
(study. cf. *pour*.)
po·rif′er·ous
pork′er
por′poise
por′ridge
port′a·ble
por′tage
por′tal
por·tend′
por′tent
por·ten′tous
por′ter
por′ter·age
por′ter·house′
port·fo′li·o
port′hole′
por′ti·co
por′ti·coes
por·tiere′
por′tion
port′li·ness
port′ly
port·man′teau
port·man′teaus
Port–au–Prince, Haiti
por′trait
por′trai·ture
por·tray′
por·tray′al
Por′tu·guese
Por′tu·la′ca
po·si′tion
pos′i·tive
pos′se
pos·sess′
pos·ses′sion
pos·ses′sive
pos·ses′sor
pos·ses′so·ry
pos′si·bil′i·ty
pos′si·ble
post′age
post′al
post card
post′date′
post′di·lu′vi·an
post′er
pos·te′ri·or
pos·ter′i·ty
pos′tern
post·grad′u·ate
post′haste′
post′hu·mous
post′man
post′mark′
post′mas′ter
post′me·rid′i·an
post′–mor′tem
post′–o′bit
post′paid′
post·pone′
post·pone′ment
post′script
pos′tu·lant
pos′tu·late
pos′tu·la′tion
pos′ture
po′sy
po′ta·ble
pot′ash′
po·tas′si·um
po·ta′tion
po·ta′to
po·ta′toes
pot′bel′ly
pot′boil′er
pot′boy′
po′ten·cy
po′tent

po′ten·tate
po·ten′tial
po·ten′ti·al′i·ty
po·ten′tial·ly
po′tent·ly
pot′hole′
pot′hook′
pot′house′
po′tion
pot′luck′
pot shot
pot′tage
pot′ter
pot′ter·ies
pot′ter·y
Pough·keep′sie, N. Y.
poul′ter·er
poul′tice
poul′try
pound′age
pound′cake′
pound′er
pound′–fool′ish
pour
(rain. cf. *pore.*)
pour′er
pov′er·ty
pow′der
pow′der·y
pow′er
pow′er·ful
pow′er·less
pow′wow′
prac′ti·ca·bil′i·ty
prac′ti·ca·ble
prac′ti·cal
prac′ti·cal′i·ty
prac′ti·cal·ly
prac′ti·cal·ness
prac′tice
prac′ticed
prac′tic·er
prac·ti′tion·er
prag·mat′ic
prag·mat′i·cal
prag′ma·tism
prag′ma·tist
prai′rie
praise′wor′thy
pra′line
prank′ish
prat′tle
prayer
prayer book
prayer′ful
preach′er
preach′ing
preach′ment
pre′am′ble
pre·car′i·ous
prec′a·to′ry
pre·cau′tion
pre·cau′tion·ar′y
pre·cau′tious
pre·cede′
pre·ced′ence
pre·ced′en·cy
pre·ced′ent, *adj.*
prec′e·dent, *n.*
pre·ced′ing
pre′cept
pre·cep′tive
pre·cep′tor
pre·cep′to·ry
pre·ces′sion
pre·ces′sion·al
pre′cinct
pre′cious
prec′i·pice
pre·cip′i·tance
pre·cip′i·tan·cy
pre·cip′i·tant
pre·cip′i·tate
pre·cip′i·tate·ly
pre·cip′i·tate·ness
pre·cip′i·ta′tion
pre·cip′i·ta′tor
pre·cip′i·tous
pre·cise′
pre·ci′sion
pre·clude′
pre·clu′sion
pre·clu′sive
pre·co′cious
pre·coc′i·ty

pre′con·ceive′
pre′con·cep′tion
pre′con·cert′
pre·cur′sive
pre·cur′sor
pre·cur′so·ry
pred′a·to′ry
pre′de·cease′
pred′e·ces′sor
pre·des′tine
pre′de·ter′mine
pre·dic′a·ment
pred′i·cate
pred′i·ca′tion
pred′i·ca′tive
pred′i·ca·to′ry
pre·dict′
pre·dict′a·ble
pre·dic′tion
pre·dic′tive
pre·dic′tor
pre′di·lec′tion
pre′dis·pose′
pre′dis·po·si′tion
pre·dom′i·nance
pre·dom′i·nant
pre·dom′i·nate
pre·dom′i·na′-
tion
pre–em′i·nence
pre–em′i·nent
pre–empt′
pre–emp′tive
pre–emp′to·ry
pref′ace
pref′a·to·ry
pre′fect
pre′fec·ture
pre·fer′
pref′er·a·ble
pref′er·ence
pref′er·en′tial
pre·ferred′
pre·fer′ring
pre·fix′, *v.*
pre′fix, *n.*
preg′na·ble
preg′nan·cy
preg′nant
pre′his·tor′ic
prej′u·dice
prej′u·di′cial
prel′a·cy
prel′ate
pre·lim′i·nar′y
prel′ude
pre′ma·ture′
pre′ma·tu′ri·ty
pre·med′i·tate
pre′med·i·ta′tion
pre′mi·er
prem′ise, *n.*
pre·mise′, *v.*
pre′mi·um
pre′mo·ni′tion
pre·mon′i·to′ry
pre·na′tal
pre·oc′cu·pan·cy
pre·oc′cu·pa′tion
pre·oc′cu·pied
pre·oc′cu·py
pre·paid′
prep′a·ra′tion
pre·par′a·tive
pre·par′a·to′ry
pre·pare′
pre·par′ed·ness
pre·par′er
pre·pay′
pre·pay′ment
pre·pon′der·ance
pre·pon′der·ant
pre·pon′der·ate
pre·pon′der·at′-
ing
prep′o·si′tion
prep′o·si′tion·al
pre′pos·sess′
pre′pos·sess′ing
pre′pos·ses′sion
pre·pos′ter·ous
pre·po′ten·cy
pre·req′ui·site
pre·rog′a·tive
pres′age, *n.*
pre·sage′, *v.*

Pres′by·te′ri·an
pre′sci·ent
pre·scribe′
pre·scrip′ti·ble
pre·scrip′tion
pre·scrip′tive
pres′ence
pres′ent, *adj.*
pre·sent′, *v.*
pre·sent′a·ble
pres′en·ta′tion
pre·sent′a·tive
pres′en·tee′
pre·sent′er
pre·sen′ti·ment
pres′ent·ly
pre·serv′a·ble
pres′er·va′tion
pre·serv′a·tive
pre·serve′
pre·side′
pres′i·den·cy
pres′i·dent
pres′i·den′tial
pre·sid′er
press′–a′gent
press′board′
press′er
press gang
press′ing
press′man′
press′mark′
press′room
pres′sure
pres′sur·ize
press′work′
pres′ti·dig′i·ta′-
tion
pres′ti·dig′i·ta′-
tor
pres·tige′
pre·sum′a·ble
pre·sume′
pre·sum′ed·ly
pre·sum′er
pre·sump′tion
pre·sump′tive
pre·sump′tu·ous
pre′sup·pose′
pre′sup·po·si′-
tion
pre·tend′
pre·tend′ed
pre·tend′er
pre·tense′
pre·ten′sion
pre·ten′tious
pret′er·it
pre′text
pret′ti·ly
pret′ti·ness
pret′ty
pret′zel
pre·vail′
pre·vail′ing
prev′a·lence
prev′a·lent
pre·var′i·cate
pre·var′i·ca′tion
pre·var′i·ca′tor
pre·vent′
pre·vent′a·ble
pre·vent′er
pre·ven′tion
pre·ven′tive
pre′vi·ous
pre·vi′sion
prey
Pri′am
price′less
prick′er
prick′le
prick′ly
priest′ess
priest′hood
priest′ly
pri′ma·cy
pri′ma don′na
pri′ma fa′ci·e
pri′ma·ri·ly
pri′ma·ry
prime′ly
prime′ness
prim′er
pri·me′val
prim′i·tive

pri′mo·gen′i·ture
pri·mor′di·al
prim′rose′
prince′dom
prince′ly
prin′cess
prin′ci·pal
(chief)
prin′ci·pal′i·ty
prin′ci·pal·ly
prin′ci·pal·ship′
prin′ci·ple
(rule)
print′a·ble
print′er
print′er·y
print′ing
print′less
pri′or
pri′or·ate
pri′or·ess
pri·or′i·ty
pri′or·ship
prism
pris·mat′ic
pris′on
pris′on·er
pris′tine
pri′va·cy
pri′vate
pri′va·teer′
pri′vate·ly
pri′vate·ness
pri·va′tion
priv′a·tive
priv′i·lege
priv′i·ly
priv′i·ty
priv′y
prize fight
prize ring
prob′a·bil′i·ty
prob′a·ble
prob′a·bly
pro′bate
pro·ba′tion
pro·ba′tion·al
pro·ba′tion·ar′y
pro·ba′tion·er
pro′ba·tive
pro′ba·to′ry
prob′lem
prob′lem·at′ic
prob′lem·at′i·cal
pro·bos′cis
pro·ce′dure
pro·ceed′
pro·ceed′ing
proc′ess
pro·ces′sion
pro·ces′sion·al
pro·claim′
proc′la·ma′tion
pro·cliv′i·ty
pro·cras′ti·nate
pro·cras′ti·na′-
tion
pro·cras′ti·na′tor
pro′cre·a′tion
pro′cre·a′tive
proc′tor
proc·to′ri·al
proc′tor·ship
pro·cur′a·ble
proc′u·ra′tion
proc′u·ra′tor
proc′u·ra·to′ry
pro·cure′
pro·cure′ment
pro·cur′er
pro·cur′ess
prod′i·gal
prod′i·gal′i·ty
pro·di′gious
prod′i·gy
pro·duce′, *v.*
prod′uce, *n.*
pro·duc′er
pro·duc′i·ble
prod′uct
pro·duc′tion
pro·duc′tive
pro′duc·tiv′i·ty
prof′a·na′tion
pro·fan′a·to′ry
pro·fane′

pro·fan'i·ty
pro·fess'
pro·fess'ed·ly
pro·fes'sion
pro·fes'sion·al
pro·fes'sion·al-
ism
pro·fes'sion·al·ly
pro·fes'sor
pro'fes·so'ri·al
pro·fes'sor·ship
prof'fer
pro·fi'cien·cy
pro·fi'cient
pro'file
prof'it
prof'it·a·ble
prof'it·eer'
prof'it·less
prof'li·ga·cy
prof'li·gate
pro·found'
pro·fun'di·ty
pro·fuse'
pro·fu'sion
pro·gen'i·tor
prog'e·ny
prog·no'sis
prog·nos'tic
prog·nos'ti·cate
prog·nos'ti·ca'-
tion
pro'gram
prog'ress, *n.*
pro·gress', *v.*
pro·gres'sion·al
pro·gres'sion·ist
pro·gres'sive
pro·hib'it
pro'hi·bi'tion
pro'hi·bi'tion·ist
pro·hib'i·tive
pro·hib'i·to'ry
pro·ject', *v.*
proj'ect, *n.*
pro·jec'tile
pro·jec'tion
pro·jec'tive
pro·jec'tor
pro'late
pro'le·tar'i·an
pro'le·tar'i·at
pro'le·tar'y
pro·lif'ic
pro·lix'
pro·lix'i·ty
pro'logue
pro·long'
pro·lon'gate
pro'lon·ga'tion
prom'e·nade'
prom'e·nad'er
Pro·me'theus
prom'i·nence
prom'i·nent
prom'is·cu'i·ty
pro·mis'cu·ous
prom'ise
prom'is·ee'
prom'is·er
prom'is·ing
prom'is·so'ry
prom'on·to'ry
pro·mote'
pro·mot'er
pro·mo'tion
pro·mo'tive
prompt
prompt'er
promp'ti·tude
prompt'ly
prompt'ness
pro·mul'gate
pro'mul·ga'tion
pro'noun
pro·nounce'
pro·nounce'a·ble
pro·nounced'
pro·nounce'ment
pro·nun'ci·a'tion
proof'read'er
prop'a·ga·ble
prop'a·gan'da
prop'a·gan'dist
prop'a·gate
prop'a·ga'tion

prop'a·ga'tive
prop'a·ga'tor
pro·pel'
pro·pel'lant
pro·pelled'
pro·pel'lent
pro·pel'ler
pro·pel'ling
pro·pense'
pro·pen'si·ty
prop'er
prop'er·ly
prop'er·tied
prop'er·ty
proph'e·cies
proph'e·cy, *n.* (a prediction)
proph'e·si'er
proph'e·sy, *v.* (to predict)
proph'et
pro·phet'ic
pro·phet'i·cal
pro'phy·lac'tic
pro·pin'qui·ty
pro·pi'ti·ate
pro·pi'ti·a'tion
pro·pi'ti·a'tor
pro·pi'ti·a·to'ry
pro·pi'tious
pro·po'nent
pro·por'tion
pro·por'tion·a-ble
pro·por'tion·al
pro·por'tion·ate
pro·pos'al
pro·pose'
prop'o·si'tion
prop'o·si'tion·al
pro·pound'
pro·pri'e·tor
pro·pri'e·ty
pro·pul'sion
pro·pul'sive
pro ra'ta
pro·rat'a·ble
pro'rate'
pro·sa'ic
pro·sce'ni·um
pro·scribe'
pro·scrip'tion
pro·scrip'tive
prose
pros'e·cute
pros'e·cu'tion
pros'e·cu'tor
pros'e·lyte
pro'sit
pros'pect
pro·spec'tive
pro·spec'tus
pros'per
pros·per'i·ty
pros'per·ous
pros'tate
pros'ti·tute
pros'ti·tu'tion
pros'trate
pros·tra'tion
pros'y
pro·tag'o·nist
pro·tect'
pro·tect'ing
pro·tec'tion
pro·tec'tion·ism
pro·tec'tion·ist
pro·tec'tive
pro·tec'tor
pro·tec'tor·ate
pro'té·gé
pro'te·in
pro·test', *v.*
pro'test, *n.*
prot'es·tant
prot'es·tant·ism
prot'es·ta'tion
pro'to·col
pro'to·plasm
pro'to·plast
pro'to·type
pro·tract'
pro·trac'tile
pro·trac'tion
pro·trac'tive
pro·trac'tor

pro·trude′
pro·tru′sion
pro·tru′sive
pro·tu′ber·ance
pro·tu′ber·an·cy
pro·tu′ber·ant
pro·tu′ber·ate
prov′a·ble
prov′en
prov′er
prov′erb
pro·ver′bi·al
pro·vide′
pro·vid′ed
prov′i·dence
prov′i·dent
prov′i·den′tial
pro·vid′er
prov′ince
pro·vin′cial
pro·vin′cial·ism
pro·vin′ci·al′i·ty
pro·vin′cial·ly
pro·vi′sion
pro·vi′sion·al
pro·vi′sion·ar′y
pro·vi′sion·er
pro·vi′so
pro·vi′so·ry
pro·vi′sos
prov′o·ca′tion
pro·voc′a·tive
pro·voke′
pro·vok′ing
prow′ess
prox′ies
prox′i·mal
prox′i·mate
prox·im′i·ty
prox′i·mo
prox′y
prude
pru′dence
pru′dent
pru·den′tial
prud′ish
pru′ri·ence
pru′ri·ent
Prus′sian
pry′ing
psalm
psalm′ist
pseu′do·carp
Psy′che
psy·chi′a·try
psy′chic
psy′cho·a·nal′y-
sis
psy′cho·log′i·cal
psy·chol′o·gist
psy·chol′o·gize
psy·chol′o·gy
psy′cho·path
psy′cho·path′ic
psy·cho′sis
pu′ber·ty
pub′lic
pub′li·ca′tion
pub′li·cist
pub·lic′i·ty
pub′lic·ly
pub′lic·ness
pub′lish
pub′lish·er
puck′er·y
pud′ding
pud′dle
pud′dling
pu′den·cy
pueb′lo
pueb′los
pu′er·ile
Puer′to Ri′co
pu′gil·ism
pu′gil·ist
pu′gil·is′tic
pug·na′cious
pug·nac′i·ty
pug nose
pug′–nosed′
pu′is·sance
pu′is·sant
pul′chri·tude
pul′chri·tu′di-
nous
pul′let

pul′ley
Pull′man
pul′mo·nar′y
Pul′mo′tor
pulp′i·ness
pul′pit
pulp′y
pul′sate
pul′sa·tile
pul·sa′tion
pul′sa·tive
pul·sa′tor
pul′sa·to′ry
pul′ver·ize
pul′ver·iz′er
pum′ice
pum′per·nick′el
pump′kin
pun′cheon
punch′er
punc′tate
punc′tat·ed
punc·ta′tion
punc·til′i·o
punc·til′i·ous
punc′tu·al
punc′tu·al′i·ty
punc′tu·al·ly
punc′tu·ate
punc′tu·a′tion
punc′tu·a′tor
punc′ture
pun′gen·cy
pun′gent
pun′ish
pun′ish·a·ble
pun′ish·er
pun′ish·ment
pu′ni·tive
pun′ster
punt′er
pu′ny
pu′pil
pup′pet
pup′pet·ry
pup′py
pur′chas·a·ble
pur′chase
pur′chas·er
pure′ly
pure′ness
pur·ga′tion
pur′ga·tive
pur′ga·to′ri·al
pur′ga·to′ri·an
pur′ga·to′ry
purge
purg′er
pu′ri·fi·ca′tion
pu′ri·fi′er
pu′ri·fy
pur′ism
pur′ist
Pu′ri·tan
pu′ri·tan′i·cal
Pu′ri·tan·ism
pu′ri·ty
pur′lieu
pur·loin′
pur′ple
pur′plish
pur·port′, *v.*
pur′port, *n.*
pur′pose
pur′pose·ly
pur′pos·ive
purr
purr′ing
purs′er
pur·su′al
pur·su′ance
pur·su′ant
pur·sue′
pur·suit′
pur·vey′
pur·vey′ance
pur·vey′or
pur′view
push′ball′
push button
push′cart′
push′er
push′ing
push′o′ver
push′pin′
push′-pull′

puss′y wil'low
pus′tu·lant
pus′tu·lar
pus′tu·late
pus'tu·la′tion
pus′tule
pu'tre·fac′tion
pu'tre·fac′tive
pu′tre·fied
pu′tre·fy
pu·tres′cence
pu·tres′cent
pu′trid
putt′er
put′ty
puz′zle
puz′zler
puz′zling
pyg′my
py'or·rhe′a
pyr′a·mid
py·ram′i·dal
pyre
py·rox′y·lin
pyr′rhic
Py′thon

Q

quack′er·y
quad′ran'gle
quad·ran′gu·lar
quad′rant
quad·ren′ni·al
quad·ren′ni·um
quad'ri·lat′er·al
qua·drille′
quad·ril′lion
quad·roon′
quad′ru·ped
quad·ru′pe·dal
quad′ru·ple, *adj.*
quad·ru′ple, *v.*
quad′ru·plet
quad·ru′pli·cate
quaff
quag′mire'
Quak′er
qual'i·fi·ca′tion
qual′i·fied
qual′i·fy
qual′i·ta'tive
qual′i·ty
qualm
qualm′ish
quan′da·ry
quan′ti·ta'tive
quan′ti·ty
quan′tum
quar′an·tine
quar′rel
quar′rel·some
quar′ry
quar′ter
quar′ter·back'
quar′ter–deck'
quar′tered
quar′ter·ing
quar′ter·ly
quar′ter·mas'ter
quar·tet′
quar′to
quar′tos
quartz
qua′si
quat′rain
qua′ver
quay
(wharf)
quench′less
que′ried
quer′u·lous
que′ry

ques'tion
ques'tion·a·ble
ques'tion·er
ques'tion·ing·ly
question mark
ques'tion·naire'
quib'ble
quick'en
quick'–fire', *adj.*
quick'lime'
quick'ly
quick'ness
quick'sand'
quick'sil'ver
quick'step'
quick'–wit'ted
quid'di·ty
quid'nunc'
qui·es'cence
qui·es'cen·cy
qui·es'cent
qui'et
qui'et·ly
qui'et·ness
qui'e·tude
qui·e'tus
qui'nine
quint·es'sence
quin·tet'
quire
quit'claim'
quit'tance
quiv'er
qui vive'
quix·ot'ic
quiz
quizzed
quiz'zi·cal
quiz'zing
quo'rum
quo'ta
quot'a·ble
quo·ta'tion
quote
quo'tient

R

rab'bi
rab'bit
rab'bit·ry
rab'ble
rab'id
ra'bi·es
rac·coon'
race'course'
race horse
rac'er
race track
race'way
ra'cial
rack'et
rack rail
rac'on·teur'
ra'dar
ra'dar·scope
ra'di·al
ra'di·an
ra'di·ance
ra'di·an·cy
ra'di·ant
ra'di·ant·ly
ra'di·ate
ra'di·a'tion
ra'di·a'tive
ra'di·a'tor
rad'i·cal
rad'i·cal·ism
rad'i·cal·ly
ra'di·i, *pl.*
ra'di·o
ra'di·os
ra'di·o·ac'tive
ra'di·o·gram'

ra'di·o·graph'
ra'di·og'ra·phy
ra'di·om'e·ter
ra'di·o·phone'
ra'di·o·tel'e-
gram
ra'di·o·tel'e-
graph
ra'di·o·tel'e-
phone
rad'ish
ra'di·um
ra'di·us
raf'fle
raft'er
rafts'man
rag'a·muf'fin
rag'ged
rag'ing
rag'man'
ra·gout'
rag'pick'er
rag'time'
rag'weed'
rail'er
rail'head'
rail'ing
rail'ler·y
rail'road'
rail'way'
rai'ment
rain'band'
rain'bow'
rain cloud
rain'coat'
rain'drop'
rain'fall'
rain gauge
rain pipe
rain'proof'
rain'–swept'
rain'tight
rain water
rain'y
rai'sin
ra'ja
rake'hell'
rake'–off'
rak'ish
ral'ly
ram'ble
ram'bler
ram'bling
ram'e·kin
ram'i·fi·ca'tion
ram'i·fy
ramp'ant
ram'part
ram'rod'
ram'shack'le
ranch'man
ran'cid
ran'cor
ran'cor·ous
ran'dom
rang'y
ran'kle
ran'sack
ran'som
ra·pa'cious
ra·pac'i·ty
ra·pid'i·ty
ra'pi·er
rap'ine
rap·port'
rap'ture
rap'tur·ous
rar'e·fac'tion
rar'e·fied
rar'e·fy
rare'ly
rare'ness
rar'i·ty
ras'cal
ras·cal'i·ty
rash'ly
rash'ness
rasp'ber'ry
rat'a·ble
ratch'et
rath'er
rat'i·fi·ca'tion
rat'i·fied
rat'i·fy
ra'tio
ra'ti·oc'i·na'tion

ra′tion
ra′tion·al
ra′tion·al·ize
rat′proof′
rat′tle·snake′
rau′cous
rav′age
rav′en
rav′en·ing
rav′en·ous
ra·vine′
rav′ish
raw′boned′
raw′hide′
ray′on
ra′zor
ra′zor·back′
re·act′
re·ac′tion
re·ac′tion·ar′y
read′a·ble
read′i·ly
read′i·ness
read′ing room
re′ad·just′ment
read′y-made′
re′af·firm′
re·a′gent
re′al·ism
re′al·ist
re′al·is′tic
re·al′i·ty
re′al·i·za′tion
re′al·ize
re′al·ly
realm
re′al·ty
re·an′i·mate
re′ap·point′
rear guard
re·arm′
re′ar·range′
rea′son
rea′son·a·ble
rea′son·ing
re′as·sem′ble
re′as·sur′ance
re′as·sure′
re·bel′, *v.*
reb′el, *adj.*
re·belled′
re·bel′ling
re·bel′lion
re·bel′lious
re·birth′
re·buff′
re·buke′
re′bus
re·but′tal
re·cal′ci·trant
re·cant′
re′ca·pit′u·late
re′ca·pit′u·la′tion
re·cap′ture
re·cede′
re·ceipt′
re·ceiv′a·ble
re·ceive′
re·ceiv′er·ship
re·ceiv′ing
re′cent
re·cep′ta·cle
re·cep′tion
re·cep′tive
re·cess′
re·ces′sion·al
re·ces′sive
ré′chauf′fé′
re·cher′ché′
re·cid′i·vism
rec′i·pe
re·cip′i·ent
re·cip′ro·cal
re·cip′ro·cate
re·cip′ro·ca′tion
rec′i·proc′i·ty
re·cit′al
rec′i·ta′tion
re·cite′
reck′less
reck′on
reck′on·ing
re·claim′
rec′la·ma′tion
re·cline′
re·cluse′

rec′og·ni′tion
rec′og·niz′a·ble
re·cog′ni·zance
rec′og·nize
re·coil′
rec′ol·lect′
rec′ol·lec′tion
re′com·mence′
rec′om·mend′
rec′om·men·da′-
tion
re′com·mit′
rec′om·pense
rec′on·cil′a·ble
rec′on·cile
rec′on·cil′i·a′-
tion
rec′on·dite
re·con′nais·sance
rec′on·noi′ter
re·con′quer
re′con·sid′er
re′con·struct′
re′con·struc′tion
rec′ord, *n.*
re·cord′, *v.*
re·cord′er
re·course′
re·cov′er
re·cov′er·y
rec′re·ant
rec′re·a′tion

re·crim′i·na′-
tion
re′cru·des′cence
re·cruit′
rec′tan′gle
rec·tan′gu·lar
rec′ti·fi·ca′tion
rec′ti·fied
rec′ti·fy
rec′ti·lin′e·ar
rec′ti·tude
rec′to·ry
rec′tum
re·cum′bent
re·cu′per·ate
re·cu′per·a′tion
re·cur′
re·curred′
re·cur′rence
re·cur′rent
re·cur′ring
red′bird′
red′breast′
red′bud′
red′cap′
red′coat′
Red Cross
re·deem′
re·deem′a·ble
re·deem′er
re·demp′tion
red′head′

red heat
red herring
re′dis·trib′ute
red lead
red′–let′ter
red′o·lence
red′o·lent
re·doubt′a·ble
re·dound′
re·dress′
red′skin′
red tape
re·duce′
re·duc′tion
re·dun′dan·cy
re·dun′dant
red′wing
red′wood
re′–e·lect′
re–em·bark′
re′–en·act′
re′–en·grave′
re′–en·list′
re–en′ter
re–en′trance
re–en′try
re′–es·tab′lish
re′–ex·am′i·na′-
tion
re′–ex·am′ine
re·fer′
ref′er·ee′

ref′er·ence
ref′er·en′dum
re·ferred′
re·fer′ring
re·fine′
re·fine′ment
re·fin′er
re·fin′er·y
re·flect′
re·flec′tion
re·flec′tive
re·flec′tor
re′flex, *adj.*
re·flex′, *v.*
re·flex′ive
re·form′
ref′or·ma′tion
re·form′a·to′ry
re·frac′tion
re·frac′to·ry
re·frain′
re·fresh′
re·fresh′ment
re·frig′er·ant
re·frig′er·ate
re·frig′er·a′tion
re·frig′er·a′tor
ref′uge
ref′u·gee′
re·ful′gent
re·fus′al
re·fuse′, *v.*
ref′use, *adj., n.*
ref′u·ta·ble
ref′u·ta′tion
re·fute′
re·gain′
re′gal
re·gale′
re·ga′li·a
re·gard′
re·gard′less
re·gat′ta
re′gen·cy
re·gen′er·ate
re·gen′er·a′tive
re′gent
reg′i·cide
re·gime′
reg′i·men
reg′i·ment
reg′i·men′tal
reg′i·men·ta′tion
re′gion
re′gion·al
reg′is·ter
reg′is·trar
reg′is·tra′tion
reg′is·try
re·gres′sion
re·gret′
re·gret′ful
re·gret′ta·ble
re·gret′ted
re·gret′ting
reg′u·lar
reg′u·lar′i·ty
reg′u·lar·ly
reg′u·late
reg′u·la′tion
re·gur′gi·tate
re′ha·bil′i·tate
re·hash′
re·hears′al
re·hearse′
re′im·burse′
re′in·car·na′tion
rein′deer′
re′in·force′
re′in·force′ment
re′in·sert′
re′in·stall′
re′in·state′
re′in·sure′
re′in·vig′or·ate
re·it′er·ate
re·it′er·a′tion
re·ject′
re·jec′tion
re·joice′
re·join′
re·join′der
re·ju′ve·nate
re·lapse′
re·late′
re·la′tion

rel′a·tive
re·lax′
re′lax·a′tion
re·lay′
re·layed′
re·lease′
rel′e·gate
re·lent′
re·lent′less
rel′e·vance
rel′e·vant
re·li′a·ble
re·li′ance
rel′ic
rel′ict
re·lief′
re·lieve′
re·li′gion
re·li′gious
re·lin′quish
rel′i·quar′y
rel′ish
re·luc′tance
re·luc′tant
re·ly′
re·main′
re·main′der
re·mand′
re·mark′
re·mark′a·ble
re·me′di·al
rem′e·dy
re·mem′ber
re·mem′brance
re·mind′
re·mind′er
rem′i·nis′cence
rem′i·nis′cent
re·mis′sion
re·mit′tance
re·mit′tent
rem′nant
re·mon′e·ti·za′-
tion
re·mon′e·tize
re·mon′strance
re·mon′strate
re′mon·stra′tion
re·morse′
re·morse′less
re·mote′
re·mov′a·ble
re·mov′al
re·move′
re·mu′ner·ate
re·mu′ner·a′tion
re·mu′ner·a′tive
ren′ais·sance′
ren′der
ren′dez·vous
ren·di′tion
ren′e·gade
re·new′
re·new′a·ble
re·new′al
ren′net
re·nom′i·nate
re·nounce′
ren′o·vate
ren′o·va′tion
re·nown′
rent′al
re·nun′ci·a′tion
re·oc′cu·py
re′or·gan·i·za′-
tion
re·or′gan·ize
re·pair′
rep′a·ra′tion
rep′ar·tee′
re·past′
re·pay′
re·peal′
re·peat′
re·peat′er
re·pel′
re·pelled′
re·pel′lent
re·pel′ling
re·pent′
re·pent′ance
re·pent′ant
re′per·cus′sion
rep′er·toire
rep′er·to′ry
rep′e·ti′tion

rep′e·ti′tious
re·pine′
re·place′
re·place′a·ble
re·place′ment
re·plen′ish
re·plen′ish·ment
re·plete′
re·plev′in
rep′li·ca
re·ply′
re·port′
re·port′er
re·pose′
re·pos′i·to′ry
re′pos·sess′
rep′re·hend′
rep′re·hen′si·ble
rep′re·sent′
rep′re·sen·ta′tion
rep′re·sent′a·tive
re·press′
re·pres′sion
re·prieve′
rep′ri·mand
re·print′, *v.*
re′print′, *n.*
re·pris′al
re·proach′
re·proach′ful
rep′ro·bate
re′pro·duce′
re′pro·duc′tion
re′pro·duc′tive
re·proof′
re·prove′
rep′tile
rep·til′i·an
re·pub′lic
re·pub′li·can
re·pu′di·ate
re·pu′di·a′tion
re·pug′nance
re·pug′nant
re·pulse′
re·pul′sion
re·pul′sive
re·pur′chase
rep′u·ta·ble
rep′u·ta′tion
re·pute′
re·quest′
re′qui·em
re·quire′
re·quire′ment
re·quir′ing
req′ui·site
req′ui·si′tion
re·quit′al
re·quite′
rere′dos
re·scind′
re·scis′sion
res′cue
re·search′
re·sem′blance
re·sem′ble
re·sent′
re·sent′ful
re·sent′ment
res′er·va′tion
re·serve′
res′er·voir
re·ship′
re·side′
res′i·dence
res′i·dent
res′i·den′tial
re·sid′u·al
re·sid′u·ar′y
res′i·due
re·sid′u·um
re·sign′
res′ig·na′tion
re·sil′i·ence
re·sil′i·ent
res′in
res′in·ous
re·sist′
re·sist′ance
re·sist′ant
re·sist′less
res′o·lute
res′o·lu′tion
re·solve′
res′o·nance

res′o·nant
re·sort′
re·sound′
re·source′
re·source′ful
re·spect′
re·spect′a·bil′i·ty
re·spect′a·ble
re·spect′ful
re·spec′tive
res′pi·ra′tion
res′pi·ra′tor
re·spir′a·to′ry
res′pite
re·splend′ent
re·spond′
re·spond′ent
re·sponse′
re·spon′si·bil′-
i·ty
re·spon′si·ble
re·spon′sive
res′tau·rant
res′ti·tu′tion
res′tive
rest′less
res′to·ra′tion
re·stor′a·tive
re·store′
re·strain′
re·straint′
re·strict′
re·stric′tion
re·stric′tive
re·sult′
re·sult′ant
re·sume′
ré′su·mé′
re·sump′tion
re·sur′gence
res′ur·rect′
res′ur·rec′tion
re·sus′ci·tate
re·sus′ci·ta′tion
re′tail
re·tain′
re·tain′er
re·tal′i·ate
re·tal′i·a′tion
re·tal′i·a·to′ry
re·tard′
re′tar·da′tion
re·ten′tion
re·ten′tive
ret′i·cence
ret′i·cent
ret′i·cule
ret′i·na
ret′i·nue
re·tire′
re·tire′ment
re·tort′
re·touch′
re·trace′
re·tract′
re·trac′tile
re·trac′tion
re·treat′
re·trench′
ret′ri·bu′tion
re·triev′a·ble
re·trieve′
ret′ro·ac′tive
ret′ro·ces′sion
ret′ro·grade
ret′ro·gres′sion
ret′ro·spect
ret′ro·spec′tive
ret′rous·sé′
re·turn′
re·turn′a·ble
re·un′ion
re′u·nite′
re·vamp′
re·veal′
re·veil′le
rev′el
rev′e·la′tion
rev′eled
rev′el·ing
re·venge′
rev′e·nue
re·ver′ber·a′tion
re·ver′ber·a·to′ry
re·vere′
rev′er·ence

rev′er·end
rev′er·ent
rev′er·en′tial
rev′er·ie
re·ver′sal
re·verse′
re·vers′i·ble
re·ver′sion
re·vert′
re·vet′ment
re·vict′ual
re·view′
re·view′er
re·vile′
re·vin′di·cate
re·vise′
re·vi′sion
re·vi′so·ry
re·viv′al
re·vive′
re·viv′i·fy
re·viv′ing
rev′o·ca·ble
rev′o·ca′tion
re·voke′
re·volt′
rev′o·lu′tion
rev′o·lu′tion-
ar′y
rev′o·lu′tion·ize
re·volve′
re·volv′er

re·vul′sion
re·ward′
rhap′so·dist
rhap′so·dy
rhe′o·stat
rhet′o·ric
rhe·tor′i·cal
rheu·mat′ic
rheu′ma·tism
rhine′stone′
rhi·noc′er·os
rhu′barb
rhythm
rhyth′mic
rib′ald
rice field
ric′o·chet′
rid′dle
rid′er·less
ridge′pole′
rid′i·cule
ri·dic′u·lous
riff′raff′
ri′fle·man
rifle pit
ri′fling
right′eous
right′eous·ness
right′ful
right′–hand′ed
right of way
rig′id

ri·gid′i·ty
rig′or·ous
ring′bolt′
ring′bone′
ring′dove′
ring′lead′er
ring′side′
ring′worm′
ri′ot·ous
ri·par′i·an
rip′en
rip′ple
rip′rap′
rip′saw′
ris′qué′
ris′sole′
rit′u·al
ri′val
ri′valed
ri′val·ing
riv′er
riv′er·side′
riv′et
riv′et·ing
riv′u·let
road′bed′
road′house′
road′side′
road′stead
road′ster
road′way′
rob′ber·y

ro·bust′
rock′ing chair
rock′work′
ro·co′co
ro′dent
ro′de·o
Roent′gen
ro′guish
roll′back′
roll call
rolled
roller skate, *n.*
roller towel
roll′ing
rolling mill
rolling pin
ro·mance′
ro·man′tic
ro·man′ti·cism
roof garden
roof′less
roof′tree′
room′mate′
roost′er
rope′danc′er
rope′walk′
ro′se·ate
rose bug
rose cold
rose fever
rose′mar′y
ro·se′o·la
ro·sette′
rose water
rose window
rose′wood′
ros′ter
ros′trum
ro′ta·ry
ro′tate
ro·ta′tion
rot′ten·stone′
ro·tund′
ro·tun′da
ro·tun′di·ty
rough′age
rough′cast′
rough′dry′
rough′en
rough′hew′
rough′house′
rough′rid′er
rough′shod′
rou·lade′
rou·leau′
rou·lette′
round′a·bout′
roun′de·lay
round′house′
round′–shoul′-
dered
rounds′man
round′up′
roust′a·bout′
rou·tine′
row′boat′
row′dies
row′dy
row′el
row′lock
roy′al
roy′al·ist
roy′al·ty
Ru·bái′yát′
ru·ba′to
rub′ber
rub′ber·ize
rub′bish
rub′ble
Ru′bi·con
ru′bi·cund
ru′bric
rud′der
rud′dy
ru′di·ment
ru′di·men′ta·ry
rue′ful
ruf′fi·an
ruf′fle
rug′ged
ru′in·ous
rum′ble
ru′mi·nant
ru′mi·nate
ru′mi·na′tion
rum′mage

ru′mor
rum′ple
rum′pus
run′a·bout′
run′a·way′
run′–down′
run′ner
run′ner–up′
run′way′
ru·pee′
rup′ture
ru′ral
ru′ral·ly
rus′set
rus′tic
rus′ti·cate
rus′tle
rust′proof′, *adj.*
rust′–proof′, *v.*
ru′ta·ba′ga
ruth′less

S

Sab′bath
sab·bat′i·cal
sa′ber
sa′ble
sa′bot′
sab′o·tage′
sac′cha·rin
sac′er·do′tal
sa′chem
sack′cloth′
sac′ra·ment
sac′ra·men′tal
sa′cred
sac′ri·fice
sac′ri·fi′cial
sac′ri·lege
sac′ri·le′gious
sac′ris·tan
sac′ris·ty
sac′ro·sanct
sa′crum
sad′den
sad′dle
sad′dle·bag′
sad′dle·bow′
sad′dler
sad′i′ron
sad′ness
safe′–con′duct
safe′guard′
safe′keep′ing
safe′ty
safety match
safety pin
safety valve
saf′fron
sa′ga
sa·ga′cious
sa·gac′i·ty
sag′a·more
sage′brush′
sa′hib
sail′boat′
sail′cloth′
sail′fish′
sail′or
saint′li·ness
saint′ly
sa·laam′
sal′a·bil′i·ty
sal′a·ble
sa·la′cious
sal′ad
sal′a·man′der
sal′a·ried
sal′a·ry
sal′e·ra′tus
sales′man

sales'man·ship
sales'room
sales'wom'an
sal'i·cyl'ic
sa'li·ence
sa'li·ent
sa'line
sa·li'va
sal'i·var'y
sal'ma·gun'di
sal'mi
salm'on
sa'lon'
sa·loon'
sal'ta·to'ry
salt'cel'lar
salt marsh
salt'pe'ter
sa·lu'bri·ous
sal'u·tar'y
sal'u·ta'tion
sa·lu'ta·to'ri·an
sa·lute'
sal'vage
sal·va'tion
Sa·mar'i·tan
sam'ite
sam'o·var
sam'pan
sam'ple
sam'u·rai
san'a·to'ri·um
san'a·to·ry
(healing. cf. *sanitary.*)
sanc'ti·fi·ca'tion
sanc'ti·fied
sanc'ti·fy
sanc'ti·mo'ni·ous
sanc'tion
sanc'ti·ty
sanc'tu·ar'y
sanc'tum
san'dal
san'dal·wood'
sand'bag'
sand'blast'
sand'glass'
sand hog
sand'man'
sand'pa'per
sand'pip'er
sand'stone'
sand'wich
sang'–froid'
san'gui·nar'y
san'guine
san'i·tar'y
(hygienic. cf. *sanitory.*)
san'i·ta'tion
san'i·ty
sans'–cu·lotte'
sap'ling
sa·pon'i·fy
sap'phire
sar'a·band
sar'casm
sar·cas'tic
sar·co'ma
sar·coph'a·gi, *pl.*
sar·coph'a·gus
sar·dine'
sar·don'ic
sar'do·nyx
sar·gas'so
sar'sa·pa·ril'la
sar·to'ri·al
sas'sa·fras
sa·tan'ic
satch'el
sa·teen'
sat'el·lite
sa'ti·ate
sa·ti'e·ty
sat'in
sat'in·wood'
sat'ire
sa·tir'ic
sa·tir'i·cal
sat'i·rize
sat'is·fac'tion
sat'is·fac'to·ri·ly
sat'is·fac'to·ry
sat'is·fied
sat'is·fy

sa′trap
sat′u·rate
sat′u·ra′tion
sat′ur·nine
sat′yr
sauce′pan′
sau′cer
sauer′kraut′
Sault Sainte Ma·rie′
saun′ter
sau′sage
sau·té′
sav′age
sav′age·ry
sa·van′na
sa·vant′
sav′ing
sav′ior
sa′vo·ry
saw′dust′
saw′horse′
saw′mill′
saw′yer
sax′o·phone
scab′bard
scaf′fold
scaf′fold·ing
scal′a·wag
scal′lion
scal′lop
scal′pel
scam′per
scan′dal
scan′dal·ize
scan′dal·ous
scan′sion
scant′i·ly
scant′ling
scant′y
scape′goat′
scap′u·la
scap′u·lar
scar′ab
scarce′ly
scar′ci·ty
scare′crow′
scar′la·ti′na
scar′let
scath′ing
scat′ter
scat′ter·brain′
scav′en·ger
sce·na′ri·o
scen′er·y
sce′nic
scep′ter
sched′ule
scheme
Sche·nec′ta·dy, N. Y.
scher′zo
schism
schist
schnap′per
schol′ar
schol′ar·ly
schol′ar·ship
scho·las′tic
school bell
school′book′
school board
school′boy′
school bus
school child
school′girl′
school′house′
school′man
school′mas′ter
school′mate′
school′room
school′teach·er
school′work′
school′yard′
schoon′er
Schuyl′kill
sci·at′ic
sci·at′i·ca
sci′ence
sci′en·tif′ic
sci′en·tist
scim′i·tar
scin·til′la
scin′til·late
sci′on
scis′sors

scle·ro′sis
scor·bu′tic
scorn′ful
scor′pi·on
scoun′drel
scrap′book′
scrap′er
scratch
scratch′proof′
screech
screed
screen
screw′driv′er
scrib′ble
scrim′mage
script
scrip′tur·al
scrip′ture
scrive′ner
scrof′u·la
scroll′work′
scru′ple
scru′pu·lous
scru′ti·nize
scru′ti·ny
scuf′fle
scuf′fling
scul′ler·y
scul′lion
sculp′tor
sculp′tur·al
sculp′ture

scur·ril′i·ty
scur′ril·ous
scut′tle
scut′tling
scythe
Sea′bee′
sea′board′
sea′coast′
sea′drome
sea′far′er
sea′far′ing
sea fight
sea food
sea′fowl
sea′girt′
sea′go′ing
sea green
sea gull
sea horse
sea legs
sea level
seal′ing wax
sea lion
seal ring
seal′skin′
sea′man
seam′stress
sé′ance′
sea′plane′
sea′port′
search′light′
search warrant

sea′shore′
sea′sick′
sea′side′
sea′son
sea′son·a·ble
sea′son·al
sea′ward
sea′way′
sea′weed′
sea′wor′thy
se·ba′ceous
se′cant
se·cede′
se·ced′ing
se·ces′sion
se·clude′
se·clu′sion
sec′ond
sec′ond·ar′i·ly
sec′ond·ar′y
sec′ond–rate′
se′cre·cy
se′cret
sec′re·tar′i·al
sec′re·tar′y
se·crete′
se·cre′tion
se·cre′tive
se·cre′to·ry
sec·tar′i·an
sec′ta·ry
sec′tion

sec′tion·al
sec′tion·al·ly
sec′tor
sec′u·lar
se·cure′
se·cu′ri·ty
se·dan′
se·date′
sed′a·tive
sed′en·tar′y
sed′i·ment
se·di′tion
se·di′tious
se·duce′
se·duce′ment
se·duc′er
se·duc′tion
se·duc′tive
sed′u·lous
seed′ling
seem′ly
seep′age
seer′suck′er
see′saw′
seg′ment
seg′re·gate
seg′re·ga′tion
seis′mo·graph
seiz′a·ble
seize
seiz′ing
sei′zure

sel′dom
se·lect′
se·lec′tion
se·lec′tive
se·lect′man
se·le′ni·um
self′–con′fi·dence
self′–con′scious
self′–con-
tained′
self′–con·trol′
self′–de·fense′
self′–es·teem′
self′–gov′ern-
ment
self′–im·por′-
tance
self′ish
self′less
self′–made′
self′–pos·sessed′
self′–pro·tec′-
tion
self′–re·gard′
self′–sac′ri·fice
self′same′
self′–start′er
sel′vage
sem′a·phore
sem′blance
se·mes′ter
sem′i·cir′cle

semi′i·civ′i·lized
sem′i·co′lon
sem′i·con′scious
sem′i·de·tached′
sem′i·fi′nal
sem′i·month′ly
sem′i·nar′
sem′i·nar′y
sem′i·pre′cious
sem′pi·ter′nal
sen′ate
sen′a·tor
sen′a·to′ri·al
send′–off′
se·nes′cent
sen′es·chal
se′nile
se·nil′i·ty
sen′ior
sen·ior′i·ty
sen·sa′tion
sen·sa′tion·al
sense′less
sen′si·bil′i·ty
sen′si·ble
sen′si·tive
sen′si·tiv′i·ty
sen′si·tize
sen′so·ry
sen′su·al
sen′su·ous
sen′tence

sen·ten′tious
sen′tient
sen′ti·ment
sen′ti·men′tal
sen′ti·men·tal′-
  i·ty
sen′ti·nel
sen′try
sep′a·ra·ble
sep′a·rate
sep′a·ra′tion
sep′a·ra′tist
sep′a·ra′tor
se′pi·a
sep′sis
sep·tet′
sep′tic
sep′ul·cher
se·pul′chral
sep′ul·ture
se′quel
se·que′la
se′quence
se·quen′tial
se·ques′ter
se·ques′trate
se′quin
se·quoi′a
se·ragl′io
ser′aph
se·raph′ic
ser′e·nade′
se·rene′
se·ren′i·ty
ser′geant
sergeant at
  arms
se′ri·al
se′ries
ser′if
se′ri·ous
ser′mon
ser′mon·ize
se′rous
ser′pent
ser′pen·tine
ser·ra′tion
se′rum
serv′ant
serv′ice
serv′ice·a·ble
ser′vile
ser·vil′i·ty
ser′vi·tor
ser′vi·tude
ses′a·me
ses′sion
set·tee′
set′ter
set′tle·ment
set′up′
sev′en
sev′en·teen′
sev′en·ti·eth
sev′er
sev′er·al
sev′er·ance
se·vere′
se·ver′i·ty
sew′age
sew′er
sex′tant
sex·tet′
sex′ton
shab′bi·ness
shab′by
shack′le
shad′ow·y
shag′bark′
sha·green′
shake′down′
shak′i·ly
shal′lop
shal·lot′
shal′low
sham
sham′ble
shame
shamed
shame′faced′
shame′ful
shame′less
sham′ing
shammed
sham′ming
sham·poo′

sham'rock
shang·hai'
shan'ty
shape'less
shap'ing
share'hold'er
shar'ing
sharp'en·er
sharp'er
sharp'shoot'er
sharp'–sight'ed
shave'tail'
shawl
sheaf
shear
(cut. cf. *sheer.*)
sheathe, *v.*
sheath'ing
sheath knife
sheen
sheep
sheep'cote'
sheep dog
sheep'fold'
sheep'ish
sheep'skin'
sheep'walk'
sheer
(thin. cf. *shear.*)
shel·lac'
shel·lacked'
shel·lack'ing

shell'fish'
shell'proof'
shel'ter
Shen'an·do'ah
shep'herd
sher'bet
sher'iff
sher'ry
shib'bo·leth
shield
shift'less
shil'ling
shim'mer
shin'gle
shin'plas'ter
ship'board'
ship'build'er
ship'load'
ship'mas'ter
ship'mate'
ship'ment
ship'ping room
ship'own'er
ship'shape'
ship'wreck'
ship'wright'
ship'yard'
shiv'er
shock'proof'
shod'dy
shoe box
shoe'brush'

shoe'horn'
shoe'mak'er
shoe pol'ish
shoe store
shoe'string
sho'gun'
shop'keep'er
shop'lift'er
shop'per
shop'walk'er
shop'worn'
short'age
short'cake'
short'com'ing
short'en·ing
short'hand'
short'hand'ed
Short'horn'
short'–lived'
short'sight'ed
short'stop'
short'–wind'ed
shot'gun'
shoul'der
shoulder blade
shov'el
shov'eled
shov'el·ing
show'case'
show'down'
show'er
shower bath

show′i·ly
show′man
show′room′
show′y
shrap′nel
shrewd
shrew′ish
shriek
shrimp
shrink′age
shriv′el
shriv′eled
shrub′ber·y
shrunk′en
shuf′fle
shuf′fle·board′
shut′down′
shut′–in′
shut′off′
shut′out′
shut′ter
shut′tle·cock′
shy′ster
sib′i·lant
sib′yl
sib′yl·ine
Si·cil′i·an
sick′en
sick′ish
sick′le
sick′li·ness
sick′ness
sick′room
side′board′
side′long′
si·de′re·al
side′sad′dle
side′track′
side′walk′
side′ways′
siege
si·en′na
si·es′ta
sieve
sight′less
sight′–see′ing
sig′moid
sig′nal
sig′naled
sig′nal·ize
sig′na·to′ry
sig′na·ture
sign′board′
sig′net
sig·nif′i·cance
sig·nif′i·cant
sig′ni·fi·ca′tion
sig′ni·fied
sig′ni·fy
sign′post′
si′lage
si′lence
si′lenc·er
si′lent
si·le′si·a
si′lex
sil′hou·ette′
sil′i·ca
sil′i·cate
sil′i·con
silk′en
silk′i·ness
silk′weed′
silk′worm′
silk′y
sil′ly
si′lo
si′los
sil′ver
sil′ver·smith′
sil′ver·ware′
sil′ver·work′
sil′ver·y
sim′i·an
sim′i·lar
sim′i·lar′i·ty
sim′i·le
si·mil′i·tude
sim′mer
sim′per
sim′ple
sim′ple·heart′ed
sim′ple·ton
sim′ple–wit′ted
sim′plex
sim·plic′i·ty

sim′pli·fi·ca′tion
sim′pli·fied
sim′pli·fy
sim′ply
sim′u·la′crum
sim′u·late
sim′u·la′tion
si′mul·ta′ne·ous
sin·cere′
sin·cer′i·ty
si′ne·cure
sin′ew
sin′ew·y
sin′ful
sin′gle
sin′gle·hand′ed
sin′gle–mind′ed
sin′gle·ton
sin′gly
sing′song′
sin′gu·lar
sin′is·ter
sink′age
sink′er
sink′hole′
sink′ing fund
sin′u·ous
si′nus
Sioux City, Iowa
si′phon
si′ren
sir′loin′
si·roc′co
sir′up
sis′ter
sis′ter–in–law′
site
(place)
sit′ting room
sit′u·at′ed
sit′u·a′tion
six′fold′
sixth
six′ti·eth
siz′a·ble
siz′zle
siz′zling
Skan′e·at′e·les
skein
skel′e·ton
skep′tic
skep′ti·cal
skep′ti·cism
sketch
sketch′book′
sketch′i·ly
sketch′y
skew′er
ski
ski′ing
skill′ful
skimp′y
skin′flint′
skin′tight′
skip
skip′per
skir′mish
skit′tish
skiv′er
skulk
skull′cap′
skunk
sky′–blue′, *adj.*
sky′lark′
sky′light′
sky line
sky′rock′et
sky′scrap′er
sky′ward
sky wave
sky′writ·ing
slack′en
slan′der
slan′der·ous
slap′ping
slat′tern
slaugh′ter
slav′er·y
slav′ish
slea′zy
sledge
sledge hammer
sleep′er
sleeping car
sleep′less
sleigh

slen′der
sleuth
slide rule
slight
slime
slip′per
slip′per·y
slip′shod′
slith′er
sliv′er
slo′gan
slope
sloth′ful
slouch
slov′en·ly
sludge
slug′gard
slug′gish
sluice
sluice′way′
slum′ber
slush
small′pox′
smart′en
smash′up′
smat′ter·ing
smi′lax
smith′er·eens′
smoke′house
smoke′jack′
smoke′less
smok′er
smoke′stack′
smok′y
smol′der
smooth
smooth′bore′
smor′gas·bord′
smoth′er
smudge
smug′gle
smut′ty
snaf′fle
sna·fu′
snake′root′
snak′y
snap′drag′on
snap′shot′
snare drum
sneak′er
sneeze
snick′er
sniv′el
snob′ber·y
snob′bish
snow′ball′
snow′bank′
snow′-blind′
snow′bound′
snow′drift′
snow′drop′
snow′fall′
snow′flake′
snow line
snow′plow′
snow′shed′
snow′shoe′
snow′storm
snow′y
snub′-nosed′
snuff′box′
snuf′fle
soap′box′
soap′i·ness
soap opera
soap′stone′
soap′suds′
soap′y
so′ber
so′ber-mind′ed
so·bri′e·ty
so′bri·quet
soc′cer
so′cia·ble
so′cial
so′cial·ism
so′cial·ist
so′cial·ize
so′cial·ly
so·ci′e·ty
so′ci·ol′o·gy
sock′et
so′da
so·dal′i·ty
sod′den
so′di·um

sof′ten
soft′heart′ed
soft′–soap′, *v.*
soi′–di′sant′
so·journ′
sol′ace
so′lar
sol′der
sol′dier
sol′e·cism
sole′ly
sol′emn
so·lem′ni·ty
sol′em·nize
so′le·noid
sol·feg′gio
so·lic′it
so·lic′i·ta′tion
so·lic′i·tor
so·lic′it·ous
so·lic′i·tude
sol′id
sol′i·dar′i·ty
so·lid′i·fied
so·lid′i·fy
so·lid′i·ty
so·lil′o·quize
so·lil′o·quy
sol′i·taire′
sol′i·tar′y
sol′i·tude
so′lo
so′los
sol′stice
sol′u·ble
so·lu′tion
solv′a·ble
sol′ven·cy
sol′vent
som′ber
som·bre′ro
som·bre′ros
some′bod′y
some′how
some′one′
som′er·sault
some′thing
some′time′
some′times′
some′what′
some′where′
som′no·lent
so·na′ta
song′ster
song′stress
son′–in–law′
son′net
son′net·eer′
so·nor′i·ty
so·no′rous
soothe
sooth′say′er
soph′ism
so·phis′ti·cate
so·phis′ti·cat′ed
so·phis′ti·ca′tion
soph′ist·ry
soph′o·more
so′po·rif′ic
so·pra′no
sor′cer·er
sor′cer·y
sor′did
sor′ghum
so·ror′i·ty
sor′rel
sor′row
sor′row·ful
sor′ry
sou·brette′
soul′ful
soul′less
soup′çon′
south′east′
south′er·ly
south′ern
south′ern·er
south′ern·most
south′west′
sou′ve·nir′
sov′er·eign
sov′er·eign·ty
so′vi·et
soy
so′ya

soy′bean′
spa′cious
spa·ghet′ti
spal·peen′
span′drel
span′iel
spar′kle′
spar′row
spas·mod′ic
spas′tic
spat′ter
spat′u·la
speak′er
spear′fish′
spear′head′
spear′mint′
spe′cial
spe′cial·ist
spe′cial·ize
spe′cial·ty
spe′cie
spe′cies
spe·cif′ic
spec′i·fi·ca′tion
spec′i·fied
spec′i·fy
spec′i·men
spe′cious
spec′ta·cle
spec·tac′u·lar
spec·ta′tor
spec′ter
spec′tral
spec′tro·scope
spec′trum
spec′u·late
spec′u·la′tion
spec′u·la′tive
spec′u·lum
speech
speech′less
speed′boat
speed′i·ly
speed limit
speed·om′e·ter
speed′way′
spell′bound′
spend′thrift′
spher′i·cal
sphinc′ter
sphinx
spic′ule
spic′y
spi′der
spig′ot
spike′nard
spill′way′
spin′ach
spi′nal
spin′dle
spine′less
spin′et
spin′ster
spi′ral
spir′it·ed
spir′it·less
spir′it·u·al
spir′it·u·al·ism
spir′it·u·al′i·ty
spir′it·u·ous
spite′ful
spit′fire′
spit·toon′
splen′did
splen′dor
sple·net′ic
splin′ter
splurge
spoil′age
spoils′man
spoke′shave′
spokes′man
spo′li·a′tion
spon′dee
sponge
spon′gy
spon′sor
spon′ta·ne′i·ty
spon·ta′ne·ous
spoon′ful
spo·rad′ic
spor′tive
sports′man
sports′man·ship
spot′less
spot′light′

spring′board′
spring′bok′
spring′i·ness
spring′time′
sprin′kle
sprock′et
sprout
spruce
spu′ri·ous
sput′nik
sput′ter
spu′tum
spy′glass′
squab′ble
squad′ron
squal′id
squall
squal′or
squan′der
square dance
square′head′
square knot
square′–rigged′
square root
squash
squat′ter
squaw
squawk
squeak
squeam′ish
squee′gee
squir′rel
squirt
sta·bil′i·ty
sta′bi·lize
sta′bi·liz′er
sta′ble
stac·ca′to
sta′di·um
stage′coach′
stage′craft′
stag′ger
stag′hound′
stag′nant
stag′nate
stag·na′tion
stain′less
stair′case′
stair′head′
stair′way′
sta·lac′tite
sta·lag′mite
stale′mate′
stal′lion
stal′wart
sta′men
stam′i·na
stam′mer
stam·pede′
stamp′er
stanch
stan′chion
stand′ard
stand′ard·ize
stand′–by′
stand′off′
stand′pipe′
stand′point′
stand′still′
stan′za
sta′ple
star′board
starch′y
star′fish′
star′gaz′er
star′let
star′light′
star′ling
star′lit
starred
star′ring
star′–shaped′
star shell
star′–span′gled
star′tle
star·va′tion
starve
state′craft′
state′hood
State′house′
state′ly
state′ment
state′room′
states′man
stat′ic

sta'tion
sta'tion·ar'y (fixed)
sta'tion·er
sta'tion·er'y (paper)
sta·tis'ti·cal
stat'is·ti'cian
sta·tis'tics
stat'u·ar'y
stat'ue
stat'u·esque'
stat'u·ette'
stat'ure
sta'tus
stat'ute
stat'u·to'ry
stay'sail'
stead'fast
stead'i·ly
stealth
steam'boat'
steam boiler
steam'car'
steam engine
steam'er
steam fitter
steam'–roll'er
steam'ship'
steam table
steam'tight'
steel'work'
steel'yard
stee'ple
stee'ple·chase'
steer'age
steer'age·way
steers'man
sten'cil
ste·nog'ra·pher
sten'o·graph'ic
ste·nog'ra·phy
sten·to'ri·an
step'child'
step'fa'ther
step'lad'der
step'moth'er
step'ping·stone'
ster'e·op'ti·con
ster'e·o·type'
ster'ile
ste·ril'i·ty
ster'i·lize
ster'ling
ster'num
ster'nu·ta'tion
ster'to·rous
steth'o·scope
ste've·dore'
stew'ard
stew'pan
stick'ful
stick'i·ness
stiff'en
sti'fle
stig'ma
stig'ma·tize
still'born'
still hunt
stim'u·lant
stim'u·late
stim'u·la'tion
stim'u·li, *pl.*
stim'u·lus
stin'gi·ness
stin'gy
stink'weed'
sti'pend
sti·pen'di·ar'y
stip'ple
stip'u·late
stip'u·lat'ing
stip'u·la'tion
stir
stirred
stir'ring
stir'rup
stock·ade'
stock'bro'ker
stock'hold'er
stock'ing
stock'man
stock'–still'
stock'yard'
sto'ic

stoke′hold′
stol′id
stom′ach
stom′ach–ache′
stone′boat′
stone crush′er
stone′cut′ter
stone′ma′son
stone proof
stone′ware′
stone′work′
stone′yard′
ston′i·ly
stop′cock′
stop′gap′
stop′page
stop′per
stop watch
stor′age
store′house′
store′room′
storm′–tight′
sto′ry
stove′pipe′
stow′age
stow′a·way′
stra·bis′mus
strag′gle
straight
(direct)
straight′a·way′
straight′edge′
straight′for′-
ward
strait
(narrow)
strait jacket
stran′ger
stran′gle
stran′gu·late
strat′a·gem
stra·te′gic
strat′e·gist
strat′e·gy
strat′i·fy
stra′to·sphere
stra′tum
straw′ber′ry
straw′board′
stream
stream′lined
strength
strength′en
stren′u·ous
strep′to·coc′cus
stri·a′tion
stric′ture
stri′dent
strin′gent
strip′ling
strong′hold′
strong′–mind′ed
strong′room
stro′phe
struc′tur·al
struc′ture
strug′gle
strug′gling
strych′nine
stub′born
stuc′co
stuc′co·work′
stud′book′
stu′dent
stud′ied
stu′di·o
stu′di·ous
stud′y
stuff
stuff′i·ness
stuff′ing
stul′ti·fy
stum′ble
stu′pe·fy
stu·pen′dous
stu′pid
stu·pid′i·ty
stu′por
stur′dy
stur′geon
stut′ter
Styg′i·an
styl′ish
sty′lo·graph′ic
sty′lus
sty′mie

styp′tic
sua′sion
suave
suav′i·ty
sub·al′tern
sub′cel′lar
sub′com·mit′tee
sub·con′scious
sub′con·trac′tor
sub′cu·ta′ne·ous
sub′di·vide′
sub′di·vi′sion
sub·due′
sub·ed′i·tor
sub′head′
sub′ject, *adj.*
sub·ject′, *v.*
sub·jec′tion
sub·jec′tive
sub′ju·gate
sub·junc′tive
sub′lease′
sub′li·mate
sub′li·ma′tion
sub·lime′
sub·lim′i·nal
sub·lim′i·ty
sub′ma·rine′
sub·merge′
sub·mers′i·ble
sub·mer′sion
sub·mis′sion
sub·mis′sive
sub·mit′
sub·nor′mal
sub·or′di·nate
sub·or′di·na′tion
sub·orn′
sub·poe′na
sub·scribe′
sub·scrip′tion
sub′se·quent
sub·ser′vi·ent
sub·side′
sub·sid′ence
sub·sid′i·ar′y
sub′si·dize
sub′si·dy
sub·sist′
sub·sist′ence
sub′stance
sub·stan′tial
sub·stan′ti·ate
sub′stan·tive
sub′sti·tute
sub′ter·fuge
sub′ter·ra′ne·an
sub′tle
sub′tle·ty
sub′tly
sub·tract′
sub·trac′tion
sub′tra·hend′
sub·treas′ur·y
sub·trop′i·cal
sub′urb
sub·ur′ban
sub·ven′tion
sub·ver′sion
sub·ver′sive
sub′way′
suc·ceed′
suc·cess′
suc·cess′ful
suc·ces′sion
suc·ces′sive
suc·ces′sor
suc·cinct′
suc′cor
suc′co·tash
suc′cu·lent
suc·cumb′
suc′tion
sud′den
su′dor·if′ic
sue
(*sued, suing*)
su′et
suf′fer
suf′fer·ance
suf′fer·ing
suf·fice′
suf·fi′cien·cy
suf·fi′cient
suf′fix
suf′fo·cate

suf′fo·ca′tion
suf′fra·gan
suf′frage
suf′fra·gette′
suf′fra·gist
suf·fuse′
suf·fu′sion
sug′ar
sugar beet
sugar cane
sug′ar–coat′, *v.*
sug′ared
sug′ar·house′
sugar maple
sug′ar·plum′
sug·gest′
sug·ges′tion
sug·ges′tive
su′i·cid′al
su′i·cide
su′ing
suit′a·ble
suit′case′
suit′or
sulk′i·ness
sul′len
sul′phate
sul′phide
sul′phite
sul′phur
sul·phu′ric
sul′phu·rous
sul′tan
sul·tan′a
sul′try
su′mac
sum′ma·ri·ly
sum′ma·rize
sum′ma·ry
sum·ma′tion
sum′mer
sum′mer·house′
sum′mit
sum′mon
sum′mons
sump′tu·ar′y
sump′tu·ous
sun′beam′
sun′bon′net
sun′burn′
sun′burst′
sun′di′al
sun′down′
sun′dries
sun′dry
sun′fast′
sun′fish′
sun′flow′er
sun′glass′
sunk′en
sun lamp
sun′light′
sun′ning
sun′ny
sun′rise′
sun′room′
sun′set′
sun′shade′
sun′shine′
sun′shin′y
sun′stroke′
su′per·a·bun′dant
su′per·an′nu·ate
su·perb′
su′per·car′go
su′per·cil′i·ous
su′per·fi′cial
su′per·flu′i·ty
su·per′flu·ous
su′per·heat′
su′per·hu′man
su′per·im·pose′
su′per·in·duce′
su′per·in·tend′
su′per·in·tend′ent
su·pe′ri·or
su·pe′ri·or′i·ty
su·per′la·tive
su′per·man′
su·per′nal
su′per·nat′u·ral
su′per·nu′mer·ar′y
su′per·scrip′tion

su′per·sede′
su′per·sti′tion
su′per·sti′tious
su′per·struc′ture
su′per·vise′
su′per·vi′sion
su′per·vi′sor
su·pine′, *adj.*
sup′per
sup′per·time′
sup·plant′
sup′ple
sup′ple·ment
sup′ple·men′tal
sup′ple·men′ta·ry
sup′pli·ance
sup′pli·ant
sup′pli·cant
sup′pli·cate
sup′pli·ca′tion
sup·pli′er
sup·ply′
sup·port′
sup·port′er
sup·pose′
sup′po·si′tion
sup·pos′i·ti′tious
sup·press′
sup·pres′sion
sup′pu·ra′tion
su′pra·re′nal
su·prem′a·cy
su·preme′
su·preme′ly
sur′base′
sur·cease′
sur·charge′, *v.*
sur′charge′, *n.*
sur′cin′gle
sure′–foot′ed
sure′ly
sure′ty
sur′face
sur′feit
sur′geon
sur′ger·y
sur′gi·cal
sur·mise′
sur·mount′
sur′name′
sur·pass′
sur′plice
sur′plus
sur′plus·age
sur·prise′
sur·ren′der
sur′rep·ti′tious
sur′ro·gate
sur·round′
sur′tax′
sur·veil′lance
sur·vey′, *v.*
sur′vey, *n.*
sur·vey′or
sur·viv′al
sur·vive′
sur·vi′vor
sus·cep′ti·ble
sus′pect, *n.*
sus·pect′, *v.*
sus·pend′
sus·pense′
sus·pen′sion
sus·pi′cion
sus·pi′cious
sus·tain′
sus′te·nance
sut′ler
sut·tee′
su′ture
su′ze·rain
swad′dle
swag′ger
swal′low
swamp
swarth′y
swas′ti·ka
sweat′er
sweep′stakes′
sweet′bread′
sweet′bri′er
sweet corn
sweet fern
sweet flag
sweet′heart′
sweet′meat′

sweet pea
sweet′shop′
sweet William
swel′ter
swerve
swim′ming·ly
swin′dle
swin′dler
swine′herd′
swin′ish
switch
switch′back′
switch′board′
switch′man
swiv′el
swoon
swoop
sword
sword′fish′
sword grass
sword knot
sword′play′
swords′man
syc′a·more

syc′o·phant
syl·lab′ic
syl·lab′i·cate
syl′la·ble
syl′la·bus
syl′lo·gism
sylph
syl′van
sym′bol
(emblem)
sym·bol′ic
sym′bol·ism
sym′bol′ize
sym·met′ri·cal
sym′me·try
sym′pa·thet′ic
sym′pa·thize
sym′pa·thiz′er
sym′pa·thy
sym·phon′ic
sym′pho·ny
sym·po′si·um
symp′tom
syn′a·gogue

syn′chro·nism
syn′chro·nize
syn′chro·nous
syn′co·pate
syn′co·pa′tion
syn′co·pe
syn′dic
syn′di·cate
syn·ec′do·che
syn′od
syn′o·nym
syn·on′y·mous
syn·op′sis
syn′tax
syn′the·sis
syn′the·size
syn·thet′ic
syr′inge
sys′tem
sys′tem·at′ic
sys′tem·a·tize
sys′to·le
syz′y·gy

T

tab′ard
Ta·bas′co
tab′er·nac′le

ta′ble
tab′leau
tab′leaux, *pl.*

ta′ble·cloth′
table cover
ta′ble d'hôte′

ta'ble·land'
ta'ble·spoon'
ta'ble·spoon'ful
tab'let
ta'ble·ware'
tab'loid
ta·boo'
ta'bor
tab'o·ret
tab'u·lar
tab'u·late
tab'u·la'tor
ta·chom'e·ter
ta·chyg'ra·phy
tac'it
tac'i·turn
tack'le
tact'ful
tac'ti·cal
tac·ti'cian
tac'tics
tac'tile
tact'less
tad'pole'
taf'fe·ta
taff'rail
tail'board'
tail'less
tail'light'
tai'lor–made'
tail'piece'
tail'race'
tail spin
tail'stock'
tail wind
take'down'
take'–off
tak'ing
talc
tale'bear'er
tal'ent
tales'man
tal'is·man
talk'a·thon
talk'a·tive
Tal'la·has'see, Fla.
Tal'mud
tal'on
ta·ma'le
tam'a·rack
tam'a·rind
tam'bou·rine'
tam'per
tam'pon
tan'bark'
tan'dem
tan'gent
tan'ge·rine'
tan'gi·ble
tan'gle
tan'go
tank'ard
tan'ner·y
Tann'häu·ser
tan'nic
tan'ta·lize
tan'ta·mount'
tape'line'
ta'per
tap'es·try
tar'an·tel'la
ta·ran'tu·la
tar'di·ness
tar'dy
tar'get
tar'iff
tar'la·tan
tar'nish
tar·pau'lin
tar'pon
tar'tan
tar'tar
tar·tar'ic
Tar'ta·rus
task'mas'ter
tas'sel
taste'ful
taste'less
tast'y
tat'ter·de·mal'ion
tat·too'
taunt
tau·tol'o·gy
tav'ern
taw'dry

taw'ny
tax'a·ble
tax·a'tion
tax'–ex·empt'
tax'i·cab'
tax'i·der'my
tax'i·me'ter
tax'pay·er
teach'a·ble
teach'er
team'mate'
team'ster
team'work
tea'pot'
tear'ful
tear gas
tear sheet
tea'room
tea'spoon·ful
tea'time'
tea wagon
tech'ni·cal
tech'ni·cal'i·ty
tech·ni'cian
Tech'ni·col'or
tech·nique'
tech·nol'o·gy
te'di·ous
te'di·um
tee'ter
tee·to'tal·er
tel·au'to·graph
tel'e·gram
tel'e·graph
te·leg'ra·pher
tel'e·graph'ic
te·lep'a·thy
tel'e·phone
tel'e·phon'ic
te·leph'o·ny
tel'e·scope
tel'e·vi'sion
tell'tale'
te·mer'i·ty
tem'per
tem'per·a·ment
tem'per·ance
tem'per·ate
tem'per·a·ture
tem'pest
tem·pes'tu·ous
tem'plate
tem'ple
tem'po
tem'po·ral
tem'po·rar'y
tem'po·rize
tempt
temp·ta'tion
tempt'ress
ten'a·ble
te·na'cious
te·nac'i·ty
ten'an·cy
ten'ant
ten'ant·a·ble
tend'en·cy
tend'er, *n.*
ten'der, *adj., v.*
ten'der·foot'
ten'der·heart'ed
ten'der·loin'
ten'don
ten'dril
Ten'e·brae
ten'e·ment
ten'nis
ten'on
ten'or
ten'pin'
ten'sile
ten'sion
ten'–strike'
ten'ta·cle
ten'ta·tive
ten'ter·hook'
ten·u'i·ty
ten'u·ous
ten'ure
te'pee
tep'id
ter·cen'te·nar'y
te·re'do
ter'gi·ver·sa'tion
ter'ma·gant
ter'mi·nal

ter′mi·nate
ter′mi·na′tion
ter′mi·ni, *pl.*
ter′mi·nol′o·gy
ter′mi·nus
ter′mite
Terp·sich′o·re
ter′race
ter′ra cot′ta
ter′ra fir′ma
ter·rain′
ter′ra·pin
Ter′re Haute′, Ind.
ter·res′tri·al
ter′ri·ble
ter′ri·er
ter·rif′ic
ter′ri·fied
ter′ri·fy
ter′ri·to′ri·al
ter′ri·to′ry
ter′ror
ter′ror·ism
ter′ror·ist
ter′ror·ize
terse
ter′ti·ar′y
tes′sel·la′tion
tes·ta′cean
tes′ta·ment
tes′ta·men′ta·ry
tes·ta′tor
tes′ti·fy
tes′ti·mo′ni·al
tes′ti·mo′ny
test tube
tet′a·nus
tête′–à–tête′
te·tral′o·gy
te′trarch
Teu·ton′ic
text′book′
tex′tile
tex′tu·al
tex′ture
than′a·top′sis
thank′ful
thank′less
thanks·giv′ing
the′a·ter
the·at′ri·cal
the′ism
thence′forth′
the·od′o·lite
the′o·lo′gi·an
the′o·log′i·cal
the·ol′o·gy
the′o·rem
the′o·ret′i·cal
the′o·rize
the′o·ry
the·os′o·phy
ther′a·peu′tics
there·af′ter
there·by′
there′fore
there′up·on′
there·with′
ther′mal
ther′mite
ther·mom′e·ter
ther′mo·stat
the·sau′rus
the′sis
thick′et
thick′set′
thick′–skinned′
thief
thieves
thiev′ish
thim′ble
thin′–skinned′
thirst′y
this′tle
thith′er
tho·rac′ic
tho′rax
tho′ri·um
thor′ough
thor′ough·bred′
thor′ough·fare′
thought′ful
thou′sand
thrall′dom
thra·son′i·cal

thread′bare′
thread′worm′
threat′en
three′fold′
three′-ply′
three′score′
three′some
thren′o·dy
thresh′old
thrift′less
thrive
throat
throm·bo′sis
throng
through·out′
thumb′screw′
thun′der·bolt′
thun′der·cloud′
thun′der·head′
thun′der·ous
thun′der·show′er
thwart
thyme
thy′mus
thy′roid
tib′i·a
tick′er
tick′et
tick′le
tick′ler
tid′al
tide′wa′ter
ti′di·ly
tie′-in′
tie′-up′
ti′ger
til′bu·ry
tim′bale
tim′ber
tim′ber·man
tim′ber·work′
time′-hon′ored
time′keep′er
time′less
time′ly
time′piece′
time′ta′ble
tim′id
ti·mid′i·ty
tim′or·ous
tim′o·thy
tinc′ture
tin′der
tin′gle
tink′er
tin′smith′
tin′type′
tin′ware′
ti′ny
tip′ple
tip′staff′
tip′ster
tip′sy
tip′toe′
tip′top′
ti′rade
tire′some
tis′sue
Ti′tan
ti·tan′ic
tit′bit′
tithe
tith′ing
tit′il·late
tit′i·vate
ti′tle
tit′mouse′
ti′trate
ti·tra′tion
tit′u·lar
toad′stool′
toast′mas′ter
to·bac′co
to·bac′cos
to·bac′co·nist
to·bog′gan
toc·ca′ta
toc′sin
to·day′
tod′dy
tof′fee
to′ga
to·geth′er
tog′gle
toi′let
toil′some

to′ken
tol′booth′
tol′er·a·ble
tol′er·ance
tol′er·ant
tol′er·ate
tol′er·a′tion
toll′gate′
tom′a·hawk
to·ma′to
to·ma′toes
tom′boy′
tomb′stone′
tom′cat′
to·mor′row
ton′al
to·nal′i·ty
tone
tongue
ton′ic
to·night′
ton′nage
ton·neau′
ton′sil
ton′sil·li′tis
ton·so′ri·al
ton′sure
ton′tine
tool bag
tool chest
tool′hold·er
tool kit
tool rack
tool′–us′ing, *adj.*
tooth′ache′
tooth′brush′
tooth′pick′
tooth pow′der
tooth′some
tooth′wash
to′paz
top boot
top′coat′
top′flight′
top hat
top′ic
top′i·cal
top′knot′
top′mast′
top′most
to·pog′ra·pher
to·pog′ra·phy
top′ping
top′sail′
top′side′
top′soil′
top′sy–tur′vy
torch′light′
tor′e·a·dor′
tor·ment′, *v.*
tor′ment, *n.*
tor·men′tor
tor·na′do
tor·na′does
tor·pe′do
tor·pe′does
torpedo boat
tor′pid
tor′por
torque
tor′rent
tor·ren′tial
tor′rid
tor′sion
tor′so
tor·til′la
tor′toise
tor′tu·ous
tor′ture
toss′up′
to′tal
to′taled
to′tal·ing
to·tal′i·ty
to′tal·ize
to′tal·ly
to′tem
touch′down′
touch′i·ly
touch′i·ness
touch′stone′
tough′en
tou·pee′
tour′ist
tour′ma·line
tour′na·ment

tour′ney
tour′ni·quet
tow′age
to′ward
to′wards
tow′boat′
tow′el
tow′er
tow′head′
tow′line′
towns′folk′
town′ship
towns′man
towns′peo′ple
tow′path′
tow′rope′
tox·e′mi·a
tox′ic
trace′a·ble
trac′er·y
tra′che·a
tra·cho′ma
trac′ing
track′age
track′less
track′man
track′walk′er
trac′ta·ble
trac′tion
trac′tor
trade′–in′
trade′–last′
trade′–mark′
trade name
trade school
trades′man
trade wind
tra·di′tion
tra·duce′
traf′fic
trag′a·canth
tra·ge′di·an
tra·ge′di·enne′
trag′e·dy
trag′ic
trail′er
train′er
train′man
trait
trai′tor
trai′tor·ous
trai′tress
tra·jec′to·ry
tram′mel
tram′ple
tram′way′
tran′quil
tran·quil′li·ty
trans·act′
trans·ac′tion
trans′at·lan′tic
tran·scend′
tran·scend′ent
tran·scribe′
tran′script
tran·scrip′tion
tran′sept
trans·fer′, *v.*
trans′fer, *n.*
trans·fer′a·ble
trans·fer′ence
trans·fig′u·ra′-
tion
trans·fig′ure
trans·fix′
trans·form′
trans′for·ma′tion
trans·form′er
trans·fuse′
trans·gress′
trans·gres′sion
trans·gres′sor
tran′sient
tran·sis′tor
trans′it
tran·si′tion
tran′si·tive
tran′si·to′ry
trans·late′
trans·la′tion
trans·la′tor
trans·lit′er·ate
trans·lu′cent
trans·mi′grate
trans·mis′si·ble
trans·mis′sion

trans·mit′
trans·mit′tal
trans·mit′ter
trans′mu·ta′tion
trans·mute′
tran′som
trans·par′ent
tran·spire′
trans·plant′
trans·port′, *v.*
trans′port, *n.*
trans′por·ta′tion
trans·pose′
trans′po·si′tion
trans·ship′
tran′sub·stan′ti-
a′tion
trans·verse′
trap door
tra·peze′
trap′per
Trap′pist
trash′y
trau′ma
trav′ail
trav′el
trav′eled
trav′el·er
trav′el·ing
trav′erse
trav′er·tine
trav′es·ty
treach′er·ous
treach′er·y
trea′cle
tread′mill′
trea′son
treas′ure
treas′ur·er
treas′ure–trove′
treas′ur·y
treat
trea′ties
trea′tise
treat′ment
trea′ty
tre′ble
tree fern
tree′nail′
tree′top′
tre′foil
trel′lis
trem′ble
tre·men′dous
trem′o·lo
trem′or
trem′u·lous
trench
trench′an·cy
trench′ant
trench′er
tre·pan′
tre·phine′
trep′i·da′tion
tres′pass
tres′pass·er
tres′tle
tres′tle·work′
tri′ad
tri′al
tri′an′gle
tri·an′gu·lar
tri·an′gu·la′tion
tribe
trib′u·la′tion
tri·bu′nal
trib′une
trib′u·tar′y
trib′ute
trick′er·y
trick′i·ly
trick′i·ness
trick′le
tri′col′or
tri′cy·cle
tri′dent
tri·en′ni·al
tri′fle
tri·fo′cal
trig′ger
trig′o·nom′e·try
tril′lion
tril′li·um
tril′o·gy
trin′i·ty
trin′ket

tri·par′tite
triph′thong
tri′ple
tri′plet
tri′plex
trip′li·cate
trip′li·ca′tion
tri′pod
trip′tych
tri′reme
tri′sect′
tri′umph
tri·um′phal
tri·um′phant
tri·um′vi·rate
triv′i·al
triv′i·al′i·ty
tro′car
tro′che
(lozenge)
tro′chee
(poetic term)
trog′lo·dyte
trol′ley
trom′bone
trope
tro′phy
trop′ic
trou′ba·dour
trou′ble
trou′ble·some
trou′blous
trou′sers
trous′seau′
tro′ver
trow′el
tru′an·cy
tru′ant
truck′le
truck′man
truc′u·lence
truc′u·lent
truf′fle
tru′ism
trump′er·y
trum′pet
trum′pet·er
trun′cate
trun′cheon
trun′dle
trunk room
trun′nion
trus·tee′
trus·tee′ship
trust′ful
trust′wor′thy
truth′ful
try′sail′
try square
tryst
tset′se
tu′ba
tu′ber
tu·ber′cu·lar
tu·ber′cu·lin
tu·ber′cu·lo′sis
tu·ber′cu·lous
tu′bu·lar
Tu′dor
tug of war
tu·i′tion
tu′lip
tu′lip·wood′
tulle
tum′ble
tum′bler
tum′ble·weed′
tum′brel
tu′mult
tu·mul′tu·ous
tune′ful
tune′less
tung′sten
tu′nic
tun′ing fork
tun′nel
tur′ban
tur′bid
tur′bine
tur′bot
tur′bu·lence
tur′bu·lent
tur′gid
tur′key
tur′keys
tur′mer·ic

tur′moil
turn′buck′le
turn′coat′
turn′cock′
turn′down′
tur′nip
turn′key′
turn′out′
turn′o′ver
turn′pike′
turn′screw
turn′spit′
turn′stile′
turn′ta′ble
tur′pen·tine
tur′pi·tude
tur′quoise
tur′ret
tur′tle
tur′tle·dove′
tus′sle
tus′sock
tu′te·lage
tu′tor
tut′ti–frut′ti
tu′yère′
twi′light′
twitch
tym′pa·num
type′cast′
type founder
type metal
type′script′
type′set′ter
type′write′
type′writ′er
type′writ′ing
ty′phoid
ty·phoon′
ty′phus
typ′i·cal
typ′i·fy
typ′ist
ty·pog′ra·pher
ty′po·graph′i·cal
ty·pog′ra·phy
ty·poth′e·tae
ty·ran′ni·cal
ty·ran′ni·cide
tyr′an·nize
tyr′an·nous
tyr′an·ny
ty′rant
ty′ro

U

u·biq′ui·tous
u·biq′ui·ty
ud′der
ug′li·ness
ug′ly
uh′lan
u·kase′
u′ku·le′le
ul′cer
ul′cer·a′tion
ul′cer·a′tive
ul′cer·ous
ul′na
ul′ster
ul·te′ri·or
ul′ti·mate
ul′ti·ma′tum
ul′ti·mo
ul′tra·ma·rine′
ul′tra·vi′o·let
ul′u·la′tion
U·lys′ses
um·bil′i·cal
um·bil′i·cus
um′brage
um·bra′geous
um·brel′la

um′laut
um′pire
un·a′ble
un′ac·count′a·ble
un′ac·cus′tomed
un′af·fect′ed
un′al·loyed′
un′–A·mer′i·can
u′na·nim′i·ty
u·nan′i·mous
un′as·sum′ing
un′a·void′a·ble
un′a·ware′
un·bal′anced
un′be·com′ing
un′be·lief′
un′be·liev′er
un·bend′
un·bi′ased
un·bid′den
un·bound′ed
un·but′ton
un·called′–for′
un·cer′tain
un·char′i·ta·ble
un·civ′i·lized
un′cle
un·clean′
un·com′fort·a·ble
un′con·cerned′
un′con·di′tion·al
un·con′scion·a-
ble
un·con′scious
un·couth′
un·cov′ered
unc′tion
unc′tu·ous
un′de·ni′a·ble
un′der·brush′
un′der·clothes′
un′der·cov′er
man
un′der·cur′rent
un′der·dose′
un′der·glaze′
un′der·go′
un′der·hand′ed
un′der·line′
un′der·mine′
un′der·neath′
un′der·rate′
un′der·score′
un′der·sell′
un′der·shirt′
un′der·sized′
un′der·slung′
un′der·stand′
un′der·stood′
un′der·stud′y
un′der·tak′er
un′der·tone′
un′der·tow′
un′der·val′ue
un′der·wa′ter
un′der way
un′der·wear′
un′der·weight′
un′der·world′
un′der·write′
un·doubt′ed·ly
un′du·la′tion
un·du′ly
un·earned′
un·earth′ly
un·eas′y
un′em·ployed′
un·e′qual
un′e·quiv′o·cal
un·err′ing
un′ex·pect′ed
un′fa·mil′iar
un·fa′vor·a·ble
un′for·get′ta·ble
un·for′tu·nate
un·furl′
un·gain′ly
un·god′ly
un′guent
u′ni·cam′er·al
u′ni·fi·ca′tion
u′ni·form
u′ni·form′i·ty
u′ni·fy
u′ni·lat′er·al

un′im·proved′
un·in′ter·est·ed
un′ion
un′ion·ize
u·nique′
u′ni·son
u′nit
u·nite′
u′ni·ty
u′ni·ver′sal
u′ni·ver·sal′i·ty
u′ni·verse
u′ni·ver′si·ty
un·kempt′
un·law′ful
un·leash′
un·less′
un·let′tered
un·like′ly
un·lim′it·ed
un·man′ly
un·nat′u·ral
un·nec′es·sar′y
un·nerve′
un·oc′cu·pied
un·par′al·leled
un·pleas′ant
un·prec′e·dent′ed
un·prej′u·diced
un′pre·med′i-
tat′ed
un·prin′ci·pled

un·qual′i·fied
un·ques′tion·a-
ble
un·rav′el
un·re′al
un·rea′son·a·ble
un′re·gen′er·ate
un′re·mit′ting
un·right′eous
un·sa′vor·y
un·scru′pu·lous
un·seem′ly
un·skill′ful
un·so′cia·ble
un′so·phis′ti-
cat′ed
un·speak′a·ble
un·strung′
un·ti′dy
un·tie′
un·til′
un·time′ly
un·told′
un·to′ward
un·truth′ful
un·tu′tored
un·u′su·al
un·var′nished
un·want′ed
(undesired)
un·war′y
un·wield′y

un·wont′ed
(unaccustomed)
un·wor′thy
un·writ′ten
up·braid′
up·heav′al
up·hold′
up·hol′ster
up·hol′ster·er
up·hol′ster·y
up′keep′
up·lift′, *v.*
up′lift′, *n.*
up·on′
up′per
up′per·cut′
up′per·most
up′right′
up·ris′ing
up·roar′i·ous
up·root′
up·set′, *v.*
up′set′, *n.*
up′shot′
up′stairs′, *adv.*
up′stairs′, *adj.*
up·start′, *v.*
up′start′, *n.*
up′stroke′
up′–to–date′
up′ward
u·ra′ni·um

ur′ban
ur·bane′
ur·ban′i·ty
ur′chin
ur′gen·cy
ur′gent
u′ric
Ur′su·line
ur′ti·ca′ri·a
U′ru·guay′an
us′a·ble
us′age
us′ance
use′ful
use′ful·ness
use′less
ush′er
u′su·al
u′su·fruct
u′su·rer
u·su′ri·ous
u·surp′
u′sur·pa′tion
u·surp′er
u′su·ry
u′ter·ine
u·til′i·tar′i·an
u·til′i·ty
u′ti·lize
ut′most
ut′ter
ut′ter·ance
ux·o′ri·ous

V

va′can·cy
va′cant
va′cate
va·ca′tion
va·ca′tion·ist
vac′ci·nate
vac′ci·na′tion
vac′cine
vac′il·late
vac′il·la′tion
va·cu′i·ty
vac′u·ous
vac′u·um
va′de me′cum
vag′a·bond
va·gar′y
va′gran·cy
va′grant
vague
vain′glo′ri·ous
vain′glo′ry
vain′ness
val′ance
val′e·dic·to′ri·an
va′lence
val′en·tine
val′et
val′e·tu′di·nar′i·an
Val·hal′la
val′iant
val′id
val′i·date
val′i·da′tion
va·lid′i·ty
va·lise′
val′ley
val′leys
val′or
val′or·i·za′tion
val′or·ous
val′u·a·ble
val′u·a′tion
val′ue
val′ue·less
val′vu·lar
vam′pire
van′guard′

va·nil′la
van′ish
van′i·ty
van′quish
van′tage
vap′id
va′por
va′por·i·za′tion
va′por·ize
va′por·iz′er
va′por·ous
va·que′ro
var′i·a·ble
var′i·ance
var′i·ant
var′i·a′tion
var′i·col′ored
var′i·cose
var′ied
var′i·e·gate
var′i·e·ga′tion
va·ri′e·ty
var′i·o′rum
var′i·ous
var′nish
var′y
vas′cu·lar
vas′e·line
vas′sal
Vat′i·can
vaude′ville
ve·dette′
veg′e·ta·ble
veg′e·tar′i·an
veg′e·tar′i·an·ism
veg′e·tate
veg′e·ta′tion
veg′e·ta′tive
ve′he·mence
ve′he·ment
ve′hi·cle
ve·hic′u·lar
vel′lum
ve·loc′i·pede
ve·loc′i·ty
ve·lure′
vel′vet
vel′vet·een′
ve′nal
vend·ee′
ven·det′ta
ven′dor
ve·neer′
ven′er·a·ble
ven′er·ate
ven′er·a′tion
Ve·ne′tian
venge′ance
venge′ful
ve′ni·al
ven′i·son
ven′om
ve′nous
ven′ti·late
ven′ti·la′tion
ven′ti·la′tor
ven′tral
ven′tri·cle
ven·tril′o·quism
ven·tril′o·quist
ven′ture·some
ven′tur·ous
ven′ue
ve·ra′cious
ve·rac′i·ty
ve·ran′da
ver′bal
ver′bal·ly
ver·ba′tim
ver·be′na
ver′bi·age
ver·bose′
ver·bos′i·ty
ver′dant
ver′dict
ver′di·gris
ver′dure
ver′ger
ve·rid′i·cal
ver′i·fi·ca′tion
ver′i·fied
ver′i·fy
ver′i·ly
ver′i·si·mil′i·tude
ver′i·ta·ble
ver′i·ty

ver′mi·cel′li
ver′mi·cide
ver′mi·form
ver′mi·fuge
ver·mil′ion
ver′min
ver′min·ous
ver·nac′u·lar
ver′nal
ver′ni·er
ver′sa·tile
ver′sa·til′i·ty
ver′si·fi·ca′tion
ver′si·fy
ver′sion
ver′sus
ver′te·bra
ver′te·brae, *pl.*
ver′te·bral
ver′te·brate
ver′tex
ver′ti·cal
ver′ti·cal·ly
ver·tig′i·nous
ves′i·cle
ves′pers
ves′sel
ves′tal
ves′ti·bule
ves′tige
ves·tig′i·al
vest′ment
ves′try
ves′try·man
vet′er·an
vet′er·i·nar′y
ve′to
ve′toed
ve′toes
ve′toing
vex·a′tion
vex·a′tious
vi′a·ble
vi′a·duct
vi′and
vi′brant
vi′brate
vi·bra′tion
vi·bra′to
vic′ar
vi·car′i·ous
vice′–ad′mir·al
vice′–chan′cel-
lor
vice′–con′sul
vice′–pres′i·dent
vice′re′gal
vice′roy
vi′ce ver′sa
vi′chys·soise′
vic′i·nage
vi·cin′i·ty
vi′cious
vi·cis′si·tude
vic′tim
vic′tim·ize
vic′tor
vic·to′ri·a
vic·to′ri·ous
vic′to·ry
vict′ual
vid′e·o
vig′il
vig′i·lance
vig′i·lant
vi·gnette′
vig′or·ous
vil′i·fy
vil′lain
vil′lain·ous
vil′lain·y
vin′ai·grette′
vin′cu·lum
vin′di·cate
vin′di·ca′tion
vin·dic′tive
vin′e·gar
vine′yard
vin′tage
vint′ner
vi′ol
vi·o′la
vi′o·late
vi′o·lence
vi′o·lent
vi′o·let

vi′o·lin′
vi′per
vir′gin
vir′ile
vi·ril′i·ty
vir′tu·al
vir′tue
vir′tu·os′i·ty
vir′tu·o′so
vir′tu·ous
vir′u·lence
vir′u·lent
vi′rus
vis′age
vis′–à–vis′
vis′cer·a
vis′cid
vis·cos′i·ty
vis′count′
vis′cous
vi′sé
vis′i·bil′i·ty
vis′i·ble
vi′sion
vi′sion·ar′y
vis′it·ant
vis′it·a′tion
vis′i·tor
vis′or
vis′ta
vis′u·al
vis′u·al·ize
vi′tal
vi·tal′i·ty
vi′tal·ize
vi′ta·min
vi′ti·ate
vit′re·ous
vit′ri·fy
vit′ri·ol
vi·tu′per·a′tion
vi·tu′per·a′tive
vi·va′cious
vi·vac′i·ty
viv′id
viv′i·sec′tion
vix′en
vi·zier′
vo·cab′u·lar′y
vo′cal
vo′cal·ist
vo′cal·ize
vo·ca′tion
vo·ca′tion·al
voc′a·tive
vo·cif′er·ous
vod′ka
voice′less
vol′a·tile
vol′a·til′i·ty
vol·can′ic
vol·ca′no
vol·ca′noes
vo·li′tion
vol′ley
volt′age
vol′u·bil′i·ty
vol′u·ble
vol′ume
vo·lu′mi·nous
vol′un·tar′i·ly
vol′un·tar′y
vol′un·teer′
vol·up′tu·ar′y
vo·lup′tu·ous
vom′it
vo·ra′cious
vo·rac′i·ty
vor′tex
vo′ta·ry
vo′tive
vouch·safe′
vow′el
voy′age
vul′can·ize
vul′gar
vul′gar·ism
vul·gar′i·ty
vul′ner·a·ble
vul′ture

W

wa'fer
waf'fle
wa'ger
Wag·ne'ri·an
wag'on
wain'scot
waist'band'
wait'ing room
wait'ress
waive
waiv'er (abandonment. cf. *waver*.)
walk'a·way
walk'ie–talk'ie
walk'out'
walk'o'ver
walk'–up'
wal'let
wall'flow'er
wal'low
wall'pa·per
wal'nut
wal'rus
wam'pum
wan'der
wan'ton
wap'i·ti
war'bler
ward'en
ward'robe'
ward'room'
ware'house'
ware'room'
war'fare'
war'i·ly
war'i·ness
war'like'
warmth
warp
war'rant
war'ran·tor
war'ran·ty
war'ren
war'ri·or
War'saw, Ind.
war'ship'
war'time'
war'y
wash'a·ble
wash'board'
wash'bowl'
wash'cloth'
wash'er
wash'out'
wash'stand'
was'sail
wast'age
waste'bas'ket
waste'ful
waste·pa'per
wast'rel
watch'case'
watch'dog'
watch'ful
watch'mak'er
watch'man
watch'tow'er
watch'word'
watch'work'
wa'ter
water blister
water bug
water color
wa'ter course'
wa'ter·fall'
wa'ter·fowl'
water front
water gap
water gas
water jump
water level
water lily
wa'ter·log'
wa'ter·logged'
water main
wa'ter·man

wa'ter·mark'
wa'ter·mel'on
water meter
water pipe
water polo
water power
wa'ter·proof'
wa'ter·shed'
wa'ter·side'
water snake
wa'ter·spout'
water table
wa'ter·tight'
water tower
water vapor
water wagon
water wave
wa'ter·way'
wa'ter·works'
wa'ter·y
Wau'sau, Wis.
wa'ver
(hesitate. cf. *waiver.*)
wax'en
wax pa'per
wax'weed
wax'work'
way'bill'
way'far'er
way'lay'
way'side'

way'ward
weak, *adj.*
(feeble. cf. *week.*)
weak'fish'
weak'ling
weak'ness
wealth
weap'on
wear'a·ble
wea'ri·less
wea'ri·ly
wea'ri·ness
wea'ri·some
wea'ry
wea'sand
wea'sel
weath'er
weath'er·proof'
weav'er
wedge–shaped
wed'lock
week, *n.*
(7 days. cf. *weak.*)
week'day
week'end'
wee'vil
weigh
weight
weight'y
weird
wel'come
wel'fare'

wel'kin
well
(Most combinations with *well* take the hyphen before a noun [*the well-known man*] but drop the hyphen after the noun [*the man is well known*]. There are exceptions like *well-read,* in which the hyphen is always retained, and *wellborn,* written as one word.)
well'–be'ing
well'born'
well'–bred'
well'–nigh'
well'spring'
wel'ter
were'wolf'
West Ches'ter, Pa.
West'ches'ter, N. Y.
west'er·ly
west'ern
west'ern·er
west'ward
whale'boat'
whale'bone'
wharf
wharf'age
wharf'in·ger
what·ev'er
what'not'

what'so·ev'er
whee'dle
wheel'bar'row
wheel'house'
wheel'wright'
whence
when·ev'er
when'so·ev'er
where'a·bouts'
where·as'
where·at'
where·by'
where'fore
where·in'
where·in'to
where·of'
where'so·ev'er
wher·ev'er
where·with'
wher'ry
wheth'er
whet'stone'
whey
which·ev'er
which'so·ev'er
while
whi'lom
whim'per
whim'si·cal
whip'cord'
whip hand
whip'lash'
whip'pet
whip'ping
whip'poor·will'
whip'stitch'
whirl'i·gig'
whirl'pool'
whirl'wind'
whisk'er
whis'ky
whis'per
whist
white'bait
white'beard
white book
white'cap'
white'–col'lar
white feather
white'fish
white flag
white'–head'ed
white'–hot'
white lead
white paper
white'wash'
white'wood'
whith'er
whit'ing
whit'low
whit'tle
who'dun'it
who·ev'er
whole'heart'ed
whole'sale'
whole'some
whoop
who'so·ev'er
wick'ed·ness
wick'er·work'
wick'et
wide'spread'
wid'ow
wield
wig'wag'
wig'wam
wild'cat'
wil'der·ness
wild'fire'
will'ful
will'–o'–the–wisp'
wind'age
wind'break'
wind'fall'
wind'jam'mer
wind'lass
wind'mill'
win'dow
win'dow·pane'
wind'pipe'
wind'shield'
wind'ward
wine'glass'
wine'glass·ful'
wine'skin'

win'now
win'some
Win'ston–Sa'-
lem, N. C.
win'ter
win'ter·green'
win'ter·ize
win'ter·time'
wire'less
wire'pull'ing
wire'weed'
wis'dom
wise'a'cre
wise'ly
wish'bone'
wish'ful
wis·ta'ri·a
wist'ful
witch'craft'
witch'er·y
with·al'
with·draw'
with·draw'al
with·hold'
with·in'
with·out'
with·stand'
wit'ness
wit'ti·cism
wit'ti·ly
wit'ting·ly
wit'ty

wiz'ened
wolf'hound'
wom'an
wom'an·hood
wom'an·ish
wom'an·kind'
wom'an·like'
wom'an·ly
won'der·ful
won'der·ment
won'der–
strick'en
won'der·work'
won'drous
wood'chuck'
wood'craft'
wood'cut'
wood'en
wood'en·ware
woon'land
wood lot
wood'man
wood'peck'er
wood'pile
wood pulp
wood'shed
woods'man
wood'work'
wool'en
wool'gath'er·ing
wool'ly
wool'sack'

Woos'ter, Ohio
Worces'ter,
Mass.
work'a·ble
work'a·day'
work'bag'
work'bench'
work'book'
work'box'
work'day'
work'house'
work'ing·man'
work'man
work'man·like'
work'man·ship
work'out'
work'room
work'shop'
work'ta'ble
work'week'
world'li·ness
world'ly
world'ly–wise'
world'–wide'
worm'eat'en
worm'hole'
worm'wood'
worn'–out'
wor'ri·ment
wor'ship
wor'ship·ful
wor'sted

wor′thi·ly
worth′less
wor′thy
wound
wraith
wran′gle
wrap′per
wrath′ful
wreath, *n.*
wreathe, *v.*
wreck′age
wrench
wres′tle
wres′tler
wretch′ed
wrig′gle
wrig′gly
wring′er
wrin′kle
wrist′band'
wrist′let
wrist′lock'
wrist pin
wrist watch
writ′er
write′–up'
writ′ing
writ′ten
wrong
wrong′do'er
wrong′ful
wrought
Wy·o′ming

X

Xan·thip′pe
xe′non
xe·rog′ra·phy
X ray, *n.*
X-ray, *adj.*, *v.*
xy′lo·phone

Y

yacht
yachts′man
yak
yam
Yan′kee
yard′age
yard′arm'
yard′stick'
yar′row
yat′a·ghan
yawl
yawn
year′book'
year′ling
year′ly
yearn
yeast
yel′low
yeo′man
yeo′man·ry
yes′ter·day
yew
Yid′dish
yield
yoke
yo′kel
yolk

yon′der
yore
young
young′ster
your·self′
youth′ful
yt·ter′bi·um
yt′tri·um
yule

Z

za·min′dar′
za′ny
zeal′ot
zeal′ot·ry
zeal′ous
ze′bra
ze′bu
ze·na′na
ze′nith
zeph′yr
Zep′pe·lin
ze′ro
zest
zig′gu·rat
zig′zag′
zinc
Zi′on
Zi′on·ism
zir′con
zir·co′ni·um
zith′er
zo′di·ac
zo·di′a·cal
zo′o·log′i·cal
zo·ol′o·gy
Zou·ave′
Zu′ñi
zwie′back′
zy′mase
zy·mot′ic

SPELLING HELPS

English spelling being what it is, no rule will enable the learner to spell correctly. The rules given below will help. Often, however, to guard against error, reference must be made to the alphabetic list in this book.

1 Words ending in silent *e* drop the *e* before a suffix beginning with a vowel.

reducing	refining	desirable
troubling	inducing	ensuing
arguing	debatable	sponging

2 Words ending in silent *e* retain the *e* before a suffix beginning with a consonant.

completeness	careful	enforcement
engagement	genuineness	statement
resourceful	advertisement	management

3 Exceptions to final *e* rules.

traceable	enforceable	peaceable
serviceable	noticeable	courageous
manageable	exchangeable	chargeable
mileage	dyeing	duly
truly	wholly	argument
abridgment	judgment	acknowledgment

4 Final *y* preceded by a *consonant* is changed to *i* before every suffix except *ing*.

Final *y* preceded by a *vowel* is *not* changed before a suffix.

heaviest	salaried	steadily
carrier	pitiful	trying
satisfied	accompanying	journeying
necessarily	supplying	conveyance
copying	livelihood	delayed
hurried	dutiful	annoyance

5 Monosyllables, and also words of more than one syllable accented on the last syllable, ending in a single consonant preceded by a single vowel, double the final consonant before a suffix beginning with a vowel.

referred	expelling	remittance
compelling	occurring	permitting
transferred	regrettable	committed

6 Words of more than one syllable ending in a single consonant preceded by a single vowel, but not accented on the last syllable, do *not* double the final consonant before a suffix beginning with a vowel.

solicited	modeled	unequaled
benefited	limited	canceled
offered	profited	opened
credited	debited	labeled

7 The majority of adverbs are formed from adjectives by adding the suffix *ly*.

external-ly	accurate-ly	appropriate-ly
conclusive-ly	separate-ly	respective-ly
total-ly	occasional-ly	adequate-ly

8 "Put *i* before *e*
Except after *c*,
Or when sounded like *a*,
As in *neighbor* and *weigh:*
And except *seize* and *seizure*,
And also *leisure*,
Weird, height, and *either*,
Forfeit and *neither*."

ie

achieve	apiece	believe
brief	chief	yield

ei

ceiling	conceit	either
freight	receipt	receive

The word *Celia* may often be used as the key. Thus, *c* is followed by *e* and *l* by *i*, as re*ceive*, be*lieve*.

9 The plurals of nouns ending in *y* preceded by a *consonant* are formed by changing *y* to *i* and adding *es*.

varieties	prophecies	monopolies
authorities	companies	necessities

10 The plurals of nouns ending in *y* preceded by a *vowel* are formed by adding *s* to the singular.

holidays	moneys	galleys
journeys	attorneys	surveys

11 The plurals of most nouns ending in *o* are formed by adding *s* to the singular.

pianos	provisos	quartos
folios	mementos	ratios

12 The plurals of some nouns ending in *o* are formed by adding *es* to the singular.

potatoes	vetoes	embargoes
cargoes	mottoes	tomatoes

13 The plurals of most nouns ending in *f* are formed by adding *s* to the singular.

sheriffs	plaintiffs	beliefs
briefs	proofs	staffs

14 Some nouns ending in *f* or *fe* form their plurals by changing *f* or *fe* into *v* and adding *es.*

knives	halves	shelves
leaves	thieves	wharves

15 In some nouns the plural is formed by a vowel change instead of by the addition of a suffix.

geese	mice	men
women	feet	teeth

16 Some words of foreign origin retain their original plural form.

bases	memoranda	data
phenomena	parentheses	stimuli

17 In compound nouns the plural sign is usually added to the last member, but sometimes to the first member.

cupfuls	mouthfuls	stand-bys
bills of lading	notes receivable	sons-in-law

18 Some nouns are rarely or never used in the singular.

annals	proceeds	clothes
scissors	spectacles	obsequies

19 The possessive singular of nouns is formed by adding an apostrophe and an *s*. In proper names ending in *s*, the authorities favor adding the apostrophe and *s* to monosyllables, and the apostrophe only to words of more than one syllable.

auditor's	broker's	consignee's
Jones's	Frances'	month's

20 Plural nouns not ending in *s* form the possessive in the same way as singular nouns.

children's	mice's	men's

21 Plural nouns ending in *s* add only the apostrophe for the possessive.

witnesses'	students'	mothers'
stationers'	customers'	creditors'

22 Possessive forms of pronouns are written without the apostrophe. (*Its*, the possessive, should be differentiated from *it's*, the contraction for *it is*.)

yours	hers	its
his	theirs	ours

DIVISION OF WORDS

1 Words should be divided only between syllables.

de-part-ment	ab-surd	proc-ess

2 Monosyllables should never be divided.

which	through	passed

3 A single letter should not be separated from the rest of the word.

enough	among	enor-mous

4 Avoid two-letter divisions, and never carry over two letters only.

only	until	every

5 Diphthongs and digraphs cannot be divided.

build-ing	buoy-ant	peo-ple

6 When a final consonant is doubled before a suffix, the additional consonant goes with the suffix.

run-ning	bid-ding	control-ling

7 When two consonants come together between two vowels, divide between the consonants.

mil-lion	struc-ture	advan-tage

No rules that can be given will guide the writer unerringly in the division of words. If a word must be divided, consult the list given in this book.

The secretary, stenographer, and typist will find, however, that it is possible to learn to maintain satisfactory right-hand margins without dividing words. The slight extra effort required to learn to obtain good margins without word division will be more than repaid by the time saved that would otherwise be spent looking for the correct division. Don't be discouraged if you have trouble at first—it can be done.

HOMONYMS

Two or more words that are pronounced alike, but used and spelled differently, are called "homonyms." Other groups of words not strictly homonyms, but which are often confused because of their similarity in sound, have also been included under this heading.

accede	To comply with.
exceed	To surpass.
accept	To take, receive.
except	To exclude.
access	Admittance, admission.
excess	Surplus.
aloud	Audibly; with a loud voice.
allowed	Permitted; sanctioned.
altar	A place of worship.
alter	To change.
ascent	Act of rising; motion upward.
assent	Consent.
aught	Anything; slightest thing (poetic).
ought	Should; obliged.
calendar	Record (of time).
calender	Finishing machine used in the manufacture of paper, cloth, etc.

canvas	A strong cloth.
canvass	To solicit thoroughly; to scrutinize.
capital	Seat of government of a state or country; money invested.
capitol	Government building.
cede	To grant; give up.
seed	That from which anything is grown.
cereal	Any grain food.
serial	Arranged in a series; appearing in successive numbers of a magazine.
choir	A group of singers.
quire	Twenty-four sheets of paper.
coarse	Rough; large.
course	Direction; part of a dinner; action.
correspondence	Letters.
correspondents	Letter writers.
council	An assembly of men or women summoned for deliberation.
counsel	An attorney; advice.
currant	A small fruit.
current	Tide; electricity; belonging to the present.
complement	That which fills or completes.
compliment	To congratulate.

confidant	Friend; adviser.
confident	Sure; positive.
deference	Respect; courteous regard for another's wishes.
difference	Contrary; not like.
decent	Proper; right; suitable.
descent	Going down; coming down.
dissent	Difference of opinion; disagreement.
die	To cease to breathe; finish; tool with depressed design.
dye	To change the color of.
elusive	Tantalizing; hard to catch.
illusive	Misleading; deceiving; unreal.
eminent	Well known; prominent.
imminent	Very near; impending; threatening.
fair	Beautiful; blonde; just.
fare	Cost of travel.
grate	A frame of iron bars holding the fuel in a furnace; to produce a harsh sound; to reduce to small particles by rubbing.
great	Eminent; foremost; large; many.
hear	To perceive by the ear; to listen to.
here	This place.

indict	To consider guilty.
indite	To compose and write (a document).
incite	To cause trouble, uprising.
insight	An inner knowledge; understanding.
lead	A metal.
led	Guided; past tense of the verb "lead."
load	To lay a burden on or in.
lode	A vein (of ore).
loan	That which one lends or borrows.
lone	Solitary.
miner	An underground worker in a mine.
minor	Under full age or majority; less.
plain	Simple; flat land.
plane	A tool for smoothing a surface.
ordinance	A local law enacted by a municipal government.
ordnance	Arms; munitions.
precedence	Priority; superior rank.
precedents	Previous acts used as guides.
principal	Chief; the original sum; the head of a school.
principle	A fundamental truth; a settled rule of action.

residence A home; dwelling place.
residents Those living in a place.

right Correct; privilege.
rite Ceremony.
write To inscribe by hand.

rôle A part in a play; a function assumed by anyone.
roll To cause to revolve by turning over and over.

sight Vision.
site Place to build on.
cite To make a reference to something previously written.

stationary Staying in one place.
stationery Writing supplies.

stile A step, or set of steps.
style Fashion.

straight Not crooked or curved.
strait Narrow strip of water connecting two large bodies of water.

suite A number of things used or classed together; a company of attendants.
sweet Having an agreeable taste; pleasing to the eye or ear.

tare The allowance made by the seller for the weight of a container.
tear To rip.

to	Preposition.
too	More than enough.
two	One and one.
waist	Part of the body; garment.
waste	Needless destruction; useless consumption.

PUNCTUATION SIMPLIFIED

The great majority of all questions about punctuation may be answered with a knowledge of a few simple principles. Those principles are given here. No attempt is made to give the principles covering the occasional rare and difficult problems that arise.

The few grammatical terms required in these explanations are defined and illustrated in the explanations. The brief comparative review of the uses of the comma and the semicolon (page 247) will be found to be especially helpful.

COMMA

Parenthetical comma. In order to make his meaning clearer, a writer sometimes inserts a comment or explanation that could be omitted without changing the meaning of the sentence. These added comments and explanations are called parenthetical and are separated from the rest of the sentence by parentheses, dashes, or commas. Ordinarily, the comma is preferable.

> You owe us the $25, however, and you have not paid.
> You should remember us, too, with a payment.

A special type of parenthetical expression is called appositive and is explained below.

Comma in apposition. Sometimes a writer mentions a certain person or thing and then, in order to make his meaning perfectly clear to the reader, says the same thing in different words.

> Call Miss Hall, our assistant manager, at Main 6000.
> Here it is Friday, May 23, and we have not . . .

In many cases these constructions in apposition resemble the constructions in which the commas are used to set off parenthetical expressions. It is really immaterial whether a writer thinks he is using the commas to set off an apposition or to set off a parenthetical expression. They are substantially the same thing and the result is identical.

An apposition may occur at the end of a sentence, in which case only one comma is needed.

> Send us your check for $18.20 by Friday, January 12.

Comma in series. When three or more similar expressions (words, phrases, or clauses) occur in a series with a conjunction before the last expression, a comma should be placed before the conjunction.

> . . . provide the envelopes, letterheads, and cards that . . .
> . . . goods shipped on March 10, April 7, and May 4.
> The Mutual Insurance Company found the plan she wanted, set it up for her, and made her happy.

Comma after introductory expressions. A comma is used after an introductory expression, such as *for instance* or *on the contrary*. A comma is also used after an *if* clause, a *when* clause, an *as* clause, or any similar dependent clause at the beginning of a sentence.

The dependent, or subordinate, clause signals the coming of another clause with a relative pronoun or a subordinate conjunction. The relative pronouns are *that, who, what, which, whoever, whatever, whichever.* The commonest subordinating conjunctions are *if, though, although, whether, unless, as, because, when, since, while, where, after, wherever, until, before, how, however.*

If, when, and *as* are the three commonest subordinating conjunctions found in business correspondence.

> If there is any error, please let us know.
> When many customers owe us small balances, the total amounts to a surprising sum.
> As I am leaving for a two months' vacation abroad, I should like to rent my apartment.

The rule covering the group of introductory dependent clauses is that a comma is used to separate a subordinate clause from a *following* main clause. If the main clause comes first, no comma is required. A comma was placed in the preceding sentence after the subordinate clause (*if the main clause comes first*) because that clause came before the main clause. No comma would be required if the position of the two clauses were reversed so that that sentence read: *No comma is required if the main clause comes first.*

Thus the comma is required when the subordinate clause introduces the main clause. Similarly a comma is required after other introductory or explanatory expressions, such as *on the contrary, in brief, for instance.*

> Supplementing the annual report, I have occasionally written to the members of our company . . .
> In brief, our plan is to . . .

It is safe to use a comma after any introductory or explanatory expression or after any element of a sentence that is used at the beginning of the sentence out of its natural word order. The writer whose judgment has been formed by constant practice may omit the comma after a short introductory expression that seems to flow into the rest of the sentence without a break.

Comma with nonrestrictive expressions. Nonrestrictive clauses and phrases are set off by commas. A nonrestrictive clause or phrase is one that may be omitted without changing the meaning of the sentence. The nonrestrictive clause or phrase might be classified as parenthetical. It is important to follow the meaning of the copy in order to be able to identify the restrictive and the nonrestrictive clauses and phrases and to punctuate them correctly.

> Restrictive—no commas: The automobile that was speeding was completely destroyed.
>
> Nonrestrictive—commas: The automobile, which was speeding, was completely destroyed.

In the first sentence above, *that was speeding* is a restrictive clause and must not be set off by commas. The expression *that was speeding* identifies the particular automobile that was destroyed. In the second sentence, *which was speeding* is a nonrestrictive or descriptive or parenthetical clause that must be set off with commas. It does not identify the particular automobile that was destroyed; it merely describes further an automobile that has already been identified. Notice in the examples given above that the careful writer uses *that* to introduce a restrictive clause and *which* to introduce a nonrestrictive clause. Many writers fail to observe this distinction, however.

Restrictive—no commas: The girl standing in the garden waved to him.
Nonrestrictive—commas: The girl, standing in the garden, waved to him.

In the first sentence above, *standing in the garden* is a restrictive phrase and must not be set off with commas. The expression *standing in the garden* identifies the particular girl who waved to him. In the second sentence, *standing in the garden* is a nonrestrictive or descriptive or parenthetical phrase that must be set off with commas. It does not identify the girl who waved. The girl has already been identified by a previous sentence or by a gesture of the speaker; the nonrestrictive phrase *standing in the garden* merely describes where she stood when she waved.

The use of the commas is determined by the meaning of the sentence. It is almost always possible to decide from the context whether an expression was intended to be nonrestrictive or restrictive—whether it should be transcribed with or without commas.

Comma to indicate omission of "and." Usually two adjectives preceding a noun are separated by a comma.

It is a clear, bright day.

The comma is not used if the first adjective modifies the second adjective and the noun as a unit.

She wore a beautiful green dress.

SEMICOLON

Comma or semicolon between independent clauses. Although in some ways this is one of the easiest punctuation problems, and certainly one of the most frequent, few writers seem to be able to solve it rapidly and accurately.

A comma is used to separate two independent clauses that are joined by one of the conjunctions *and, but, or, for, neither, nor.* If the two independent clauses are not joined by one of those conjunctions, the clauses are separated by a semicolon.

An independent clause (sometimes called a *main* or *principal* clause) is one that has a subject and predicate and could stand alone as a separate sentence.

> We have to meet all our bills, but we cannot do so until we collect what is due from our customers.

The first independent or principal or main clause is

> We have to meet all our bills . . .

because that could stand as a separate sentence. The second independent clause, which could also stand as a separate sentence, is

> . . . we cannot do so until we collect what is due from our customers.

These could be written as two separate sentences with a period after each. Because the thought of the two sentences is closely related, it seemed better to the writer to put them into one sentence. Because the two independent clauses are connected by the coordinating conjunction *but,* a comma is used between them. The writer could have said:

> We have to meet all our bills; we cannot do so until we collect what is due from our customers.

In this case the semicolon would be used to separate the two independent clauses because there is no conjunction.

Semicolon required because of comma. If the comma were always used between independent clauses connected by a conjunction, and if the semicolon were always used between independent clauses not connected by a conjunction, the writer would have little trouble becoming accustomed to the correct punctuation. The one exception referred to by the above heading serves to confuse the learner. The exception is that the semicolon is used instead of the comma if a comma is found within either of the independent clauses joined by a conjunction.

The reason for this change from comma to semicolon is simple enough. If there are other commas in the sentence, something stronger than a comma is required to separate the two parts of the sentence. For example, the following sentence uses a comma to separate the two independent clauses joined by the conjunction *but:*

> We have to meet all our bills, but we cannot do so until we collect what is due from our customers.

When the sentence is changed by the addition of one word and a comma, as shown below, the comma after the word *bills* must be changed to a semicolon.

> Moreover, we have to meet all our bills; but we cannot do so until we collect what is due from our customers.

It is clear that the punctuation between the two independent clauses, the two main parts of the sentence, must be of greater strength than the punctuation within the first clause. Therefore, the semicolon is used instead of the comma.

Here is the same sentence with a parenthetical phrase added in the second clause, necessitating the change from a comma to a semicolon before the *but*.

> We have to meet all our bills; but we cannot do so, as a practical matter, until we collect what is due from our customers.

Comparative review of uses of comma and semicolon. 1. Comma between preceding dependent (subordinate) clause and following independent (main) clause:

> If we are to meet our bills, we must collect what is due from our customers.

2. No punctuation at all if the dependent (subordinate) clause comes after the main clause:

> We must collect what is due from our customers if we are to meet our bills.

3. Comma between two independent (main) clauses joined by the conjunctions *and, but, or, for, neither, nor:*

> We have to meet our bills, but we cannot do so until we collect what is due from our customers.

4. Semicolon between two independent (main) clauses joined by the conjunctions *and, but, for, or, neither, nor* if there is a comma in either clause:

a. Moreover, we have to meet our bills; but we cannot do so until we collect what is due from our customers.
b. We have to meet our bills; but we cannot do so, as a practical matter, until we collect what is due from our customers.
c. Moreover, we have to meet our bills; but we cannot do so, as a practical matter, until we collect what is due from our customers.

5. Semicolon between two independent (main) clauses that are not joined by the conjunctions *and, but, or, for, neither, nor:*

We have to meet our bills; we cannot do so until we collect what is due from our customers.

COLON

A colon is used after an expression that is an introduction to some following material, such as a long quotation, an explanation of a general statement, a list, or an enumeration.

There are three requirements: speed, accuracy, and artistry.
The new plate has this advantage: You can use it in any of the ten stores listed on the enclosed card.

QUOTATIONS

Several punctuation usages in regard to quotations are summarized under this heading.

1. Short quotations are introduced by a comma.

The boy said, "Help me, sir."

2. Long quotations are introduced by a colon.

The boy said: "I have studied for many years to prepare for this work, and I hope that you are willing to help me find a place either here or in some neighboring city."

3. The comma and the period are always typed inside the final quotation mark; other punctuation marks are placed inside or outside the final quotation mark, according to the sense of the sentence.

"I cannot believe," she said, "that he has left."
She asked, "Why did he go?"
Why did she say, "He has left"?

HYPHENATION

The use or omission of the hyphen in expressions like *worth while* and *up to date* is a problem largely because of the infrequency of its occurrence. The principle is extremely simple. If a noun follows the expression, the hyphens are inserted—no following noun, no hyphen.

> The book is up to date. (No noun after the expression.)
> The up-to-date book . . . (Noun follows the expression.)

An exception is that no hyphen is used when the first element of the modifier ends in *ly*. Therefore, there would be no hyphen in *skillfully planned campaign*.

DATES

The correct form is *March 20*, without the *th* after the figure.

The year figure is set off by commas.

> It was in June, 1949, that I first met him.

FIGURES

The correct form for even amounts of dollars is *$83* with no decimal point and no ciphers.

> . . . remittance of $25 or return the merchandise.
> . . . your overdue account of $25.
> The amount, as you know, is $166; and . . .
> Was your first remittance $37?

As may be seen in the examples above, sometimes the figures representing the amount will be followed by a period, a semicolon, or another mark of punctuation required by the context of the sentence.

Amounts indicating *cents* and *per cent* are written as shown in the examples. Notice that *per cent* is written as two words without a following period but that *percentage* is one word.

It is true that 98 per cent of the items may be purchased for 7 cents or less. A small percentage may cost 8 cents or more.

PERIOD AFTER A COURTEOUS REQUEST

This usage is seldom found except in business correspondence. The businessman is always trying to persuade the customer or prospective customer to take some action desired by the businessman. The customer might take offense if the businessman were to say directly, *I want to hear from you by return mail.* Therefore, the businessman says:

May we hear from you by return mail.

The question must be followed by a question mark; the courteous request, by a period.

The courteous request always calls for an answer in the form of an action; the question calls for an answer in the form of words.

The businessman who said *May we hear from you by return mail* did not expect the answer to be *yes.* He expected the answer to be a letter by return mail.

The small things are the ones that we overlook, aren't they?

The question mark is used in the above sentence because the only possible answer would be the word *yes.*

— Cheryl —

6505 58 St No

Corner of 58 & 63

Green VW